THE GENERAL STRIKE

THE
GENERAL STRIKE

A Historical Portrait

by

JULIAN SYMONS

*With 8 pages
of plates*

READERS UNION
THE CRESSET PRESS
LONDON 1959

By the same author

BIOGRAPHY AND CRITICISM

A. J. A. SYMONS, HIS LIFE AND SPECULATIONS

CHARLES DICKENS

THOMAS CARLYLE: THE LIFE AND IDEAS OF A PROPHET

HORATIO BOTTOMLEY

CRIME NOVELS

THE IMMATERIAL MURDER CASE

A MAN CALLED JONES

BLAND BEGINNING

THE THIRTY-FIRST OF FEBRUARY

THE BROKEN PENNY

THE NARROWING CIRCLE

THE PAPER CHASE

THE COLOUR OF MURDER

THE GIGANTIC SHADOW

© JULIAN SYMONS, 1957

This RU edition was produced in 1959 for sale to its members only by Readers Union Ltd at 38 William IV Street, Charing Cross, London, and at Letchworth Garden City, Hertfordshire. Full details of membership may be obtained from our London address. The book has been reset in 10 point Baskerville, and printed by The Aldine Press, Letchworth. It was first published by the Cresset Press in 1957.

PREFACE

'The General Strike was an important event in British history, but I am not aware that there exists any full historical account of it,' I read in Duff Cooper's autobiography, *Old Men Forget*. 'Yet it continued for ten days, it divided the people into two camps, it threatened the survival of parliamentary government, and it brought the country nearer to revolution than it has ever been.' There was indeed, as a little investigation showed me, only a hazy idea of the strike's character and objects in the minds of many people; Duff Cooper's own remarks testify to that haziness, for the strike lasted not for ten days but for nine. It began at midnight on 3rd May 1926, and ended at noon on 12th May.

It is true that no full account of the strike exists. This book attempts to fill that small gap in history. The way in which it has been put together may be of some interest. I began by consulting the printed sources: books, strike newspapers and periodicals. The newspapers and periodicals give a bare account of incidents, without elucidating motives or conveying much about the feelings aroused by the strike in different parts of the country, or among different sections of the community. Political memoirs written after the strike are of some help, but many of them merely repeat legends which gained currency during the strike period, and few have much that is fresh to say. It became obvious that the printed material was of only limited use in catching the flavour and feeling of the nine days. The most important printed source which I have used is Professor W. H. Crook's account of the strike in his book, *The General Strike: A Study of Labour's Tragic Weapon in Theory and Practice*, published in 1931. Professor Crook, an American historian, visited England shortly after the strike, and talked to many trade union and some Government leaders. The two hundred pages given to the British General Strike in his book are based largely on these interviews and conversations, and what he has to say must be important for any later historian.

Most of my own material, however, came from three sources outside the existing printed books and papers. First, from the Trades Union Congress, who very generously gave me permission to use the papers in their library relating to the General Strike. Here I found the heart of the strike, on the trade union side: the reports and discussions of the Intelligence, Press and Publicity, and other committees, and – even more important – hundreds of reports and queries from local Strike Committees and Councils of Action on almost every conceivable aspect of the strike. Examination of this material which, the librarian thought, had not been looked at by anybody since 1926, led me to certain conclusions which the TUC are not likely to share. The fact that they have given me permission to use the material in their library does not, I must emphasize, imply their agreement with any of the opinions I have expressed.

Second, a number of people more or less closely connected with the strike have offered information or answered what must often have been tiresomely detailed questions, either in conversation or by correspondence. I am sincerely grateful to Mr A. W. Baldwin, Mr G. D. H. Cole, Mr Tom Driberg, Viscount Davidson, Sir Patrick Duff, Mr Hugh Gaitskell, Sir Patrick Gower, Lord Lawson, Mr Raymond Postgate, Lord Reith, Viscount Samuel, Sir Henry Slesser, Mr John Strachey, Viscount Waverley and Sir Horace Wilson for the information they have given me about various aspects of the strike. I must acknowledge also my debt to the Conservative Party Research Bureau and to the Labour Party for the help they have given me, and to Mr F. G. Prince-White and the *Daily Mail* for information about the '*Daily Mail* incident'.

The third source of information was perhaps the most valuable. From a letter which appeared in several newspapers and periodicals, asking for personal experiences of the strike, I received some hundreds of replies. Several correspondents sent extracts from diaries kept at the time; many sent letters written to their families during the strike; and I have made much use of this material, which gives just the direct, first-hand view of the strike for which I was looking. For the most part I have let these correspondents speak for themselves, believing that what they had to say was more interesting, even when it was demonstrably wrong or partial, than any paraphrase; but sometimes I have blended the remarks of half a dozen correspondents into an observation of my own.

Most of these correspondents are unnamed in the text, but I acknowledge most gratefully my debt to them all, and in particular to Miss D. M. Adams, Miss D. Austen-Leigh, Mr A. M. Bell, Mr I. C. Berry, Mrs Olga Ball, Mr G. Bird, Mr W. T. Bett, Lieut.-Col. P. R. Butler, Lady Brooke, Miss E. I. Blake, Dr J. H. Beilby, Sir Lewis Casson, Mr R. Capper, Mr James Champion, Mr W. G. Campbell, Mr R. H. Cobbold, Mr H. W. C. Christmas, Mr Walter Duncan, Mr Frank Dawtry, Mr D. O. Dixon, Mr John Ellis, Mr R. Endall, Miss A. Fowler, Miss Elsie Fox, The Reverend P. Gardner-Smith, Miss M. Gosset, Lieut.-Col. A. M. Garnett, Mr R. F. Homeyard, Canon R. W. Howard, Mr F. T. Hawkins, Mr Paul Swain Havens, Mr F. P. Howard, Mr Harold Harris, Mr J. B. Harvey, Brigadier R. Johnston, Mrs P. F. Jones, Mr C. Malcolm Johnstone, Group Captain F. F. Kennedy, Lieut.-Col. C. A. G. Keeson, Mr F. F. M. Lee, Mr Evan Lewis, Sister M. Lewis, Mr A. J. Land, Sir William Lawther, Brigadier F. H. Maynard, Mr John E. Morgan, Miss G. Heather Meadows, Mr S. Matthewman, Miss L. M. Norton, Mr Frank Newell, Mr John O'Leary, Mrs Dorothy Perkins, Mr R. W. Plummer, Mr G. K. D. Pontifex, Mrs K. M. Patterson, Mr H. C. Robinson, Mr F.

Dudley Rose, Brigadier R. B. Rathbone, Mr A. T. Rowland, Commander F. M. Simon, Mr Sydney Smith, Mr B. W. Smith, Mr R. S. Stanier, Mr H. Stephenson, Mr R. W. Skirving, Mr Charles Saunders, Sir William Seeds, Mrs Ursula Stanton, Mr W. H. S. Truell and Miss E. M. Walker.

Finally, I owe further debts of gratitude to Mr Raymond Postgate for reading the proofs, and for correcting some at least of my errors, and to Lord Samuel for permitting me to reproduce in full his previously unpublished letter to the Prime Minister, Stanley Baldwin, about his negotiations with the trade union leaders.

Out of it all I have tried to make a historical portrait: a picture of an event, done in places with Frithian detail, and of the famous or forgotten people who were involved in it.

April 1957   JULIAN SYMONS

CONTENTS

*

LIST OF ILLUSTRATIONS

ACKNOWLEDGMENTS

All the plates are reproduced by permission of
Picture Post.

PART I
THE YEARS BEFORE

I
BLACK FRIDAY

The General Strike, which lasted from 3rd–12th May 1926, was, Leopold Amery said afterwards, thirty years out of date. The emergence of the small private car and the development of wireless, he thought, had tilted the scales so decisively in favour of the middle class and of the Government that the strike had no chance of success. The miners' leader, Will Lawther, who was arrested for his part in the strike, said epigrammatically that in 1926 the coal-owners dug their own graves. Yet the strike was not, as Amery implied, a gesture self-evidently absurd; nor was it true, as Lawther suggested, that it could have been averted by a little good sense on the part of the coal-owners. The complex of feelings and attitudes that caused the strike had their roots in the events of Black Friday and Red Friday, as 15th April 1921 and 31st July 1925 were respectively called in the trade union movement. After these black- and red-letter days some such struggle as the General Strike was inevitable.

The coal question, as it was called, was symbolic of the battle between capital and labour in the period after the First World War; and this was so not merely because the Miners' Federation emerged from the war as by far the strongest trade union in the country, but because the miner's work, by its unpleasant and dangerous nature, gained him the respectful sympathy of people unconnected with the industry, who felt no such sympathy with the wage claims of shop assistants, or even railwaymen. People felt that miners should be well paid, and were uneasily conscious that, with wages at an average of 50s to 60s a week, they were not.

To strengthen their bargaining hand the miners had in 1914 sponsored the formation of a Triple Industrial Alliance, of miners, railwaymen and transport workers. The idea behind this alliance was that the three bodies should act together in making wage agreements and settling hours of work. Obviously the alliance was, at least potentially, a very powerful industrial instrument. In 1919, when the miners threatened to strike, the other members of the Triple Alliance joined with them in support of the miners' demand for more money and shorter hours. The strike was postponed when the Government agreed to set up a Royal Commission.

The Sankey Commission issued a report almost wholly in favour of the miners; that fact has been mentioned in every argument about the coal industry during the last thirty odd years. The composition of the commission has been less frequently remarked: since the miners were allowed to nominate four members and approve two (R. H. Tawney and Sidney Webb), and upon the other side the Government and the coal-owners nominated three apiece, obviously a great deal depended upon the chairman. By what one feels to have been a Government oversight the chairman appointed, a judge of the King's Bench Division named Sir John Sankey, proved distinctly sympathetic to the miners' aspirations. The commission recommended wage increases of 2s a shift, a seven- instead of an eight-hour day, and a system of public ownership for the coal industry. On this last point the six representatives of the miners and Sankey were on one side, the three coal-owners' representatives and two of the Government nominees on the other; the last member, Sir Arthur Duckham, proposed a scheme of his own, based on a system of economic checks and balances. Bonar Law, for the Government, expressed its intention of carrying out 'in

the spirit and in the letter' the recommendations of the Sankey Report. When the strike notices had been withdrawn,
however, the miners got their seven-hour day, and some
wage increases, but in the House of Commons the Prime
Minister, Lloyd George, flatly rejected the idea of nationalization as impractical.

The events of 1919 thus provided no test for the Triple
Alliance. When it was tried it failed. During the war, and for
some time after it, the mines had been under the direct control of the Government. In the spring of 1921 it suddenly announced that this control would be terminated at the end of
March. The owners and miners had been discussing the
question of a permanent agreement on wages when the
Government announcement was made. While Parliament
was still debating the Decontrol Bill the owners announced
sweeping wage reductions, and lockout notices were posted
at all collieries. At the end of March the lockout began, and
on 8th April the leaders of the Triple Alliance issued a call
for a railway and transport strike, to begin in four days' time.

It is interesting to compare the reactions of Lloyd George's
Coalition Government with those of Baldwin's Conservative
Government five years later, when faced with the threat of a
national strike. In 1921 the military preparations to combat
the strike were plain for all to see. A state of emergency was
declared, reservists were called to the colours, machine-guns
were posted at pitheads, and troops in battle order were sent
to many working-class areas. Compared with this display of
militancy the Government's attitude in 1926 was positively
pacific.

The leaders of the Triple Alliance sat in continuous session
at the railwaymen's headquarters. Like most men who have
reached important positions in the trade union movement,
they preferred negotiations to fighting. Frank Hodges, who
held the key position of secretary to the Miners' Federation,
had presented the miners' case to the Sankey Commission
with a skill and sympathy that earned him great respect. Since

then he had moved steadily away from a belief in militant policies. Within a few years he was to be appointed by a Conservative Government as a member of the National Electricity Board. Later he became a director of several colliery and iron and steel companies, and at his death in 1947 left an estate of more than £100,000. The secretary of the Transport Workers' Federation, Robert Williams, was a former dock labourer and coal trimmer, who after the war became a member of the recently founded Communist Party. Williams's influence in the Federation, however, had declined as that of the assistant secretary increased. This was Ernest Bevin, a rising figure in the Labour movement, powerful in the federation through his ascendancy in his own dockers' union. But beyond doubt the most popular and influential leader in the Triple Alliance was the railwaymen's leader Jimmy Thomas, the greatest buffoon the Labour movement has known, a man who dropped his aitches as eagerly as he put on a dinner jacket, the personification of the beery, cheery, plain-speaking man that music hall comedians felt the British working man to be; an image of this imaginary working man, also, for the employers with whom he dined and negotiated so zestfully, and for the aristocrats who enjoyed his frank and unabashable social climbing; a man loved, finally, by the railway workers he represented because, by his humour and his good humour, his virtues and even his amiable failings, he seemed to be more thoroughly one of themselves than any other British labour leader. Of Thomas's influence during the General Strike there will be much more to say. In 1921 his role was that of peacemaker, of a man who felt that any kind of settlement was preferable to a transport strike.

The hint of such a settlement came when, on the night before the strike was due to begin, two private meetings of members of Parliament were held in the committee rooms of the House of Commons. The first of these meetings was addressed by Evan Williams, chairman of the Mining Association, and the second by Frank Hodges. In the course of his speech Hodges proposed a scheme for a temporary settlement of the wage issue, on a district basis – an idea quite opposed to the Miners' Executive's insistence that a wage settlement must be national, that is, applicable to the whole country. Keenly questioned by several members Hodges said blithely that he thought this scheme would provide an acceptable basis for negotiation. Hodges had no authority to speak on behalf of his Executive, which immediately disowned him; but the damage was done. The other leaders of the alliance thankfully threw in their hands, not because they objected to Hodges's suggestions, but because they said that by disowning him the miners had rejected the chance o a settlement. At three o'clock in the afternoon of 15th April, Jimmy Thomas came out of the conference room at Unity House, ran down the steps, and handed reporters an announcement that the strike was off.

Such was the day known in the Labour movement as Black Friday, which marked the end of what was bitterly called the Cripple Alliance. It would be difficult to exaggerate the effect of Hodges's slip. Thomas often afterwards met on the platform the cry: 'Who sold us on Black Friday?' Hodges was accused of deliberate betrayal, but there is no evidence that he realized the likely effect of his remarks. His resignation from the position of secretary was tendered but not accepted. Ernest Bevin said that there had been a grave lack of preparation and co-ordination on the part of the unions; and it is true that the basic defect of the Triple Alliance was that the transport workers and railwaymen had at this time no demands of their own, but were placing their own livelihoods in jeopardy simply for the sake of the miners. The practical results of the Triple Alliance's defeat were, in any case, very great. The miners had to resume work on the owners' terms, although they received help from a £10 million Government subsidy, and during the following year wage cuts were forced on many trades and industries, including engineers, shipyard workers and cotton operatives. No further attempt was made by the unions to act in concert, although at a distance this seems the lesson most obviously to be learned from Black Friday.

II
RED FRIDAY

The rise of the General Council of the Trades Union Congress was a logical result of Black Friday. The collapse of the Triple Alliance left the way open for any other body that could claim to speak for a mass of trade unionists: but although the idea of such a body was constantly discussed, for a long time the discussions had no practical result. Although the General Council had a mandate to act in trade union disputes, it was by no means certain that the bigger trade unions would be willing to accept the council's authority. Ernest Bevin, for one, did not like the idea of such a central authority, and he made an attempt to organize an Industrial Alliance, which would revive the Triple Alliance in a new form. Arguments about this were still going on when action was demanded by the mining crisis of 1925.

The French occupation of the Ruhr in 1923 had greatly eased the miners' position. Coal exports were, for a short time, higher than they had ever been, and the Miners' Federation was able to negotiate a new national agreement which provided for a substantially higher minimum wage. It is likely that the owners agreed to this as a temporary measure, because a Labour Government was in power and was threatening to bring in an Act which would have raised the miners' wages by law. A year later the boom was over; the Labour Government was out of office; and Baldwin's

Conservative Government had decided to return to the gold standard, thus forcing up the value of sterling in world markets and producing (as J. M. Keynes put it) 'an atmosphere favourable to the reduction of wages'. It was in such an atmosphere that the coal-owners proposed a joint inquiry with the miners into the 'extremely serious condition of the coal industry'.

The owners' position was simply stated. The export market for coal had dropped disastrously; prices were falling, and must fall further; and they suggested that a return to the wage structure of 1921, and the resumption of the eight-hour day, were essential. The miners' position was equally simple. The problem was, they said, one of 'under-consumption' caused by 'the general crisis of the capitalist world'. The short-term cure for it was more efficient production and cutting away of 'the waste and parasitic growth of profits'; and 'in any case, whether the price of coal to the consumer is lowered or not, the living wage of the miners (together with hours and conditions) must be *untouchable.* . . . The present wage is not a living wage'.

Two propositions so different were easily enough supported by pages of statistics – when, indeed, were these ever lacking to support any thesis? At last the owners broke this long-range shadow boxing by giving a month's notice that they were terminating the National Wages Agreement of 1924. They referred pointedly to the miners' refusal to consider an extension of the seven-hour day, and proposed a new wage structure which would have cut all wages very considerably, and abolished the minimum wage altogether. Because of the industry's complicated structure, and the variation in wages in different districts, it is difficult to express the exact financial meaning of the proposed wage cuts, but they were between 10 per cent and 25 per cent of the wages earned, and these wages varied between £2 and £4 a week.

The terms were thought harsh: but, as *The Times* said in a

sage editorial, sacrifices must be made all round, and the proposals were made in no spirit of hostility to the Miners' Federation. The suggestions might, indeed, be the only means of saving the industry and its workers from practical extinction. In a day or two *The Times* was tut-tutting over the miners' response. The terms suggested, they had said, gave no ground for discussion or negotiation, since the miners could not entertain the idea of any reduction of wages, or any lengthening of hours.

There are times when such intransigence is merely foolish; there are other times when, carefully calculated, it may yield good results; but there is every indication that the refusal of the Miners' Federation even to discuss the owners' terms was much influenced by the personalities of its president and secretary. Herbert Smith, who had become president of the Miners' Federation in 1922, was a remarkable character. He was a blunt, tough Yorkshireman, who had come up from the pits, and was in conference brusque and even rude; a man not pliable, who made up his mind to a course of action and stuck to his decision, almost regardless of consequences. Smith distrusted all mine-owners' representatives, most Tories, and even perhaps some of his own trade union colleagues. His concern for the miners was so deep and strong that it was sometimes felt that his interest in other trade unions was limited to the amount of support they were prepared to give the miners in their struggle for improved conditions. 'Git on ta t'field,' he urged the other representatives of the Triple Alliance, when they temporized before Black Friday. 'Git on ta t'field.' When in London for conferences Smith ate by preference at coffee stalls rather than at restaurants, and he attended meetings with his cloth cap in his pocket. He was not a negotiator. While argument went on about the possibility of accepting this or that compromise, Herbert Smith sat silent. If his opinion was asked directly he would often reply in two words: 'Nowt doin'.'

Smith's incapacity or unwillingness for argument was

over-amply compensated by the eloquence of the secretary, Arthur James Cook. When the Labour Government took office early in 1924 Frank Hodges was appointed Civil Lord of the Admiralty. Hodges was immensely ambitious, and he was still a young man, in his late thirties. He stood for election to Parliament under two misapprehensions: he thought that the Miners' Federation would relax in his case the rule by which the secretary must give his full time to the job, and he expected to be offered a Cabinet post. In the event the rules were not relaxed, in spite of an appeal made by Arthur Henderson, and Hodges did not get into the Cabinet. When the Labour Government fell later in the year he found himself out of office and out of Parliament.

The coal-owners had found it possible to negotiate with Hodges. They liked him personally, and felt him to be, by their standards, a reasonable man. Cook was anathema to them. He had entered the South Wales pits direct from his elementary school, and worked in them for twenty-one years. In youth he had been a preacher, and later he brought a revivalist flavour to the expression of left-wing opinions. He had been twice imprisoned for the part he played in strikes and lockouts, and his election to succeed Hodges was regarded as a triumph for the left-wing elements among the miners. Rightly so: for Cook's public speeches were full of violent rhetoric. He was proud, he said, to be a follower of Lenin; he was one of the Big Five in politics, and he would be more important yet; he looked forward with pleasure to the end of the British Empire. Government officials found it difficult to talk to him, for he persisted in ignoring the subject nominally under discussion while he harangued them about the miners' hardships. He spent almost every weekend making speeches to the pitmen, who loved him as they loved none of their other leaders. When Smith and Cook were brought to the conference table, however, it was Cook who was the easier to deal with.

As the July days passed it seemed unlikely that they would

be brought to the conference table. The Prime Minister, Stanley Baldwin, conferred with Colonel Lane-Fox, who was Secretary for Mines, and with W. C. Bridgeman, who had also held that post. About one thing the Government was quite firm: there could be nothing in the way of a subsidy to the miners. 'Speaking with a sense of extraordinary difficulty,' said the Minister of Labour, Sir Arthur Steel-Maitland, 'I can say quite openly and categorically that I do not think the coal industry ought to look for a subsidy to carry on.' With this said, Bridgeman was appointed as mediator. The owners firmly refused to withdraw the notices given to the men; Smith and Cook insisted that the notices must be withdrawn before negotiations took place. Long letters from Bridgeman were answered in single sentences by Cook; and when at last he managed to get owners and miners into the same room, it was to find Herbert Smith insisting that the Government must be a third party to the negotiations. Smith reminded them crudely that the miners wanted nationalization, but that Lloyd George's Coalition Government had refused it. 'You believe in private enterprise,' he said, 'although private enterprise has failed to function. It is your baby, which you must supply with milk.' Faced with such obstinacy, what could a poor Government do? Why, appoint a Court of Inquiry.

The Court of Inquiry met, the second in a year. Its members listened to the owners stating their case and asked some pointed questions. They had no chance to hear the miners because, as Cook said in a telegram, they could accept no Court of Inquiry that even considered the questions of reduction of wages or lengthening of hours. The sittings of the inquiry, at which not a single miner was present, had about them something slightly farcical; yet about the miners' absence there was also something ominous, a threat of concerted action.

Smith and Cook worked desperately to achieve such concerted action during these days of mid July. A sub-com-

mittee had been set up to work out the constitution of the
projected Industrial Alliance, but it was useless to rely for
support upon an organization that did not yet exist. The
miners therefore put their case to the General Council of the
TUC, and the General Council, seizing the chance to exert
authority in the whole trade union movement – and having
in mind, no doubt, that prompt action might scotch the
Industrial Alliance which would be in some sense its rival –
expressed whole-hearted support of the miners. This support
was to take a very practical form: the three-year-old Transport and General Workers' Union, acting in consultation
with the General Council, agreed to call a strike if necessary,
in support of the miners. The Associated Society of Locomotive Engineers and Firemen made a similar promise. The
miners, perhaps with a slight shiver of distrust when they
remembered the Triple Alliance, 'placed their case un-
reservedly in the hands of the General Council of the Trades
Union Congress as the supreme trade union committee',
and the General Council placed a complete embargo on the
movement of coal, to operate from 31st July, the day when
the employers' notices terminated.

Now at last Baldwin was compelled to enter the negotiations personally, and to engage in activities which must have
offended alike his desire for a peaceful life and his belief that
the Government should not interfere with industry. He met
a TUC deputation, which urged that the notices should be
withdrawn; he met the mine-owners, who refused to do any
such thing. On Wednesday, 29th July, he spent a weary and
fruitless day, talking all the morning to the miners and telling them that the Government could give no subsidy, talking all the afternoon to the owners (at one point taxis were
sent to bring the full committee of the owners to meet him),
and talking at nine o'clock that night to the General Council.

On this day the almost-forgotten Court of Inquiry issued
its report, which infuriated the owners and must have gravely
disconcerted the Government. The report came down

strongly in favour of a fixed minimum wage, and said that there was considerable room for improving the management, organization and development of the industry, and thus giving some aid to its economic position. That, *The Times* thought in its well-bred way, really settled the matter. The owners had no alternative but to suspend the notices and to withdraw their proposals. The paper expressed both surprise and distaste when the angry owners passed a resolution criticizing the Court of Inquiry, and flatly refusing to accept its report. King George V noted in his diary: 'I fear a strike now is inevitable at the end of the week. It will play the devil in the country.' It must have been with the feeling that he was being badly treated by those who should have been his best friends, that Baldwin resumed his discussions on Thursday.

Again he saw the miners in the morning. This time he offered an overall inquiry into the condition of the industry, in which they agreed to participate. What about a subsidy? they asked. No, he said, the Government could not give a subsidy. There followed a dialogue about which there was afterwards some dispute. Baldwin was said to have urged the miners to make some contribution towards meeting the nation's difficulties, and was asked if he meant a reduction of wages.

'Yes,' he said. 'All the workers in the country have got to face a reduction of wages.'

'What do you mean?'

'I mean all the workers of this country have got to take reductions in wages to help put industry on its feet.'

These statements were afterwards denied, and the official minute made at the time records that he did not use precisely these words, although he said something very similar in what was meant to be a confidential discussion. The miners, however, went back that day and gave their version of what Baldwin had said to a special Conference of Trade Union Executives which was meeting at Central Hall, Westminster.

The effect of this report was decisive. The conference not only approved the TUC embargo on coal, but empowered the TUC to give financial support to the strikers.

In the afternoon Baldwin was seen smoking his pipe on the balcony at the back of the Ministry of Labour, where these meetings were taking place, and talking to Steel-Maitland. Back to the owners, from whom he extracted some concessions, including agreement that there should be a minimum wage. Back again to the miners. 'What have you to give?' he asked, after telling them of the owners' concession.

'Nowt,' said Herbert Smith. 'We have nowt to give.'

'I can only repeat and emphasize', Baldwin said to them, 'that the Government can give no subsidy.'

When the miners left the ministry Cook said that they took the Prime Minister's statement as a declaration of war. That evening the instructions for the embargo on coal were given. They concerned railways, docks and wharves, waterways and locks and road transport, and amounted to a complete stoppage of the nation's transport. The Government had no effective organization to counter this embargo, and when the order went out Baldwin must have known that he was beaten.

At a quarter past five he left the Ministry of Labour for the House of Commons, and at six-thirty a vital Cabinet meeting began. What was said there remains unknown, but several members of the Cabinet must have been extremely reluctant to accept the course insisted on by Baldwin. Some three hours later Baldwin, the Chancellor of the Exchequer, Winston Churchill, and the Minister of Health, Neville Chamberlain, left the House of Commons and went back to the Ministry of Labour. There Baldwin saw first the miners, then the owners, and told them of the Government's decision. Fumbling in his pocket for his pipe when he saw the miners, and saying, 'Let's smoke, shall we?' he told them that the Government would give a subsidy to the industry until 1st May 1926. During that period there would be a full inquiry into the conditions of the industry, in which they had already agreed to participate. The owners, on their side, must withdraw the notices.

Discussion went on until after midnight on Thursday, and the terms were finally accepted by both sides at a quarter to four on Friday afternoon. With both owners and miners immovable, the Government had given way, buying nine months' peace in the mines with a subsidy that was estimated to cost £10 million and in fact cost £23 million. At four o'clock telegrams were sent out to the general secretaries of all district organizations in the coal industry:

Notices suspended. Work as usual. Cook. Secretary.

This was Red Friday.

III
REPERCUSSIONS

'So, thank God,' the king wrote in his diary, 'there will be no strike now.' *The Times* remarked calmly that the Government's decision was 'a victory for common sense, not for any of the parties concerned'. Thankfulness, however, was not the feeling uppermost in the minds of Tory members of Parliament. They had relied upon their leaders, and those leaders had allowed themselves to be blackmailed into submission. Members of the Cabinet had said again and again, in public speeches, that no question of a subsidy could be considered; Baldwin had repeated it as late as Thursday afternoon; and by Thursday evening, why, the subsidy had been granted. It would be hard to say whether the rank and file Tories were more distressed at the departure from the principles of private enterprise implied in the grant of a subsidy, or humiliated by the Government's sudden capitulation: but distress, humiliation and anger were theirs in full measure. The *Daily Express*, in an editorial headed 'Dane-geld', and the *Daily Mail*, in one headed 'A Victory for Vio-lence', expressed the feelings of the Tory back-benchers. Mis-taken steps can be retraced, the *Daily Express* warned, bad Governments can be dismissed; and it said, probably with truth, that 300 of the Government's supporters in the House of Commons condemned its action. The *Daily Mail*, with that eagerness for simplification, and for dealing with events in terms of personalities, characteristic of the popular press at all times, said that this had been a trial of strength between A. J. Cook and Stanley Baldwin, and that so far Cook had prevailed.

More important voices sang the same tune. The king's pri-vate secretary, Lord Stamfordham, said that he thought Baldwin had given way to syndicalist agitation. The Home Secretary, Sir William Joynson-Hicks, hinted at a split in the Cabinet. 'I say, coming straight from the Cabinet Coun-cils, that the danger is not over. Is England to be governed by Parliament and the Cabinet or by a handful of trade union leaders?' The coal-owners, although they would not suffer financially under the settlement, agreed with Joynson-Hicks. It was, said W. North Lewis, chairman of the South Wales Coal-owners' Association, a terrible disaster. A small minority of important Tories was in favour of the subsidy. Thus Neville Chamberlain noted in his diary that 'a stop-page of such magnitude and accompanied by such bitterness would inflict incalculable and irreparable damage upon the country', and that the subsidy was therefore justified. Besides, he thought that public opinion was inclined to sympathize with the miners.

On the other side feelings were, at first sight surprisingly, a little mixed. The TUC was naturally exultant; Ramsay MacDonald, the leader of the Parliamentary Labour Party, who was in constant touch with Lord Stamfordham, wrote to him of its triumphant mood. This was the first time that the General Council had acted on behalf of the trade union movement as a whole in such an emergency. Its tactics had been wholly successful, the announcement of the embargo on coal perfectly timed. The architects and organizers of victory on the trade union side were the Special Committee of the General Council, of which the chairman was A. B. Swales of the Engineers. Swales, who was also chairman of the TUC this year, was a powerful force in pushing through left-wing policies. Other members of the Special Committee who belonged to the left-wing of the General Council were George Hicks of the Building Trade Workers, and Alfred Purcell of the Furnishing Trades.

The miners owed much, also, to Smith and Cook, whose absolute refusal to make concessions of any kind had been abundantly justified. At their Delegate Conference in August, however, there was little tendency to self-congratulation. 'We have no need to glorify about a victory. It is only an armistice,' Herbert Smith said dourly in his opening speech, but he added that it was 'one of the finest things ever done by an organization'. Some delegates asked what had been the practical result of the struggle? Why, simply that there had been no *reduction* in what was still not a living wage. Had Cook asked for an increase, to meet the increased cost of living? one of the delegates asked Cook. And when he said he had, the delegate interjected: 'You did ask for the cost of living; then for God's sake give over talking about a glorious victory.' So differently can things look to those with opposed interests that these men were actually dissatisfied with the agreement, so fiercely fought for and with such difficulty obtained, by which their wages remained for nine months untouched.

Most of the criticism from the labour side, however, came from those right-wingers who saw in the temporary settlement a victory for what Ramsay MacDonald called 'the very forces that sane, well-considered, thoroughly well-examined Socialism feels to be probably its greatest enemy'. Incautious words these, for any 'victory' achieved had certainly been won by the General Council; and MacDonald hastily explained that his words had been intended to refer to the Communists, who were active at this time in the Miners' Minority Movement, but had no members on the General Council. Thomas, although his union had supported the coal embargo, said outright that the subsidy was wrong, and would prove a disaster to the country. Frank Hodges thought it 'a sure step in the direction of national bankruptcy', and in general the Parliamentary Labour Party felt little enthusiasm for a victory with which it had had nothing to do.

A week after the settlement Baldwin made a lame defence of his actions in the House of Commons. He anticipated his critics' complaints that 'the Government had a pistol put to their heads, and no Government ought to accept that', and replied that a spirit of higher statesmanship demanded that a subvention should be given to the industry while a committee or commission reported on it. He ended with a warning to those trade unionists who had 'the will to strife':

> If the will to strife should overcome the will to peace temporarily . . . let me say that no minority in a free country has ever yet coerced the whole community. The community will always protect itself, for the community must be fed, and it will see that it gets its food. And let me just say this, too: I am convinced that, if the time should come when the community has to protect itself, with the full strength of the Government behind it, the community will do so, and the response of the community will astonish the forces of anarchy throughout the world.

After the surprisingly mild debate that followed, Baldwin went off for his usual holiday at Aix-les-Bains.

Several years later Baldwin's biographer, G. M. Young, asked why he gave the subsidy. 'We were not ready,' he replied. This simple answer embodies the essential truth of the situation. The Government seems to have been quite unprepared for the unity shown by the trade unions in support of the miners. There was no organization for feeding the people or for arranging emergency transport, and an embargo on the movement of coal would quickly have strangled the whole of Britain's industrial life. Baldwin's aloofness from the struggle until the last week, and his insistence up to the last hours that a subsidy would not be given, may be seen as the result of genuine impercipience or as an attempt to carry through a gigantic bluff. When the time came he had no doubt of what must be done, and he convinced what Young calls 'an anxious and distrustful Cabinet' that his view must be accepted.

Those remarks about the community protecting itself were a warning. The organization to deal with the threat of another sympathetic strike, should it occur, was now to be created.

IV

THE GOVERNMENT PREPARES

Less than two months after the July settlement came the public announcement of the Government's first step. It was evident, said the statement which appeared in the press, that a movement was being organized to take advantage of difficulties in the coal industry.

> Numerous suggestions have since been made from various quarters for organizing those citizens who would be prepared to volunteer to maintain supplies and services in the event of a general strike.
>
> It seems, therefore, that the moment has come to announce publicly that such an organization has already been constituted and is at work in many metropolitan boroughs, while steps are being taken to create corresponding organizations in all the principal centres of the kingdom.

The president of the Organization for the Maintenance of Supplies, as it was called, was Lord Hardinge of Penshurst. Lord Ranfurly, Lord Jellicoe, Lord Falkland, Sir Rennell Rodd, Sir Alexander Duff, Sir Francis Lloyd, and other men who had at one time given notable service to the Government but had now retired from official participation in public affairs, were on the council. From such an arrangement the Government derived many advantages. Since the OMS (as it soon came to be called) was unofficial, and employed nobody in Government service, the Government could not be accused of acting provocatively: yet the names of the council members and of the president, who had been Viceroy of India, were sufficient guarantee that their unofficial activities had an official blessing. Committees had been formed in twenty-two of the twenty-eight metropolitan boroughs, and it was expected that the movement would spread almost at once to the provinces. Volunteers in five categories were called for: special constables (under forty-five years of age); workers to maintain public services; transport drivers; messengers and cyclists; and an unclassified group who would do clerical work or anything else not requiring technical skill.

In case some further assurance of Government sympathy might be required, Joynson-Hicks provided it with a letter to an unnamed, and perhaps fictional, correspondent, who had expressed doubts about the propriety of joining the OMS. If and when an emergency came, Joynson-Hicks said, the Government would discharge the responsibility which was theirs, and theirs alone, 'but it would be a very great assistance to us to receive from the OMS, or from any other body of well-disposed citizens, classified lists of men in different parts of the country who would be willing to place their services at the disposal of the Government'.

A statement was made, also, to allay labour suspicions. The OMS was strictly non-political and non-party in character, it was said, and had no aggressive or provocative aims.

It was not formed with the idea of opposing the legitimate efforts of trade unions to better the conditions of their members, and it was 'in complete sympathy with any constitutional action to bring about a more equitable adjustment of social or economic conditions'. It is doubtful if the organizers of the movement expected many labour or trade union leaders to be impressed by these good words: and, sure enough, all of them expressed an opposition to it which varied from the cloudy rhetoric of MacDonald and the cautious mistrust of Thomas to the outspoken denunciation of John Bromley and C. T. Cramp, the industrial secretary of the National Union of Railwaymen. Cramp, by no means a left-wing trade unionist, said sarcastically: 'Personally I have not the slightest fear of these jokers. They are people who have never worked in their lives. If they started to do it in a strike they would make a very poor job of it.'

'Certain funds', the original statement said, 'have been placed by a few patriotic citizens at the disposal of the council', and an appeal was made for public support, which was provided by contributions from many small and large firms. The OMS was launched.

The precise degree of success it achieved is not known, but it is said that a register of approximately 100,000 volunteers had been made when, just before the outbreak of the General Strike, the organization was handed over to the Government. It is said also that some factories possessing private railways put locomotives at the disposal of the OMS for training purposes, and that the organization bought several omnibuses to train drivers. If these stories are true, the training given must have been rudimentary, to judge from results; and it is a striking fact that among several hundred letters recounting strike experiences received by the writer, there is not one from anybody who had this kind of preliminary training.

Indeed, there are grounds for doubting whether the OMS register was as large as was afterwards stated. From an appeal for further volunteers made by Lord Hardinge in February

1926, in which he emphasized again that the OMS was 'no blackleg organization' and that 'its objective is the general strike – a wholly indefensible weapon', it would seem that the response was not at that time very satisfactory. An appeal to enrol for the purpose of dealing with some future, hypothetical danger is never one calculated to arouse enthusiasm, and it is likely that the number of volunteers in industrial areas, where they would be most needed, was comparatively small. Nevertheless the OMS list of volunteers was obviously useful; and it took the limelight in a way that tended to conceal the Government's own unobtrusive activities.

A disproportionate amount of attention was also given at this time to the proclamations of the British Fascists. The Fascists were not a political party, but a quasi-military group of the extreme right, headed by a retired brigadier-general and rear-admiral. They made a night raid on Communist headquarters in London, kidnapped Harry Pollitt, and engaged in other exploits. Before the outbreak of the strike, however, most of the Fascists merged with the OMS. Like the OMS they served as a smoke-screen for more serious preparations.

When the railway workers struck in 1919 an elaborate emergency supply and transport system was worked out under the control of Sir Eric Geddes, at that time Minister of Transport. This system was not fully tested at the time, and in the following years it lapsed almost completely. In 1923 the task of reviving it was put into the hands of J. C. C. Davidson, Chancellor of the Duchy of Lancaster. A groundwork had been laid, no more, when the first Labour Government came to power, and Davidson, handing over to Josiah Wedgwood, asked him not to destroy what had been done. The Labour Government was immediately confronted with a railway strike, and the Labour leaders were appalled by the inadequacy of the existing arrangements for handling supplies. Wedgwood was appointed Civil Commissioner with responsibility for inaugurating a supply and transport

B

system, and an emergency proclamation was drafted. The strike ended within a few days; the emergency proclamation was never issued and the project was allowed to lapse. When, after a few months, the Labour Government went out of office and Wedgwood handed over again to Davidson, he said: 'I haven't destroyed any of your plans. In fact I haven't done a bloody thing about them.' The plan remained a skeleton until Red Friday taught the Government a lesson.

Immediately after the settlement it was decided that an organization similar to that of 1919 must be set up; and not merely set up, but kept in readiness in case of trouble, not this month or next month, but this year or next year. The choice of a man to administer the scheme is interesting for the light it casts upon the difference in temperament and methods between Churchill and Baldwin. Churchill wanted to recall Geddes, who had resigned from public office in 1922, and put him in the position of supreme co-ordinator of a widely publicized organization. Geddes was a man of great energy and ability, as he had shown during his term of office as Minister of Labour: but such an appointment must have aroused the most violent trade union hostility, for Geddes's work as chairman of the committee on national expenditure, and the employment of what was called 'the Geddes axe' in cutting wages, had made his name hated by the organized workers. Baldwin preferred that the whole thing should be done as quietly as possible, and the chairman of the small Emergency Committee which met every week was a civil servant, at that time unknown to the public, named John Anderson.

Anderson was Permanent Under-Secretary to the Home Office. He was in his early forties, and had already a distinguished career in the Civil Service behind him. His mind was logical, orderly and clear; his capacity as an organizer immense; his temperament impatient of rhetoric, whether Churchillian or other; his expression of opinion brisk to the point of curtness, with none of the hesitations and dubieties attributed (perhaps inaccurately) to civil servants: a man, certainly, eager to take rather than to avoid responsibility and for that reason as well as others congenial to Baldwin. At the weekly meetings of the Emergency Committee on supply and transport, on which all the departments likely to be concerned in a general strike were represented (including the services departments), a complete scheme was worked out to keep the food and transport services of the country in operation throughout any period of stoppage. Before the end of November the general outline of this scheme was made clear by the issue of Circular 636 from the Ministry of Health to local authorities. England and Wales were to be divided into ten divisions (there was a separate scheme for Scotland), each under a civil commissioner. These civil commissioners were generally junior ministers. Each had a principal officer attached to him, and each commissioner had a large measure of autonomy in his own area. Each section had also a coal, finance and food officer. The local authorities were to operate in conjunction with these commissioners in the event of a stoppage, to control road transport, food and fuel supplies. Each commissioner was deputed to maintain law and order in his own area, and to recruit 'able-bodied citizens of good character to serve as special constables'. Lord Winterton, one of the commissioners, says, 'We were given further instructions in the event of a complete breakdown, to take drastic action of a comprehensive character.' Since the complete breakdown never came, the nature of these instructions is matter for conjecture.

The most important part of the scheme concerned road transport. The haulage contractors of the nation were organized into 150 local committees, and the Government arranged to relieve all haulage contractors of their existing contracts by declaring legal priority in the transport of essential commodities. The road commissioners and road officers in each district had requisitioning powers, but by making business men themselves responsible for the operation of haulage committees, the Government hoped to avoid the bad feeling that would be caused by requisitioning.

The circular outlining this scheme received remarkably little notice; Parliamentary comment was confined to questions asked by the Labour member for Lincoln, who complained that town clerks in various places were receiving letters marked 'Secret', and that in these letters they were asked to accept posts, or recommend suitable people for posts, in the organization. (Perhaps this request for recommendations was prompted by an uncomfortable memory of the way in which volunteers had driven away trucks and vans in 1919, never to be seen again.) Joynson-Hicks replied, almost casually, that these letters no doubt came from the local representatives of the Government departments concerned, and that he rather agreed with the questioner in thinking that they should not be marked 'Secret'. The leaders of the Labour Party seem to have been unaware of the preparations being made: or perhaps, of course, they silently approved of them.

As the weeks of winter and spring passed, the general outline of the circular was filled in, with such details as the special air service arranged for important documents, the plans for naval personnel to move into power stations where necessary, and the detailed organization of a convoy system for food. Stocks of food, coal and fuel were built up. By the spring of 1926 the Government was ready for any trouble that might be coming.

With such elaborate preparations made, it was possible that trouble might not come. Is it not always said that the strongest assurance of peace is to be well armed? At a dinner-party given early in the new year by Sir Arthur Steel-Maitland, the possibilities of a general strike were discussed, and both Steel-Maitland and the Minister for Mines, Colonel Lane-Fox, said that they feared a coal strike was likely. Baldwin and Churchill were also present at the dinner-party.

The Prime Minister's remarks are not remembered, but Churchill at least was optimistic. In the intervals of gnawing the cutlet which he held in his fist he told the assembled company that their fears were groundless, and that 1926 would be the most prosperous year Britain had seen since the war.

V

THE TRADE UNIONISTS TALK

The miners' reaction to the July settlement has already been shown. They were pleased, but they were aware also that this famous victory had not put a penny into their pockets. Smith and Cook made no pretence that the struggle was over. 'The fight is only beginning,' Cook said in a speech made two days after the settlement, and he warned the Government that although the miners had agreed to a Royal Commission they would not be satisfied with one 'composed of politicians, economists, lawyers, and captains of industry'. The General Council, in a letter sent out on Red Friday, also stressed that the trade union movement must remain alert, 'in case the necessity should again arise for it to act in defence of its standards'. Purcell, a left-wing member of the council, who had recently headed a delegation to the Soviet Union, said that 'at the end of nine months we shall have prepared for the struggle to come'.

With all this awareness of the coming struggle, how did it happen that in the nine months between Red Friday and the General Strike the trade unions made no effective preparations at all? The answer lies in the struggle for power which was being waged by the General Council during the whole period, in the changed character of the TUC after the Scarborough Congress of September 1925, and in the inherent difficulty of making such preparations.

At the Scarborough Congress Swales made a powerful speech in favour of a militant policy, which he called 'the only policy that will unify, consolidate and inspire our rank and file'. He also repeated the General Council's claim to act as a central controlling body in settling disputes, and urged that it should be given 'full powers to create the necessary machinery to combat every movement by our opponents'. These powers had by no means been granted. Red Friday had been a trial run, and a highly successful one: but the big unions were still very reluctant to abandon their right to individual action, and with it inevitably some of their power. The idea of the Industrial Alliance was still in the air, and although there was in theory no reason why the General Council and the Industrial Alliance should not co-operate, in practice such co-operation was unlikely. A paragraph about the eventual fate of the Industrial Alliance will indicate the pitfalls in the way of those who wished to organize the unions for joint action.

The basic idea of the alliance had been accepted before Red Friday, but it was not until September that the Miners, Foundry Workers, Electrical Trades Union and ASLEF agreed to it. Two months later a Delegate Conference of the various unions concerned met, and accepted the draft constitution. Was the alliance, then, an accomplished fact? Not at all. Several of the unions had to take ballots of their membership, and the results of these ballots were not known until February or March. Thomas's NUR caused trouble by suggesting the fusion of different unions in any given industry. This was resented by ASLEF as a blow at its individual existence. All these delays killed the alliance. It was still not ready for action when the General Strike came, and thereafter no more was heard of it.

The left-wing policies endorsed at the Scarborough Congress were mostly verbal, like the expression of 'complete opposition' to imperialism, and the motion supporting the right of all peoples in the British Empire to self-determination, with the right of secession; and such effect as they had was negated by changes in the balance of the council after Scarborough. Swales resigned as chairman, and his place was taken by Arthur Pugh, who was further to the right of the movement than Swales had been to the left. With the Labour Party out of office J. H. Thomas returned to the council, from which he had been absent for two years, and Ernest Bevin was elected to it for the first time. These last two changes were particularly significant, because of the esteem in which Thomas and Bevin were held.

The Industrial Committee of the TUC was told to keep in touch with the situation. No doubt it did so: but it did nothing more. Nothing whatever was being done in the way of preparation during weeks in which Cook was rushing up and down the country, making speeches that must have deeply alarmed the middle class. 'I don't care a hang for any government, or army or navy,' he said. 'We have already beaten, not only the employers, but the strongest government in modern times.' He went on: 'We shall prepare the machine and prepare a commissariat department. I am going to get a fund, if I can, in London that will buy grub, so that when the struggle comes, and indeed before it comes, we shall have that grub distributed in the homes of our people.' His own mother-in-law, Cook told a meeting at TUC headquarters in Eccleston Square, had been taking in an extra tin of salmon for weeks past. There was silence while this information was absorbed. Then Thomas said: 'By God! A British revolution based on a tin of salmon.'

So the weeks and months of 1925 passed, with the Industrial Committee keeping in touch with the situation, the Industrial Alliance still in embryo, and Cook making speeches that had no relation to facts. Such unpreparedness is pathetic: yet it is true that, as an American historian has said, there were great difficulties in the way of taking positive action. It is certain that no action thought of as 'provocative' would have been tolerated. Several left-wing groups proposed that Workers' Defence Corps should be formed in opposition to the OMS and the Fascists. The idea was condemned by the General Council and by the Labour Party, and no proposition of this sort had the slightest chance of acceptance by the trade union movement as a whole. The organization of many unions, also, was so cumbrous that (as has been seen in relation to the Industrial Alliance) speedy decisions were almost impossible. Nobody knew when an industrial stoppage might come, or what unions might be involved in it. Cook's speeches, however much they may have inspired the miners, infuriated other sections of the Labour movement. When he airily said that in the coming struggle the Co-operative movement would be 'the victualling movement for the fighting forces of labour', the secretary of the Co-operative Union denied that any such arrangement had been made and said that it was a pity Cook could not be muzzled.

Yet, when everything has been said, it does seem extraordinary that the General Council made no attempt to work out the skeleton plan of an organization dealing with food and transport, or even to consider how communications might be maintained between various parts of the country, in case of an industrial crisis. The signs of Government preparations were plain to see, although their full extent was hidden: in face of them the Industrial Committee contented itself with a pious statement, made after a meeting with the miners, that the position of the trade union movement was that 'there was to be no reduction in wages, no increase in working hours, and no interference with the principle of national agreements'. In effect the trade union leaders, like the leaders of the Parliamentary Labour Party, pinned their faith to the Royal Commission on the Coal Industry, rather in the spirit of impresarios who believe that, however unfortunate may have been the incidents at rehearsal, everything will be all right on the night.

VI

THE SAMUEL COMMISSION

It was in August, while Baldwin was at Aix-les-Bains, that he sent a telegram to Sir Herbert Samuel and asked him to be chairman of the proposed Royal Commission. Samuel had held many governmental and Cabinet posts, in the Liberal Government of 1905 and later, and had only recently returned from Palestine, where he had been British High Commissioner since 1919. He had looked forward to a period of retirement from active life, in which he could write a philosophical work about the failure of belief in the modern world. This was a subject that much occupied him. He believed that if he could clear his own mind of the doubts that assailed it, and arrive at some definite basis of belief, what he wrote could hardly fail to be helpful to others.

When Baldwin represented to Samuel, however, that his lack of any special knowledge of the coal industry was a qualification for chairmanship of the commission rather than the reverse, because 'fresh minds should be brought to bear', he accepted the position. It was possibly also a qualification that he was known to be opposed to nationalization of the mines. Nor were his three colleagues likely to be more kindly disposed towards the solution recommended by the majority vote of the Sankey Commission. Sir William Beveridge was already known as an orthodox Liberal economist; he had resigned recently from the Civil Service to become director of

* B

the London School of Economics. Sir Herbert Lawrence, who had been Haig's chief of staff during the war, was a managing partner in the banking house of Glyn, Mills. Kenneth Lee was a cotton manufacturer, chairman of the cotton firm of Tootal, Broadhurst & Lee, and also of the District Bank. It will be seen that the Government had avoided the mistake made by Lloyd George's administration in 1919. The new Royal Commission included no representative of labour, nor any person who had even a remote knowledge of the coal industry.

The commission sat in a large room adjoining Westminster Hall, and its sessions were crowded with newspaper reporters and members of the public. The commissioners took evidence between 15th October 1925 and mid January of the following year. They heard nearly eighty witnesses from both sides of the industry, including Smith and Cook for the miners, and the Duke of Northumberland and the chairman of the mine-owners, Evan Williams, on the other side. They received also a great mass of written evidence, and visited twenty-five mines in various parts of Great Britain. They also received from mines inspectors special reports on over forty mines, about which complaint had been made by the Miners' Federation.

About the proceedings of such a commission there must always be something faintly absurd. Four wise men sit down to consider the workings of an immensely complicated industry: an industry which has a whole terminology of its own; in which the wage structure is so complicated that days of explanation are required before it is understood; in which local feelings, customs and conditions vary remarkably from place to place. When they have listened to what people have to say who really know something about the industry, these four wise men go away and produce a report telling miners and owners what should be done. With judgment pronounced they go back to their own concerns, to cotton or banking or economics or the construction of a system of belief: they have no further direct concern with the coal industry.

Is not this an absurd procedure? Is it not plain that Governments themselves are really the only bodies who can solve such problems as were presented by the coal industry in the nineteen-twenties, problems that had been stated and restated before this commission, and that and the other Court of Inquiry; so that the Samuel Commission, solemnly listening to them restated once again, could differ in their recommendations only by the degree of their personal prejudices? For only governments can say whether, in times of depression, they wish miners to suffer; or owners to suffer; or whether the rest of the community, or some part of it, should subsidize unprofitable mines. The deliberations of the Liberal doubter in search of a philosophy, and his fellow commissioners, could elicit nothing new. It was the philosophy of the Government that decided the fate of the mines.

The Samuel Commission's Report was published early in March, a Blue Book of some three hundred pages which cost a shilling. Interest in it was so great that the volume was reissued at threepence, and sold in all over 100,000 copies. The report, which was unanimous, made many suggestions for reorganizing the industry. It recommended, not nationalization of the mines, but state ownership of the royalties accruing from them; amalgamation of many small, unprofitable mines; research into the scientific use of coal and its derivatives; the introduction of family allowances, profit-sharing schemes and pithead baths; and many other comparatively minor but important reforms. Samuel thought the report very favourable to the miners, and when he saw it Cook said exultantly that it gave them 80 per cent of what they had asked. This 80 per cent, however, was all in the future – for instance, the amalgamation of small mines into larger, efficient units was to be carried out compulsorily only if, after some years, it was found that voluntary methods failed. All of the points favourable to the miners were

distantly beneficial in a similar way: the suggestions unfavourable to them were to be put into effect immediately.

These related to hours and wages. The commission said
that a temporary reduction of wages was inevitable. The reductions it suggested were considerably smaller than those
the owners had claimed. The question of increased hours
was left in the hands of the miners themselves, by the suggestion that it was a matter for them if they preferred increased hours to reduced wages. The commission was
strongly opposed to the continuance of the subsidy which, it
said, 'should stop at its authorized term, and should never
be repeated'.

The commissioners felt that they had dealt justly, and
even generously, with the miners; and so, in terms of figures,
they had. In a few years' time, if all the commission's recommendations were carried out, working conditions in the minefields would be greatly improved. But improved working
conditions in the future fill no stomachs now: and the miners'
case had been, all along, that their wages were already so
low that decent living was impossible for them. This case
had never been seriously disputed. Evan Williams himself
had agreed that the wages in some districts, with no lengthening of the seven-hour working day, would be miserable.
The victory of July had not raised wages anywhere by so
much as a shilling, and now they were to be appreciably reduced for an unspecified length of time. That, simply stated,
was the miners' attitude to the report. The owners' attitude
also remained unchanged. Whatever sympathy for the
miners might be implied in that remark of Evan Williams
was nullified by the hard economic facts. A large proportion
of the minefields were producing at a loss. Therefore, pend-
ing the results of the reorganizations and amalgamations
proposed by the commission (and the owners did not by any
means accept its strictures on the present organization)
wages must be reduced. It was as simple as that.

It was not Baldwin's way to hurry. The report had been

published for a fortnight before he met owners and miners and read a statement which said that, although some of the recommendations contained proposals to which the Government was opposed, it would 'be prepared to undertake such measures as may be required of the State to give the recommendations effect', provided that both owners and miners accepted the report and agreed 'to carry on the industry on the basis of its recommendations'. This statement might mean much or nothing; it was essentially in accordance with Baldwin's often-expressed belief that the Government should not interfere with the conduct of industry. To its cautious suggestions the owners gave cautious acceptance. They did not agree with the commission, but would 'do their utmost to give effect to the objects aimed at in the recommendations' if the miners would accept a reduction in wages at once.

The miners refused, flatly, to accept the report. 'I do not object to being plain,' Herbert Smith said to the owners at the end of March. 'We are willing to do all we can to help this industry, but it is with this proviso, that when we have worked and given our best, we are going to demand a respectable day's wage for a respectable day's work; and that is not your intention.' The slogan that Cook had coined some time before was revived: 'Not a penny off the pay, not a second on the day.'

It was thought that such statements and slogans concealed some subtle strategy. In fact Smith and Cook had no conscious strategy at all, nothing but an unshakable faith in the justice of their cause. Their strategic innocence was manifest in the firing of these first shots in the campaign. Public sympathy with the miners was very general, but it was somewhat alienated by their leaders' apparent inflexibility. The commission had made recommendations; the Government and owners had accepted them; only the miners stood out. That was not precisely the truth of the matter, but it seemed the truth to many people. The stubborn silence of Smith and the wild verbal shadow-boxing of Cook ('A strike of the miners would mean the end of capitalism,' he said in one place, and in another, '97 per cent of the new recruits to the police and armed services have come from the working classes, and thousands of them miners, who will not shoot against their kith and kin when the order comes') deepened a general impression that these were men with whom it was impossible to negotiate.

PART II
THE DAYS BEFORE

I
DEADLOCK

The first three weeks of April passed in negotiations entered with the utmost apparent seriousness, but known in advance to be almost certainly futile. Meetings of owners' and miners' representatives, miners' conferences, meetings of industrial committees, proposals about district minimums and percentages, appeals to the Prime Minister: it was the July days of 1925 over again, with the difference that this time the Government, strong in the knowledge that it was prepared for anything, was making no concessions.

In these circumstances Baldwin's not very strenuous efforts to obtain a settlement were easily defeated by the owners' and miners' pigheadedness. It is the essence of negotiation that there shall be at least the appearance of flexibility on both sides. The proposals made may be wildly impractical, the merest kites in the wind; nevertheless they provide at least the possibility of discussion and argument. All this was ruled out by the owners' rigid attitude (Birkenhead said afterwards that he thought the miners' leaders the most stupid men he had ever met, until he met the owners), by Herbert Smith's broad-bottomed refusal to budge from his original position, and by Cook's heady vision of revolution. At one conference Smith took out his dentures, cleaned them with his handkerchief, and replaced them, before saying

with his usual deliberateness, 'Nowt doin'.' Such an attitude could have its justification only in the very exceptional
circumstances of the previous July. Now Herbert Smith's incapacity for bargaining, and his belief in the efficacy of
direct trade union action, were disastrous. Beatrice Webb's
scornful dismissal of Herbert Smith as 'senile' and of Cook
as an 'inspired idiot' were wide of the mark. It was perfectly
true, however, that they lacked the easy pliability of successful trade union negotiators. Their intransigence received
encouragement from the growth of the Minority Movement
among the miners. This Communist-backed movement, of
which Harry Pollitt was the secretary, and which cook supported, held a meeting in March which claimed to represent
a million workers. Here a motion by delegate Arthur
Horner urging that each Trades Council should 'constitute
itself a Council of Action by mobilizing all the forces of the
working-class movement in its locality' and that the General
Council should convene a 'National Congress of Action'
was adopted by acclamation.

In the second week of April the Industrial Committee
arranged that Ramsay MacDonald and Arthur Henderson
should attend meetings and negotiations. This had the effect
of bringing leaders of the Parliamentary Labour Party
closely into touch with the position for the first time. All of
these leaders – MacDonald, Snowden, Thomas, Clynes,
Henderson – were unequivocally opposed to the idea of a
General Strike. Their experience of the railway strike when
taking office had given them a poor opinion of governmental ability to resist a general stoppage; and if they feared
that defeat of the strikers would be a blow for Labour, they
perhaps feared even more that a victorious strike would be
a harder blow for the Labour leadership. The Independent
Labour Party, which was then at the peak of its power, represented in theory the left-wing of the party; but in fact the
ILP, with its thousand branches and its wide membership,
was less an organization for action than a forum for ideas.

Beatrice Webb noted the fragmentation of the Labour movement very clearly in her diary:

> The leaders so seldom see each other and are so reticent when they do meet. The ILP has a life of its own: the Clyde is self-contained, the trade union officials are dispersed in their homes all over the country and live within their own occupational circles.

The entry of MacDonald and Henderson on to the scene certainly seemed to increase the likelihood of a negotiated settlement. It was widely felt that some sort of settlement was inevitable, even when the owners posted notices in most pits to end existing contracts on 30th April, the day on which the subsidy ran out. The days of April passed, however, and no settlement came.

II

THE STRIKE DECISION

On Thursday, 29th April, a Conference of Trade Union Executives met at Farringdon Hall to discuss the situation. Bevin said later that no preparations for a national strike had been made until the Tuesday of that week, when he sat down with Purcell to draft a plan of campaign – a plan which must necessarily have been tentative, because the attitude of the unions could not be known in advance. This dilatoriness (why was the conference not called a week earlier?) is attributable partly to the almost mystic faith felt in the certainty of a settlement, partly to lack of enthusiasm among the majority of the General Council for any militant action.

The conference listened to an explanation of the situation by Arthur Pugh, heard that the Industrial Committee was negotiating with the Prime Minister, heard Thomas move that they endorse the efforts of the General Council to reach an honourable settlement, and heard Ernest Bevin make a savage attack on the Parliamentary Labour Party for its cowardice in failing to make a statement in the House of Commons about miners' wages. He warned them that in twenty-four hours they might have to cease separate existence for the time and 'become one union with no autonomy'. The tone and substance of Bevin's speech roused great enthusiasm. Thomas defended the Parliamentary Party on the ground that they had been specifically asked by the miners not to interfere in an industrial dispute, and the conference adjourned until Friday.

On Friday they sang hymns and popular songs, and waited for news. From three o'clock in the afternoon until eleven o'clock at night they waited, getting occasional messages ('the Special Industrial Committee is still with the Government'). A young journalist who spent much time around the gloomy Memorial Hall found the delegates placid, pipe-smoking, genial, mostly wearing tweeds and caps from the Co-op, and very respectful of the trade union great. The journalist sensed also a fighting mood among them, a mood which infected those who stood waiting in the lobby and the street. Just before half past eleven that night the committee returned. Pugh read a letter from the Prime Minister to Herbert Smith, in which he said that the owners were prepared to offer a national minimum wage representing a 13 per cent cut in wages if the miners agreed to work an eight-hour day.

The terms, which Baldwin passed on without comment, were far worse than those suggested by the Samuel Commission. Thomas, who addressed the meeting, pointed out that it was five weeks ago that the Government had said that it accepted the commission's report, but only now, when 40,000 men were already locked out, had any definite offer been obtained from the owners. This offer he described as one which 'would have meant such degrading terms, that I refuse to believe there is any decent-minded man or woman who would tolerate it'. He continued:

> My friends, when the verbatim reports are written, I suppose my usual critics will say that Thomas was almost grovelling, and it is true. In all my long experience – and I have conducted many negotiations – I say to you – and my colleagues will bear testimony to it – I never begged and pleaded like I begged and pleaded all day today.

Thomas's eloquence had been given to asking, not for a settlement, but simply for suspension of the notices so that negotiations could go on. The Cabinet had refused to interfere. The OMS had passed over its roll of members to the Government, and one of its placards calling for recruits had been posted throughout the country. The Emergency Powers Act had been signed, and at about the time Thomas was making his speech John Reith, managing director of the BBC, received a message from Downing Street requesting that an announcement about the coal stoppage should be broadcast at once.

On Saturday morning the general secretaries of the various unions said whether or not they were prepared to hand over their autonomy to the General Council during the emergency, and whether they approved the proposal for a national strike to begin at midnight on Monday, 3rd May. (The word 'general' was not used by the unions in reference to the strike.) When the roll was called, the first on the list was the Union of Asylum Workers. They voted 'Yes' among some laughter. Great enthusiasm was shown at the result of the ballot: 3,653,527 in favour, 49,911 against. Bevin made a speech, John Bromley made a speech, Herbert Smith made a speech: very good speeches, most of them. Pugh made a short speech, pointing out that the scheme required that the Miners' Federation hand over to the General Council the conduct of the dispute: a statement accepted unquestioningly, which was to cause much argument at a later time.

MacDonald made a speech, not very good, about the sands being emptied in the glass, and the sword being drawn.

They sang the Red Flag. MacDonald, although he had often said that the tune was a very poor one, joined in. It was all over.

III
DRAMA BECOMES FARCE

But it was not all over. The Executive of the Miners' Federation were going back to their homes to mobilize the miners in support of the strike, and various unions were issuing strike orders; on the Government side departments were sending out detailed instructions, troop movements were being announced, civil commissioners and their staffs were preparing for action; May Day marchers were cheering the news, the intellectuals among them only half believingly ('It is like asking for an elephant or a dragon,' one of them wrote in his diary. 'And, lo, here it is walking up the garden path'): yet it was not all over. While these preparations were being made upon both sides the General Council was sending a message to Baldwin, saying that it was ready to see him.

Some such development might have been expected, for whereas the union representatives thought they had voted unconditionally in favour of a national strike, the General Council interpreted the vote as placing the conduct of affairs completely in its hands, to organize a strike or arrange a settlement. Nevertheless this approach was later to become the subject of harsh comment. At about half past eight on Saturday night a delegation from the General Council came to see Baldwin and they began to discuss the Samuel Report, a report which the miners had rejected and which the General Council had itself condemned. Concealing what must have been his surprise, Baldwin suggested that they might make progress with a smaller number than the nine trade unionists and six members of the Cabinet who were now talking. A small committee was then formed with three members on each side – for the Government, Baldwin, Birkenhead and Steel-Maitland, and for the General Council, Pugh, Thomas and Swales. They sat down, with Sir Horace Wilson on one side and the acting general secretary of the TUC, Walter Citrine, on the other as note-takers, to try to work out what was later called a 'formula'. After some hours of discussion they seemed to have reached one. The lock-out and strike notices should be withdrawn; the subsidy would be continued for a fortnight; and within that time the TUC representatives felt confident that a settlement could be reached on the lines of the report. It is hard to understand why they should have felt such confidence; had Thomas and Pugh let their distaste for the idea of a general strike outweigh their recollection that the miners had already rejected the report? With mutual expressions of goodwill the sub-committees parted. The trade unionists told Baldwin that they would see the miners on Sunday morning and find out their opinion of the formula. Baldwin summoned a Cabinet for midday on Sunday.

When Citrine tried to get in touch with the miners' leaders, he found that only Cook was left in London. Of the miners' two representatives on the General Council one was ill and the other, Robert Smillie, had gone to prepare for the strike in Scotland. Cook reproached the General Council violently for approaching the Government behind the miners' backs. The reproaches were mutual, for the General Council expressed itself astonished that the miners' Executive should have left London at such a time. This was the first of several misunderstandings. The miners thought that the vote at the Memorial Hall marked a final decision about the strike, and expected consultation with their Executive at every point.

The General Council, as has been seen, thought that it had a mandate to conduct negotiations and reach a settlement, using the strike weapon only as a last resort. Cook was particularly incensed by the attitudes of Thomas and Bromley, who said that the railwaymen had had to accept reductions, and that the miners must do the same.

In the meantime the Cabinet waited for word from the trade unionists. There was a good deal of uneasiness among them about the 'formula', which was felt to be suspiciously like a concession. When no word came they dispersed for lunch and met later in the afternoon. Still there was no word from Eccleston Square. The trade unionists were not locked in argument, as may have been thought. They had simply forgotten to telephone the Prime Minister.

Cook sent off telegrams summoning the Miners' Executive back to London. While waiting for the miners to return, the General Council decided to raise further unsettled matters. Back on Sunday evening went Pugh, Thomas and Swales for more talks. From these, after an hour or two, Birkenhead produced a second 'formula', in the following masterly sentence:

> We the TUC would urge the miners to authorize us to enter upon discussions with the understanding that they and we accept the report as a basis of settlement and we approach it with the knowledge that it may involve some reduction in wages.

Could anything be vaguer? One gets the impression, however, that the formula's very vagueness pleased the negotiators. 'Never mind what the miners or anybody else say, we accept it,' said Thomas. By 'we' he meant the TUC and, as he emphasized, the General Council of the TUC was the body responsible for negotiations. At the same time Pugh, rather confusingly, said that although they could negotiate, they could not take a decision without the miners. Swales, who might have been expected to protest against the formula, was the least vocal of the three. On the Government side

Birkenhead, who was regarded as one of the least conciliatory of the Cabinet, was happy with the formula.

Armed with this precious document the TUC sub-committee left the Cabinet room, where these discussions had
taken place, and went to the Treasury board-room, where it
had been arranged that they should meet the miners. Could
Smith, Cook and the others possibly have accepted the
formula? That question was not put to the test, for the
miners' leaders, who had returned to London by train and
car, never saw it. Neither, according to Citrine, did the
General Council as a body. Discussions had only just begun
when a messenger came with a request from Baldwin that
the sub-committee should return to the Cabinet room at
once.

There they found the Prime Minister, solemn-faced. He
handed Pugh a letter and said that their efforts for peace had
been unavailing, but that he had wanted to say a last personal
word. 'Goodbye, I am sorry,' he said. 'This is the end.'

IV
THE 'DAILY MAIL' LEADER

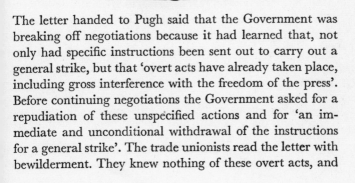

The letter handed to Pugh said that the Government was
breaking off negotiations because it had learned that, not
only had specific instructions been sent out to carry out a
general strike, but that 'overt acts have already taken place,
including gross interference with the freedom of the press'.
Before continuing negotiations the Government asked for a
repudiation of these unspecified actions and for 'an immediate and unconditional withdrawal of the instructions
for a general strike'. The trade unionists read the letter with
bewilderment. They knew nothing of these overt acts, and

were amazed by the contrast between the tone of this letter and that of their earlier conversations.

This is what had happened. The Government sub-committee retired at half past eleven at night to report progress to the rest of the Cabinet, who had by now been kicking their heels for several hours, and were not in the best of tempers. Baldwin, exhausted, dropped into an arm-chair, and Birkenhead read out the second formula, and described the negotiations. There was a sharp division of opinion. 'Some of us,' said Amery, 'would have been prepared to continue negotiations so long as there was the faintest chance of an agreement': others were determined that no concession of any kind should be made. The leaders of this second group were Churchill, Neville Chamberlain (who felt that the time had come for action) and Joynson-Hicks; on the other side it seems that Birkenhead was inclined towards a settlement, and Baldwin was thought by some of his colleagues to be more sympathetic than was proper to the cause of organized labour. While discussions were going on a telephone message came through from the *Daily Mail* with the news that the NATSOPA chapel had refused to print the paper.

This refusal was prompted by an editorial which came from the hand of the editor himself. This editor, Thomas Marlowe, was an extreme right-wing Tory (it was the *Daily Mail* that, nearly two years before, had given the news of the Zinoviev letter to the world): and his editorial, 'For King and Country', was regarded, not only by NATSOPA members, but by other union chapels at the paper, as an incitement to strike-breaking. Read thirty years later, it does not seem very provocative:

> The miners after weeks of negotiation have declined the proposals made to them and the coal-mines of Britain are idle.
> The Council of Trades Union Congress, which represents all the other trade unions, has determined to support

the miners by going to the extreme of ordering a general strike.

This determination alters the whole position. The coal industry, which might have been reorganized with good-will on both sides, seeing that some 'give and take' is plainly needed to restore it to prosperity, has now become the subject of a great political struggle, which the nation has no choice but to face with the utmost coolness and the utmost firmness.

We do not wish to say anything hard about the miners themselves. As to their leaders, all we need say at this moment is that some of them are (and have openly declared themselves) under the influence of people who mean no good to this country.

A general strike is not an industrial dispute. It is a revolutionary movement intended to inflict suffering upon the great mass of innocent persons in the community and thereby to put forcible constraint upon the Government.

It is a movement which can only succeed by destroying the Government and subverting the rights and liberties of the people.

This being the case, it cannot be tolerated by any civilized Government and it must be dealt with by every resource at the disposal of the community.

A state of emergency and national danger has been proclaimed to resist the attack.

We call upon all law-abiding men and women to hold themselves at the service of King and country.

The stereotypers had cast the plates for the article, but the machine-men refused to print it even when George Isaacs, secretary of NATSOPA, appeared in the machine-room and urged them to resume work. There was a conference between Marlowe and the paper's managing director Sir Andrew Caird on one side, and the men on the other, at which angry words passed, and the refusal was made definite. Marlowe, who would certainly have been anxious that the Government should take up the firmest possible position, telephoned to Downing Street.

The incident was trivial, and by at least one member of the Cabinet was so regarded. 'Bloody good job,' said

Birkenhead. He was at once reproved by Churchill for displaying such levity at a time of national crisis, and the feeling changed. The gravity of Churchill's mood spread to the other Cabinet members. Those in favour of a negotiated settlement were silenced, and two or three members threatened to resign if negotiations were not broken off. The Cabinet dispersed at about 12.30 am, leaving Baldwin to hand over the note.

It was a note that specifically called for a reply, since it asked for repudiation of the actions taken, as well as for the withdrawal of the General Strike instructions. After lengthy discussion a deputation went downstairs again to see the Prime Minister. To their astonishment they found the Cabinet room in darkness. A servant told them that the Prime Minister had gone to bed. As Baldwin explained later on to a friend, he had done all he could, and there was nowhere else to go.

V

THE PARTIAL GENERAL STRIKE

The idea of a general strike had for a long time been nursed by the British Labour movement. It was part of the heritage handed down from such men as the radical agitator William Benbow, who in 1832 published a pamphlet called *The Grand National Holiday and Congress of the Productive Classes*. Benbow's holiday was to last a month, paralysing production of all kinds and immobilizing the processes of Government. At the end of it the strikers would legislate for their country. 'Equal rights, equal liberties, equal enjoyments, equal toil, equal respect, equal share of production: this is the object of our holy day,' wrote Benbow. The later development of theory about the General Strike was well expressed by the syndicalist Tom Mann when he said that 'the General Strike of national proportions' would be 'the actual Social and Industrial Revolution'. The growth of revolutionary industrial unionism, which influenced most of the trade union leaders at the time, envisaged a general strike as a decisive event, which would bring down any Government.

How long such a strike should last, what should be its aims, how the population should be fed – such things were hardly ever talked about. The Labour leaders most opposed to the idea of a general strike, like Ramsay MacDonald and Snowden, who both wrote books on the subject, were those who most feared its success; they were afraid that it would destroy British civilization – by which they meant, among other things, the civilization that allowed respectable Labour leaders to argue peacefully about ways of gradually changing that civilization. Parliamentary Labour leaders and industrial unionists viewed the idea of a general strike very differently.

All this was of a mythical character. It depended upon faith, for nothing like a general strike had ever been attempted in Britain. The projected strike of the Triple Alliance in 1921, and the strike threat that led to the settlement of Red Friday, were not general in their conception, but limited to transport workers. Nor was the 'General Strike' of 1926 all-embracing, although the Government successfully labelled it so in defiance of the trade union assertion that it was a national strike. It was a partial strike of some elements in the community, with the threat that others might be called out at a later time. In making plans the General Council was torn by conflicting desires. First, it wanted to make the strike effective; second, it wanted to make certain that control of it did not pass into the hands of revolutionary agitators. 'What I dreaded about this strike more than anything else was this,' Thomas said afterwards.

'If by any chance it should have got out of the hands of those who would be able to exercise some control, every sane man knows what would have happened. . . . That danger, that fear, was always in our minds, because we wanted at least even in this struggle to direct a disciplined army.'

In the plans hastily drawn up by Bevin, Purcell and the Strike Committee, this contradiction was manifest. The trades and undertakings to stop work included all forms of transport; printing trades, including the press; iron and steel, metal and heavy chemical workers, and any others engaged in installing alternative plant to take the place of coal; building trade workers, 'except such as are employed definitely on housing and hospital work', electricity and gas workers, who were to 'co-operate with the object of ceasing to supply power' (but not light). The list is at first sight impressive, but it omits many trades and occupations: post office workers (including those handling the telephone service), engineers and electricians among others. Several members of the General Council were frightened of the genie they were ordering out of the bottle. Last July the threat of a mere transport strike had been sufficient to coerce the Government; and this was much more. They temporized, therefore, and made it a partial general strike, with electricians and woodworkers held back as a 'second line' to be called out if necessary. They might have learned something, but did not, from the Government's curt refusal of their offer to co-operate in the distribution of food. On the Government side there was a determination, even on the part of those who had once favoured conciliation, that the struggle once begun must be fought to an end. The trade unionists went into battle unreadily, and with divided leadership.

Now the last touches were put to Government preparations. The telegrams, with the code word 'Action' on them, had already been sent out. The battleships *Ramillies* and *Barham*, which had been recalled from the Atlantic fleet a week before, anchored in the Mersey. Two battalions of infantry, the South Wales Borderers and the Somerset Light Infantry, landed at Liverpool from a troopship and passed through the city in full marching order, with steel helmets, rifles and equipment. Naval contingents were sent from Portsmouth to various parts of the country for guard duty. All army and navy leave was stopped. Hyde Park was closed to serve as a food depot, and workmen could be seen erecting huts within it at frantic speed.

Now, as the individual unions sent out their strike calls to members, and more sub-committees met in a vain attempt to work out more formulas, and Churchill brusquely dismissed a final appeal by Henderson ('Have you come to say that the strike notices are withdrawn?' he asked. 'No? Then there is no reason to continue this discussion'), and Thomas left the House of Commons in tears after a speech in which he said that in any challenge to the constitution God help Britain unless the Government won, and fuel rationing was announced, and prices of retail goods were fixed, and Mr Alfred Noyes published in the *Morning Post* a timely poem called 'England First', and shopkeepers in many places posted the sign 'No Credit Allowed', there began the only strike of its kind in British history. For the Government it was a threat to the constitution; for the General Council a tiger to be ridden; for some alarmists (or optimists) the dawn of revolution. Now tens of thousands of British citizens were to confound all these views by finding the strike the most enjoyable time of their lives.

PART III
THE NINE DAYS

I
THE BEGINNING

———————————————◆———————————————

What people living in cities noticed first of all on that Tuesday morning was the peace and stillness of the streets. No trams or buses; none of the characteristic hurry and bustle of early morning. A breathless feeling of intense quietness, one observer noted, such as comes before a thunderstorm; another, in a manufacturing town, the strange clarity of air and sky.

The stillness did not last much beyond eight o'clock. The office worker, in London and other big cities, who had been told little but that he should get to work as and when he could, ate his breakfast and set off, on bicycle or by foot. The streets were crowded with bicycles, an army of people pedalling from suburbs into the middle of cities. Most of them were good-humoured, even amused; the whole thing was undeniably a lark, and the prospect of being an hour late at the office not unpleasant. Behind the bicycles came, in London particularly, the cars; old cars that were really almost beyond their last gasp, cars that had been used by their owners as purely week-end vehicles, cars that had chugged a way up from the trainless country, cars in their tens of thousands blocking the main approaches to London so that appalling traffic blocks formed across the bridges and in large squares, and many people who had started out early did not reach their offices before midday. And there were stranger vehicles:

governess carts, ponies and traps, adaptations of bicycles, including one which looked 'like a polony on four bicycle wheels with its works, like entrails, dropping out in front'. All these helped to swell the confusion. From Marble Arch to Piccadilly traffic moved at only a few yards an hour, and on the Embankment, which many drivers chose in preference to the Strand, there was at times a solid block from Blackfriars to Westminster.

The comradeship brought about by the strike was evident even on this first morning. Many of the walkers were surprised and delighted to find that cars were stopping to offer lifts; then they saw with amusement that some carried handprinted notices saying 'Ask for a lift if you want one', while others had a destination board like buses. Of trams there was no sign, and there were only a very few pirate buses operating in the West End.

When the workers had reached their offices there was not, as a rule, very much for them to do; many firms made arrangements for half their staff, or less, to come in until further notice. A seventeen-year-old boy who lived in Brixton and worked at Finsbury Circus noted in his diary that this was a satisfactory state of affairs. 'Amidst the general confusion and congestion of the main road I walked to Kennington and took refuge from the upheaval in a quiet day's cricket at the Oval. The weather was cold and the play not always exhilarating.' Walking home after the cricket this boy found the traffic congestion even worse than in the morning. This was because the journey up to London had been 'staggered' by the fact that people set out at different times, but no arrangement had been made for staggering the return.

During the day office workers became aware that the face of London was rapidly changing. Walking about in what was often by the courtesy of their firms an extended lunch hour, they looked in fascination at Hyde Park. Crowds lingered in front of the gates, staring at the self-contained small city that had sprung up in thirty-six hours. Here each railway company had its own office, equipped with gas, light and heat. A complete internal telephone system had been laid, and there was also provision for relaying messages to the central exchanges. Water mains had been put in, and the supply was adequate to meet the needs of the 'city'. In the centre of the park were canteens, rest-rooms and recreation-rooms; on the periphery, lined up two deep, were thousands of lorries to be used for milk delivery, each bearing the words: 'Foodstuff Urgent'. This vast milk pool was organized and managed by the Board of Trade, and they were lucky at the beginning, in the fact that most of the milk came into London as usual by early train on Tuesday morning. The London Haulage Committee was responsible for delivery of this milk. The committee consisted of business men with specialized food or distributive interests – Major Munro of Covent Garden (fruit and vegetables), James Paterson of Carter Paterson (provisions and groceries), Cecil Rickett of Rickett Cockerell (coal), and other members who dealt with wheat and flour, meat and fish, and newspapers – under the chairmanship of Sir Henry Maybury, Director-General of Roads in the Ministry of Transport, supported by permanent officials. From the first this committee's arrangements worked with wonderful smoothness, and the elaborate system of branch committees beneath it also functioned well. Local distribution was in the hands of Lyons. The crowds who stood and stared understood little of the organizational achievement represented by the Hyde Park pool. They simply accepted thankfully the fact that they were not short of milk.

Some newsagents, and a few other shops, posted up bulletins in their windows from the first day of the strike. Later the practice became general. Most of the morning newspapers dated 4th May could be bought on this first day, but the London evening papers had all suffered on Monday. The *Evening News* tried to quote part of the now-famous

c

Daily Mail editorial, and the NATSOPA members in the machine-room refused to print it. The *Evening Standard* failed to appear because four separate unions objected to an account of recruiting scenes in Whitehall, and the *Star* ran into trouble after the late afternoon for similar reasons. The very latest news, once the strike had started, was to be obtained through the wireless bulletins which were issued several times a day. The Government had realized the importance of the wireless at once. On the strike's first day Baldwin met John Reith in a club at lunch time, emphasized to him that the BBC was in a key position, and asked if their premises were properly protected. Reith said that they were.

Now people crowded outside the doors of shops that sold wireless sets (few shops had any sets left for sale, so great had been the demand in the previous two or three days), and listened to the news. They learned that the stoppage was practically complete, and that London was congested with traffic; that the price of milk had been raised by 2*d* a quart; that the country was quiet everywhere; that the Home Secretary appealed to householders to take in city workers; that there had been an overwhelming response to the appeal for volunteers on underground trains, that considerable services were advertised for tomorrow on the railways, that there had been 1,000 volunteers at Sheffield and 6,000 in Whitehall, but that still more were wanted.

There was a feeling of urgent excitement in the air. In London many of the people who listened to these bulletins went along to the Foreign Office quadrangle in Whitehall, formed up in fours and entered their names at a wooden hutment which served as a temporary office. There they were enrolled, as special constables or lorry drivers or dock workers or canteen assistants, or merely for unspecified general services. They were men of all kinds and political beliefs, from members of the small band of British Fascists to striking trade unionists who took the chance of earning an extra few pounds at some occupation not their own. Some enlisted for the fun of being a special constable or driving a motor-bicycle. It would probably be true to say that many of the people who volunteered were sympathetic to the miners' cause, and felt that they were being harshly treated. Overriding all sympathy, however, was the belief that, as the Prime Minister had said, the General Strike was a threat to the constitution. By their use of the strike weapon the unions had forfeited the sympathy, sincerely felt although not perhaps effectively expressed, of Liberals throughout the country. The divided view of official Liberalism well expressed the ambivalent feelings of that great body of amorphous Liberal opinion: on one hand the outright condemnation of the strike by Asquith and the Liberal Shadow Cabinet; on the other, Lloyd George's view that while the strike was a mistake the Government was partly responsible for it, and would in the end be forced to negotiate. Peace by negotiation was what these Liberals wanted, without victor or vanquished. Meanwhile they volunteered.

II
THE WHEELS STOP

The response to the strike call, the TUC said, 'surpassed all expectations'. In some cases the word 'desires' might have been added: for undoubtedly there were some members of the General Council – and not only Jimmy Thomas – who thought that the best thing for everybody concerned would be that the order to strike should meet with only a half-hearted response, so that immediate peace negotiations would be inevitable. As for the Labour Party leaders, they must have viewed the strike response with positive dismay: for, as Baldwin told the king, who had come to Buckingham

Palace from Windsor on Monday, they were eager to 'find an honourable way out of the position into which they have been led by their own folly'.

The workers' reaction to the strike call was immediate and overwhelming. There can be no doubt that its completeness surprised the Government as well as the TUC. From district after district reports came into the TUC headquarters at Eccleston Square, sending the same message in various words: the men were all out, the strike was solid. This is a very rare thing. Even in strikes which concern only a single industry there is often weakness in one place or another; a strike involving several industries, like this one, almost unprepared and imperfectly co-ordinated, might have been expected to show signs of collapse from the start. Instead the response was in effect complete.

Members of the NUR and of ASLEF were out almost to a man – many drivers of trains left them near their homes on Tuesday morning, without troubling to run them into the depots. The only hint of weakness on the railways was in relation to the Railway Clerks' Association, a union of white-collar workers. In a few districts a number of these clerks reported for duty, but they were of little direct use in getting trains running. In the twice-daily press conference given by J. C. C. Davidson at the Admiralty, the most he was able to say on Tuesday evening was that a limited railway service was being run, and that 'from the north of England a train is being run daily, which stops at every station'.

The response of the transport workers in London was such that on Tuesday the London General Omnibus Company did not move one of its 4,000 buses. They were finally taken to Regent's Park, which was used as an open-air bus garage, there to await drivers and conductors. A few pirate buses were running, but their number was insignificant. Fifteen out of London's 315 underground trains ran, and those for short distances. The transport situation in the rest of the country resembled that in London at the beginning of the strike, and nothing could show more conclusively the comparative failure of the OMS than the fact that the Government was unable to use its members immediately to any significant extent as drivers of trains, trams or buses. The docks also were silent. Only at sea was there at this time any serious weakness. The small National Union of Seamen was under the control of an extreme right-wing unionist named J. Havelock Wilson. At the Conference of Executives its vote was cast against the strike call, although no ballot had been taken.

Travellers returning home, however, had an uncomfortable time. William Seeds, British minister in Venezuela, came back with his wife and four children, to see a Plymouth apparently devoid of life. They were told that the ship's company was prepared to take them and their luggage on shore in a tender, but that if they landed they would find no porters and no transport. On the deserted quayside the passengers dragged their great wardrobe trunks and portmanteaus out of the tender and towards the customs sheds, where officers awaited them with unhelpful dignity. Seeds got back to London by hiring a private charabanc. The fate of his fellow passengers, most of them South American visitors to England, is not recorded.

The very completeness of the strike provided the TUC with problems. The General Council met each day in the morning and evening, and split into committees to carry out the hour-to-hour work of the strike. The most important of these was the Strike Organization Committee of six members, with Purcell as chairman and Bevin as secretary, which had in its hands the central direction of the strike. There were also committees for Intelligence, Publicity, General Purposes, Propaganda Speakers and Interviewing, and a Political Committee which included Thomas and Henderson. These committees were from the first embarrassed by the eagerness of many non-manual workers to join the strikers. Several others, some of them as small as the

Goldbeaters' Trade Society ('We are a small trade of 310 members'), wrote asking for advice. Instructions were given to unions, large and small, that their members should be restrained from participation in the strike at present. It was learned that the Government was going to issue an official newspaper called the *British Gazette*, and it was agreed that a paper should be issued under the auspices of the General Council, to be called the *British Worker*. Hurried preparations were made to distribute this paper in London and as far as possible in the provinces.

The problem of controlling provincial activities much engaged the General Council. It was feared that in some provincial towns and cities extreme left-wing elements might take control and conduct the strike as a purely political affair. Hence the Strike Organization Committee tried from the first to maintain a control over provincial activities which was, in the circumstances, simply unworkable, and which contrasts markedly with the Government's plan to give the greatest possible degree of autonomy to civil commissioners. One or two instances of the confusion that arose, almost from the beginning, will show the defects of this rigid centralization, blended as it was with the decision to permit each union to call out its own members.

The General Council decided that electricity could be supplied for lighting, but not for power, and sent out instructions accordingly. The Electrical Trade Union, however, had already given instructions that all of its members were to cease work except those supplying power for hospitals; and the Amalgamated Engineering Unions decided to cease work only when others had done so. The position was complicated by the fact that the original decision was impracticable. It proved impossible to separate lighting and power in the way that the General Council wished. Later in the strike the instructions about light and power grew vaguer and vaguer, like those telling local strike committees to meet local authorities and offer them power and light 'for such services as home, shop and street lighting, social services, power for food, bakeries, laundries and domestic purposes'. It is not surprising that many towns sent deputations to Eccleston Square to find out what the instructions really meant.

Difficulties of interpretation arose, also, from the General Council's decision to let each union act separately in calling out its members. Typical of these was the confusion that came from the order calling out all building workers, 'except such as are employed definitely on housing and hospital work'. What did the words mean? The various unions concerned disagreed about them, sometimes violently. The secretary of the Wellingborough Strike Committee complained, after calling a mass meeting: 'Each affiliated society secretary was on the platform with me, each with differently worded instructions, each of which called on the members to cease work, and then went on to lay down rules and regulations which no one could interpret, but which made it impossible for the members to do so.' In most cases these problems were solved by local committees, and not from Eccleston Square.

Most of these troubles, however, grew with the strike. On this first evening the TUC could be certain that the response to the strike call had been extraordinary, and that the wheels upon which the supplies of the nation move had been stopped. The feeling of the strikers is reflected in one of many similar reports from dispatch riders. This one was on the route Barking–Grays–Tilbury:

> *Barking.* Strikers' Committee meets at the Spotted Dog Tavern just beyond Barking railway station. All men (with the exception of five railway officials) on strike. All buses stopped by pickets. Spirits very high!
>
> *Grays.* All union men on strike. Non-unionists are gradually being persuaded to stop work. All buses stopped, and vans examined by pickets. Spirits high!
>
> *Tilbury.* All buses stopped. Shops shut. All men on strike. Spirits high!

III

VOLUNTEERS,
O VOLUNTEERS

The first day of the strike must have convinced the Government, if it needed convincing on the point, that the strike could be broken only by volunteer labour. Plans had been made, officials appointed; but in face of the strikers' united front the plans were useless without an army of volunteers to drive trains, trams and buses, unload ships, maintain order and do all the skilled and unskilled jobs generally carried out by the men on strike. The failure of the OMS to provide skilled technicians in any number is shown by the collapse of the railways and public services during the first forty-eight hours of the strike. On Wednesday the passenger railway service showed no substantial improvement over Tuesday, and – what was even more serious – goods services had practically stopped. The LGOC got a few buses on the road, most of them for a short time and running a short distance, and of London's 2,000 odd tramcars nine were operating. In a few towns a tram and bus service of sorts was operating. That, during the first forty-eight hours, was the limit of official achievement.

There was a group within the Cabinet, led by Churchill, which favoured the use of Draconian measures from the beginning of the strike. A parade of troops with tanks and armoured cars in the streets of big cities would, they felt, have an effect that could be achieved in no other way; and it was suggested also that troops might be used to guard food and other convoys. It was to such a prospect that Arnold Bennett referred when on Wednesday, after lunching at the Reform Club, he noted in his *Journal*: 'Most people gloomy, but all uncompromising. General opinion that the fight would be short but violent. Bloodshed anticipated next week.'

Baldwin was by temperament strongly opposed to the use of force, and he carried most of the Cabinet with him. Continual appeals were made for volunteers, and it was said that 10,000 had come forward during the strike's first thirty-six hours in the Northern Division, another 10,000 in the North-East, 4,000 in the North Midlands, and more than 6,000 in London. The BBC broadcast also, early on Wednesday, an appeal for volunteer linotype operators and stereotype hands, adding that they would be given full protection. It is clear that at this period there was official anxiety about the strike's ultimate outcome.

The volunteers came in their thousands: not only the thousands of respectable middle-aged professional men who were queueing outside recruiting stations, but medical students, law students and undergraduates from Oxford and Cambridge, to whom the strike was an exciting joke. The attitude of the university authorities varied. The Vice-Chancellor, Francis Pember, said that it was not desirable that any undergraduates should enrol for service, and that leave of absence would not be granted to any who were due to take examinations. This sentiment was far from universal. J. L. Nevinson, a student then in his third year at Exeter, noted in his diary on Monday: 'The sub-rector and the Vice-Chancellor caught the fever early, the latter urged undergraduates to enrol themselves, the former gave a discourse to a crowded and thrilled audience who were exhorted to come and sign on between ten and one tomorrow; persons with cars were needed, or those who could drive. The rest to be used as porters and shifters of goods, etc. All remarkably fatuous and quite unnecessary for the unions are maintaining essential services.' Nevinson discovered quickly that his opinion was not generally shared. Most of the college put down their names, including many who were doing schools which they hoped to

* C

avoid. 'I wonder when badges and white feathers will appear?' he asked ironically, but in fact he encountered no ill will for opposing volunteering in a college which supported it.

Elsewhere many undergraduates were swayed by advice from their elders. Those who went to see the Dean of Oriel, Doctor Wand, were strongly advised to register for national service. Similar advice was given at most of the colleges; only in one or two, among them Balliol, was the Vice-Chancellor's precept about neutrality obeyed. This official encouragement had considerable effect upon the undergraduates, some of whom felt uneasy about enlisting in a struggle against the miners.

At Cambridge one undergraduate remembers: 'The university fermented. Recruiting agencies opened all over the place, and undergraduates bicycled wildly from one to the next offering their services for such glamorous pursuits as engine driving, tram driving, or the steel-helmeted special constabulary. I don't think there was any strong political feeling. Just Hurrah Patriotismus or fun. I had my eye on the High Speed Motor Patrol, but its cars had to be genuinely capable of 60 mph and mine, like most of its contemporaries, peaked at 52.' This undergraduate went to unload bacon and margarine at Grimsby, and his ganger was Milner White, Dean of King's. Most of the undergraduates went to the docks or power stations, or to work on the railways. A smaller number were used for driving buses and trams, or for road transport. The importance of the undergraduates to the Government – and the red-brick universities provided their share of volunteers – can hardly be overestimated. They were young, strong and enthusiastic. They were prepared for hard work and long hours, and some of them positively welcomed the idea of a bit of trouble, not because they felt any particular enmity towards the strikers, but simply out of sheer high spirits. Had they been enlisted enthusiastically upon the strikers' side in large numbers, the

Government's task of keeping order with little resort to armed force would have been much more difficult.

The idea that the undergraduates might have been enlisted upon the other side is less fantastic than it may seem at first reading. Ten years later, at the height of the Popular Front movement, there would have been no such general response to a Governmental call for volunteers. In 1926, however, the University Labour Clubs were at their lowest ebb between the wars, and strong political feeling was unusual. Only a small minority reacted like Hugh Gaitskell, who records: 'I was in the middle of my second year at Oxford. Although my sympathies had always been on the left, I had not up to then taken any active part in politics. But there was never any doubt in my mind as to where I stood once the strike had begun. Most undergraduates responded to the call of the Government and left Oxford, with the permission of the authorities, to unload ships at the docks, or to drive buses and lorries. I remained behind and offered my services to the Oxford Strike Committee.'

Gaitskell, like some others, was introduced to the Strike Committee by G. D. H. and Margaret Cole; an indication of what might have been achieved at the universities had there been a number of Labour supporters in official positions. He later did useful work, and so did several others, although it must be said that the results of Cole's recruiting work were not always successful. One undergraduate, after making his way to Eccleston Square armed with an introductory note, found that the TUC had no interesting job for him, and in disgust went off to join Government volunteers unloading at the docks.

Volunteers did not lack encouragement outside Oxford and Cambridge. University College, London, for instance, exhibited a notice saying that students wishing to volunteer could do so at the college, and that 'any student who feels that he can render service at once in his own locality or elsewhere has leave of absence'. The Stock Exchange also provided a great number of volunteers; a number of large firms suggested in unmistakable terms to the younger members of their staff that they would do well to volunteer for service; and there were, naturally, a large number of casual volunteers, like the unemployed car salesman who confessed that 'the strike came as an unmixed blessing to me. Nine days' work at a good wage, and adventure thrown in. As a boy I had been mad on model railways, and of course my dream was to drive a train. I was really in my element.' It is said also that some strikers with technical skills volunteered for service away from their home districts; an engine driver on the Southern Railway, for instance, offering his services on the Great Western. This story is persistent, but investigation offers no ground for thinking that it was true of any large number of men. In some hundreds of letters received from volunteers of one kind and another, there is not one which mentions that the writer worked with a man who was pretending to be on strike. No doubt such cases occurred, but it seems likely that their number has been exaggerated.

There were union blacklegs of a different kind, like the driver for a haulage firm in Brighton, who carried a union card only because the meat humpers on various docks and wharves refused to load the lorry of any non-union driver. 'There was no likelihood of getting union rates or conditions', this driver says. 'The firm would have cancelled the contract first. My wage in fact was 1s an hour flat.' He was employed working round the clock for some days before the strike. 'Literally just that. In those days it was quite usual for a lorry driver to carry round with him full camping equipment. Living on the lorry, snatching what sleep one could while waiting turn on the loading bays, eating where and as one could was fairly common in four- or five-day stretches.'

On the first day of the strike this man was sent up to the wharves to load back with frozen mutton. He was recognized by the men on strike picket as the holder of a union card, and taken before a Strike Committee which met in a rag-and-bone shop. 'The committee sat in a large low-ceilinged first-floor room lit by one small and very dirty window. About twenty men sat around a large trestle table, all smoking – and the sort of tobacco that those meat handlers smoked has to be experienced to be understood. This, plus the stench coming up from below, with the grim lighting and even more grim faces of the men shook me rigid.' The blackleg's lorry was sent back empty, and he was told to attach himself to the Tilling's omnibus group in Brighton to draw 10s a week strike pay. On returning to Brighton, however, he went on driving.

Such were the volunteers: old and middle-aged men who felt that the strike was a threat to the constitution; undergraduates who joined in mostly from sheer exuberance; employees of various firms, men and women, who felt that they should support the Government, or were pressed into doing so; and a heterogeneous collection of old and young, including unemployed men and women and some union blacklegs. The Government's achievement was to make use of these volunteers in the organizations already created, so that a supply and transport service was provided throughout the country.

IV

THE WHEELS TURN

(i) *Trams, Buses, Underground*

First of all the volunteer bus, tram and underground drivers were trained for their jobs. This was often a formality. 'Training was brief and brisk,' an articled clerk to a firm of solicitors remembers. 'After a thorough medical examination we were just put on a bus with an instructor on the practice track. After one round the instructor was replaced by a police inspector, after which we took the bus out on the road.' Another volunteer, an undergraduate, writes: 'I was put in touch with the Atlas, a pirate company operating from Regent's Park. I was given a medical examination and shown a Leyland bus which I had to start, drive about 200 yards and bring it to a standstill, after which I was told to report to drive it at seven o'clock next morning.'

Training on trams was similarly slight – necessarily so, since it was confined within the fifty or hundred yards available within the tram depots. Outside them were pickets, and the volunteers often had difficulty in getting into the sheds. Training on the underground varied, but was generally rather more thorough.

Going out on the road in London was not pleasant, particularly in working-class districts. Strike pickets crowded round the depots, with the object of keeping trams and buses at home. They were particularly successful with trams, which were by their nature easily susceptible to interference. A typical experience is that of a volunteer tram driver who went out from Camberwell as driver of the second tram in a convoy of six. Their leader was Sir Michael Bruce, a dashing military figure, polo player and shooter of big game, and policemen rode on the front and back platforms of every tram. They drove successfully from Camberwell to Westminster. The volunteer driver had an exhilarating feeling of power, dashed slightly by Bruce's tram in front, which often came to rest on a stretch of dead line and had to be bumped off again. The journey back was more exciting. At the Elephant and Castle they were stopped by a police inspector, and told that they were not to stop, even if somebody lay down in front of the tram. The tram was packed with people, and the driver went at full speed down the street. Fortunately, perhaps, nobody lay down in front of it, and he got back to Camberwell. There he found that three of the six trams had got only a few yards from the depot. Point-rods

had been put down the centre rail, and had stopped them.
Moreover the volunteer conductors of the trams had disappeared. They were found crouched unheroically under
seats on the upper deck.

Attempts to run trams from Camberwell were abandoned,
and this particular volunteer was transferred to Hendon.
Here the trams were old and slow, with a top speed of 11
mph. Their journeys were local, and met with little opposition. But this was exceptional. A girl student at the London
School of Economics records in a letter home that she saw
the doors of a South London tram depot standing open, and
asked one of the triumphant pickets outside what had happened. 'He told me that five trams had been taken out by
order of the LCC, but that they were being brought back.
Up the Walworth Road they came like prizes in full sail with
police and mounted police keeping people from breaking
what remained of the windows. You should have heard the
booing when a few shamefaced blacklegs drove them into
the depot. I saw one man try to bash a window and the
mounted policeman hit at him with the butt of his whip. It
was all pretty exciting.' The strikers exerted a stranglehold
over London's tramway services from beginning to end of
the strike. There were never more than a hundred trams on
the roads on any one of the strike's nine days.

Bus drivers also had their difficulties. An indication of the
ironic, rather than positively hostile, spirit in which these
drivers were regarded is given by this account of an incident
at the Uxbridge Road garage of the LGOC, recorded by a
commercial artist sympathetic to the strikers:

> There was a sizable crowd of drivers and conductors
> grouped round the Garage entrance, opposite it, on the
> pavements, and along the road for some 500 yards going
> west. At longish intervals a bus would emerge from the
> Garage, driven by a Young Gentleman with a rather ob-
> trusively loud sporting hat and garish scarf round his
> neck, his course shepherded by another Y.G. walking
> backwards before the bus. At the gates a policeman, with

very solemn expression, would climb up beside the driver
and the vehicle would slowly turn into Uxbridge Road,
sporadic cheers arising from the uniformed drivers and
conductors. At about 50 yards' distance from the Garage
the bus would stop. The policeman would alight, and
walk back to the Garage. At once three uniformed men
boarded the bus, one either side of the driver, and one on
to the bonnet. There was a short struggle, some high-
voiced shouting of threats or insults, and a dishevelled
driver was dropped on to the pavement. The bonnet of
the bus was lifted, some vital part removed, labelled with
a piece of paper containing a serial number, and placed
beside a neat row of some 15 or 20 other such parts, under
a sort of picket guard of uniformed men.

So much for irony. Yet the fact was that the volunteers
slowly got a bus service moving which alleviated considerably the transport difficulties of the strike for Londoners.
There were certain areas where the buses never ran, Poplar
and Bermondsey among them. In other places they were
pelted with tomatoes, eggs and stones. Very few of them
made anything like a full route journey. There was no
driving after dark. Yet the psychological effect upon all
those who were still working in offices, and even upon
other volunteers, of seeing the red buses moving about the
streets was very considerable. By Saturday, the fifth day of
the strike, the number of buses working in Greater London
had increased only from 308 (the first day's figure) to 529;
but more than half of these were LGOC buses, whereas on
the first day the company had not a single bus on the road,
and on the second day only eighty-six. An instance of the
frequent gross inaccuracy of Government hand-outs during
the strike is provided by the fact that in the hand-out on the
second day the spokesman said that 'something like 800'
LGOC buses were running.

After a day or two few of the buses had any glass in the
windows, which were covered with wire to stop the missiles
thrown at them. The driver was encased in a wire net. One

policeman travelled at his side, while another accompanied the conductor. Many of the buses bore legends, comic or militant in tone:

'A stone in the hand is worth two in the bus.'
'Try our Fresh Air Cure.'
'Keep your bricks, please. All windows broken.'
'I have no pane, dear mother, now.'
'I'm almost done for, so they call me Mr Cook.'
'The driver of this bus is a student of Guy's Hospital. The conductor is a student of Guy's. Anybody who interferes with either is liable to be a patient of Guy's.'

Few of the bus drivers and conductors regarded their own conduct as particularly courageous. The good humour displayed upon both sides, the sense that there was something comic about the whole situation, was remarkable. Buses were overturned, drivers and conductors were forced out of them, but only rarely were they injured, or even attacked. On the other side the police, as we shall see, exercised great restraint, although the same could not always be said of the newly enrolled special constables. Among the drivers and conductors there existed a cheerful comradeship, which in many cases did not exclude the idea of having a good time. 'We drew the same pay as regular drivers – then 15s 6d a day', one volunteer says. 'The number of hours worked was left to one's enthusiasm and conscience. There were some who took their bus out early and got rid of it to another driver after one or two hours. I, and most others, worked a day which would have shamed many regular drivers. I arrived at Chiswick by car each morning at six o'clock and did not take my bus back until dusk.' Yet even this conscientious character thought it good fun to steal another driver's bus, if he was landed with one that was difficult to drive. Very few of the vehicles had self-starters, and the drivers made desperate attempts to keep the engine running, since swinging the handle often earned the swinger a mule-like kick.

The driver of one ancient pirate bus, for instance, stalled his machine on Hammersmith Broadway, on the last run of a very rainy day. Watched by an amused crowd he got down and swung the handle mightily. At the third swing it backfired and hurled him into the gutter. But the engine had started and, belching fire and smoke like a pantomime dragon, he made for Regent's Park without stopping again. Some drivers chose their own routes, strictly against instructions, and careered down unknown side streets to the alarm of the passengers.

The rigours of bus driving had their compensations. The undergraduate thrown into the gutter by the backfire, for instance, was lodged throughout the strike at a house in Cadogan Square, where Sir Ernest and Lady Moir, Admiral Royds and Mr Maugham, KC, acted as hosts to him and a number of his fellows. One of his best memories of the strike was of coming in very grubby from bus-driving and sitting down to a dinner of several courses, which ended with some 1803 Madeira.

The volunteers' greatest success in London was the service given on the underground railway. Here seventy-one trains were running by Saturday out of a normal total of 315. The underground system was much less subject to interference than trams and buses, and it had about it also a certain glamour denied to the other services. The training, as has already been said, was by comparison thorough. There were driving schools at several underground stations, and volunteer drivers spent a few hours on a dummy controller. After this, if they were satisfactory, they were put on to a train. Such a system, of course, was not proof against errors, like that committed by this volunteer:

> After half a day's instruction I was put on a train at eight o'clock the next morning and drove from Paddington to Lambeth and back, without a break, until eight that night. On my last trip, outside Lambeth, I came to a signal which was against me. Mistaking it for a type of

signal that allowed me to proceed with caution I was doing so when, ahead in the tunnel, I saw a train standing at the platform. I stopped at once, and then panic broke out. When I stopped an inspector ran up the tunnel to me and, just as if I needed humouring, gently steered me into the station. Then he said that, after driving all day, I must be very tired, and that I should go home and come down next day.

Guessing that this meant relegation to less interesting work, this volunteer asked next day for a transfer, was sent to the District Line, and for the rest of the strike drove successfully between Ealing Broadway and Whitechapel.

Many, perhaps most, other drivers had similar experiences. Trains stopped in tunnels, signals were often ignored or mistaken, enthusiastic undergraduates and medical students greatly exceeded the regular speed limits to the delight of their colleagues and the terror of the passengers. Once or twice trains crashed into each other. But there were no serious accidents, and the volunteers performed their tasks with an infectious good humour, even when those tasks were thoroughly uncongenial. One volunteer remembers greasing escalators with 'the most disgusting black graphite grease you can imagine'. The present Master of Magdalen College School, R. S. Stanier, presents a vivid picture of this sort of work:

Our work was done by gangs of four under a non-striking officer. We used to leave a cache of beer bottles at each station. When we reached the end we waited on the platform for the train that had brought us to go home and for the current to be turned off, and then we collected the tools from a little shed a few yards down the tunnel. To begin with we collected the tools without waiting for the current to be turned off, but after I had on one occasion slipped off the platform and landed astraddle of the live rail, we became more cautious. Current off, we proceeded, two down each tunnel, knocking in with a sledgehammer any of the wooden blocks which had fallen out or seemed likely to do so. This was easy enough – more unpleasant was greasing the checkrails, which involves use of the most appallingly stiff grease. One had a small bucketful of the stuff and a stick for smearing it on, but it was like trying to smear on a piece of indiarubber. However, every station was a resting-place, complete with beer. We finished about 3.30 or 4 am and were taken to Earl's Court where a vast building was used by about 500 to 1,000 volunteers and where the canteen was run, to the best of my recollection, by glamorous débutantes.

Several things about this account are typical: the hard work willingly undertaken and carried out with at least reasonable efficiency, the compensatory bottles of beer at every station (and the lack of discipline implied by them), the dormitory sleeping conditions and the débutantes running canteens. The absence of discipline was important; it gave many of the volunteers a delightful feeling of slight irresponsibility. It was important that you should do your job, but there were no real penalties for making mistakes; and, providing you did the job, nobody minded if you drank quite a lot of beer or played a few practical jokes. This feeling that the whole affair was really a holiday is expressed by a girl student at the Royal Academy of Dramatic Art, writing home to her mother in the country:

It is really fine to see how nice and good-tempered everybody is about the strike. When I arrived at Paddington there were no ordinary porters, but I had a very good-looking man, medical student he looked like, who seized my suit-cases. I wanted to get to Baker Street so he and I explored passages with locked gates to try to find Praed Street; he knew nothing about it apparently. Eventually he went outside and stood in the middle of the road and shouted 'Baker Street' to the first car that came along. And it stopped, and I got in and luggage, and went to Baker Street. There everybody carries your luggage for you, and is awfully nice. It is perfectly mad to hear, instead of "Arrer 'n' Uxbridge', a beautiful Oxford voice crying 'Harrow and Uxbridge train'. Ticket collectors say thank you very much; one guard of a train due to depart, an immaculate youth in plus-fours, waved a green flag. Nothing happened. He waved again and blew a whistle, then said to the driver in injured tones, 'I say, you might *go*.' It's all very jolly, and such an improvement on the ordinary humdrum state of things.

These good-humoured, charming and efficient young men were, it must be remembered, volunteers of exactly the same sort as the comically foolish 'young gentlemen' seen attempting to take the buses out of the garage: so different does the same activity look when seen from the other side.

(ii) *Power Stations and Docks*

The confusion caused by the General Council's attempt to separate the provision of light and power has already been shown. Nevertheless the threat to walk out of the docks and power stations was a real one. On the first day of the strike, according to the Government press officer, the Socialist Stepney Borough Council had given instructions that electricity could be supplied only from sunset to sunrise, with the result that the London Hospital and Whitechapel Infirmary had been left without electricity for operations, X-rays and other needs, and the out-patient department had been closed down for lack of electric light. This last statement was strongly denied in a local report to the TUC, 'the truth being that the majority of the medical staff have enlisted in the OMS and that some of the gentlemen received a warm reception when they endeavoured to load stores at Billingsgate'.

The Government had prepared for the abandonment of power stations. On Wednesday, for instance, indignant trade unionists saw some 200 naval ratings arrive at Lots Road Power Station, accompanied by a strong police guard. Within a short time two of the station's four chimneys were smoking. At several other London power stations naval ratings, many of them stokers, were ready to move in as the trade unionists moved out. They provided only a skeleton staff, supplemented in most cases by technicians who did not come out, but it was not long before a supply of volunteer labour had been drafted in. A Cambridge undergraduate was taken to Islington Power Station, with several companions, in a police convoy. He wrote to his mother and father:

> We arrived safely at the power station, where the gates opened and closed behind us like a prison. In all there were about 50 of us up there, 20 volunteers, 20 of the permanent staff and 10 or 12 seamen who helped with the stoking.

This boy worked on the main steam turbine for a day or two, reading gauges and meters, and then was shifted to the coaling gang:

> This new game was the goods as far as work was concerned, and although very dirty was very enjoyable. We had to climb into the grate of one of the boilers, and remove soot from the sides and from the masses of water tubes which formed the 'roof'. It was just like going up a chimney which hasn't been swept for years. However, it was an experience, and had to be done, and we all did it in good spirits, laughing about the 'soot pudding' with which it filled our mouths.

The Government's greatest stroke in supplying electricity was made at the London docks. The docks were immobilized completely from the beginning of the strike, and within twenty-four hours the representative of the Port of London Authority, Sir Ian Benn, had been told of the intention to cut off power, with the result that all perishable foodstuffs in the enormous refrigerating plant, where some three-quarters of a million carcasses were kept, would have gone bad. A member of the Science Department of the Admiralty had the ingenious idea of towing submerged submarines into the King George V Dock. Electricians cut away a small piece of the dock, put in switches and connected them to the submarines, which were coupled in series. With no more than half an hour's interval a supply of electricity was again in operation, to the astonishment of the many watching dockers.

It remained impossible, however, to use the London Docks in the first four days of the strike. The dockers surged round the gates all day, roughly turning away lorries and their drivers, and although it would have been easy to get volunteers into the docks from the river, the problem of getting the unloaded goods out of the docks and into lorries remained unsolved. On Thursday a shipload of meat reached London Docks and had to be diverted to Liverpool because it could not be unloaded and got away. The meat was then unloaded at Liverpool, and sent to London by road and rail. An attempt made to unload bacon, lard and butter on the south side of the river also failed because of faulty co-ordination with the Hyde Park transport pool. The unloaders had to wait two hours before the lorries arrived, and by that time such a large and hostile crowd had gathered that the project was given up.

Such incidents as these spurred the Government to action. Colonel Moore-Brabazon, Parliamentary Secretary to the Ministry of Transport, was appointed Special Commissioner for the London Docks, and given full powers to solve the problem quickly by any action he liked. On Friday afternoon a convoy of 150 vehicles was prepared, which was to leave Hyde Park for the docks at 4 am on Saturday, and to supply the necessary men for unloading. The convoy was to be given military protection, a measure to which Baldwin had finally and perhaps unwillingly agreed. The effect of this convoy is discussed in a later chapter.

(iii) *Outside London*

The position with regard to trams and buses in other big towns and cities varied, but was generally easier than in London. In Oxford, for instance, a good regular bus service ran throughout the strike; there was a smaller bus service in Chatham; the corporation bus services in Cardiff and Grimsby were restarted after two days' interruption, with voluntary labour; in Bristol tram and bus services were almost normal; in Southampton and Portsmouth a tram service was run with the help of some tramway employees. There were a number of places, on the other hand, where attempts to run such services failed completely. In Manchester, Newcastle, Hull and other cities, particularly in the north and north-east, there was strong and successful resistance. Trams and buses were overturned, and some were set on fire, although few people were injured.

The problems raised by the strike were felt mostly in the big towns and cities. People who lived in the small towns and villages of southern and south-west England hardly felt the impact of this great national event. Why should it affect their lives? The ubiquitous private car served them for transport or food supplies, and there was no strong feeling about the strike in these places which were still little touched by industry. For news they listened to the wireless. The crime novelist Roy Vickers remembers his stay at an hotel in Brendon, on Exmoor:

> It was a very small village. We had electricity, but no telephone in the valley. Wireless had been installed in the hotel a few weeks earlier. The strike had no perceptible effect on our lives, except that we had no newspapers – the Government sheet did not reach us. There was just that one wireless horn (like a large ear trumpet) for the whole valley. I had a dictaphone. By thrusting the mouthpiece into the horn a record could be made. My typist would take a top copy and two carbons. One copy for the hotel bar, one for the general shop-post office window, and one for the local farm. I was unable to resist the temptation to add an editorial, short and non-party.

Brendon resembled many other villages, except that few found anybody as ingenious as Vickers in circulating the news. And not merely villages. A parson's daughter of twenty-two, living at home in the Yorkshire cathedral town of Ripon, noted down local events in her diary with a naïveté which shows how little the town was touched by what she feared at first might be revolution. When the strike began she found all the shops still open, although people

were talking gravely about August 1914. She went with her
father to volunteer for service:

> Daddy ruled out forms, and I took the list of volunteers
> and picked all the 'General Labourers' to make a list of
> them. We were told we were not wanted in the afternoon,
> except for Daddy to rule another half-dozen forms, but
> of course may be asked to help at any time.

The number of volunteers in Ripon exceeded the number
of jobs. She was not called on, and spent the nine days of the
strike in cycling to nearby villages with information about
the Quiet Afternoon to be held in connection with the Church
Overseas, and in confiding rumours of trouble to her diary.
'There are some nasty people about, but they're not going to
get the upper hand by any means.' At the end of the strike
this family gave up *G.K.'s Weekly*, because they disapproved
of Chesterton's sympathy for the miners.

By considering only events in the commercial and industrial heart of the country one falsifies the total picture. In
many places the strike was no more than a mild incon-
venience, and its few supporters were regarded as mere
eccentrics. Yet although it is important to remember these
hamlets, villages and country towns, it is true also that they
played no real part in bringing the strike to an end. The pas-
sivity of the southern and western countryside is notable
chiefly because it could have had no counterpart in any
other country. In Wales, the Midlands, and north-eastern
England the position was different. Here feeling was much
stronger, both for and against the strike, as was to be expected in areas where many people earned their livings in
the mines or on the railways. A boy of seventeen, apprenticed
as a garage mechanic to a small firm in the Yorkshire village
of Kippax, eight miles east of Leeds, recollects incidents
which show the course of events in a place where tempers
had risen. His firm ran some twenty buses which carried
workers at various clothing factories, like Montague Burton,
the Fifty Shilling Tailors and Weaver to Wearer, into Leeds

and home again. On Thursday the garage proprietors were warned that things in Leeds had become difficult, and that they should suspend operations. That evening one of the buses got to Leeds, was stopped and stoned by an angry crowd, and the driver and passengers rescued by mounted police.

Shortly after dinner time on this Thursday the clothing firms closed down, and the workers began the eight-mile walk home on foot. One of the partners in the Kippax garage set out to fetch them, equipped with a revolver which he meant to use to threaten pickets. Outside the Kippax depot he drove past union men who tried to stop him, but four miles from Leeds was checked and sent back, for his own safety, by the police. In the meantime the local union leader, also armed, had gone to the Kippax bus depot. There he threatened with his revolver the inspector on duty, and said that he was taking charge of the depot, and that no more buses would leave until the strike was over. This threat was carried out, and there was no further bus service from Kippax.

Denied, or partially denied, the use of several big ports, the Government used many seaside towns round the coast for the movement of supplies. Most of those with piers were put to some sort of use, from Brighton and Margate to Scarborough and Skegness. Coal, food, petrol and other supplies were loaded on to all sorts of boats – barges, passenger steamers and a variety of small ships that had been offered or requisitioned for service – sent round to these temporary ports, and unloaded. A shuttle service of destroyers ran from the Liffey to Liverpool with yeast for bread-making, supplied by Guinness's Dublin Brewery.

Upon the whole this system, which in its general outline had been planned long in advance, worked very well. A seaside town is not an adequate substitute for a big dock, volunteer labour is neither so quick nor so efficient as that of experienced dock workers: none the less supplies were moved from place to place by sea quickly enough to avoid any risk of serious hardship. There is no doubt that the Government had confidently expected to have the support of sufficient dockers, railwaymen and other transport workers to unload ships and keep supplies moving: but it acted quickly, and with great resource, when the true position became clear. In some places, like Liverpool, 500 volunteers from the Liverpool Corn Exchange started to work at the docks on the first day of the strike, and by the following morning another 1,500 had joined them. After the first two or three days large batches of undergraduates were drafted into the dock areas of many cities. They were met with hostility, but rarely with open violence. 'Ye goa in aloive but ye'll coom aout deaad,' one striker cried to a party of undergraduates who were marching into Hull Docks under a heavy police escort. Bottles and stones were thrown, the police made a baton charge, and the crowd dispersed. The undergraduates were put on a drifter, and eventually given comfortable berths in first-class cabins. A Scottish undergraduate in this party made notes in his diary:

> We hung about all morning asking for a job but finding none. We met Playfair Price mooning about and asked him where our gang was. 'Oxford simply doesn't gang, old boy', he replied. 'Leave it to the Cantabs.' After lunch we gave up the search for work, and I read Trollope in the sun. The food is horrible and sloshed about by Lascar waiters. . . .

> Our first day's work is over and I have earned 12s. I feel fine. There's nothing like honest toil. Spent rather an idle morning carrying boxes of apples from a warehouse to waiting lorries. It was not hard work as we had frequent rests and were allowed to eat apples *ad lib*. In the afternoon the work was a little more strenuous. We wheeled boxes of apples from the warehouse along the quay, and loaded them on to lighters. We were not clever handlers of trolleys and were not actually feeding the nation, for one of the lighters we filled was for destination Hamburg, and the other destination Stockholm. The apples were from Australia.

This slightly disillusioned account should be complemented by that of another undergraduate volunteer which shows the euphoria often induced by the strike:

We set out from Oxford early in the evening in a vintage Bentley and drove at great speed through the lovely English countryside. At Doncaster our driver stood us dinner and a bottle of champagne. So far the drive had been uneventful, but from Doncaster onwards groups of strikers tried unsuccessfully to interrupt our progress by occasionally throwing stones or attempting to puncture our tyres. However, our driver remained unperturbed, and merely accelerated when he saw a hostile crowd – at times we reached eighty miles an hour. . . .

On the following day those of us who were to work on the docks received our marching orders, while others went to drive trams or work the cranes. There were sentries on duty at the dock gates and a light cruiser, HMS *Enterprise*, was berthed near by in case of disturbances. We were under the supervision of a Cambridge don, Mr Owen Morshead, now librarian of Windsor Castle, and we worked from dawn to dusk with intervals for refreshment. Our method of obtaining alcoholic refreshment consisted in asking the sentry at the gate to give an order to a small pub just outside, the bottles of beer being suspended in a large basket over a wall bounding the dock. Money was then placed in the basket, which was hoisted back over the wall.

Some of the old hands who drifted back to work were surprised by the speed with which we unloaded the ships, but we realized that it was a different story working for a few days as an adventure, compared to regular work over a period of years.

Feeling was high in Hull. A determined attempt to get the city's tramway service running met with equally determined resistance. Several trams were overturned, and one or two were burnt. The captain of the destroyer *Ceres*, which was berthed outside Hull, then made a speech from the balcony of the town hall in which he threatened to use naval ratings to run the trams if any more were burnt. The threat was effective, and although some minor incidents occurred, a skeleton tram service was organized. By the week-end several tramcars were decorated with ribbons showing the colours of their drivers' colleges. Here as elsewhere the under-graduates were a potent force.

Among other accounts of working at docks during the strike two deserve special notice, because they make claims of speedy working which are not generally borne out by the experiences of other volunteers. A Cambridge under-graduate working at Grimsby Docks claimed that boxes of margarine were unloaded faster than they had ever been un-loaded at Grimsby before, and that 'the locals were not very keen on the strike anyway'. He adds: 'I thoroughly enjoyed the strike. That and the anti-aircraft mobilization in 1938 have been the high spots of my life – much more fun than the war.' A surveyor working with Bristol University stu-dents at Avonmouth Docks, Bristol, in unloading bananas from a liner on to a GWR wagon, says that the GWR after-wards told them that the ship had been cleared in record time with less than the usual head of labour.

One must put beside these stories the account of a Labour sympathizer:

It was at Southampton that I first saw the undergrads unloading the vehicles. The poor devils were having a thin time. I had to laugh as one of the drivers, a thin weedy-looking bloke, went up to two hefty undergrads who were struggling with a case of oranges. They were sweating and swearing, trying to lift the case on to the tail of a lorry. The driver, using his loading hook, showed them the way, putting the hook into one end and slewing the main weight of the case on his right thigh and up on to the tail-board. Alone, he was loading at about four times the speed of the two undergrads working together.

By the week-end both sides were making claims which, al-though in appearance contradictory, were neither of them untrue. Thus the reports issued by the TUC stressed the soli-darity of the workers, with 97 per cent out on strike in this district and 96 per cent in that, while at the Government press conferences it was said that in many places normal services were on the way to being restored. The contradiction is simply explained: the services that should have been provided by trade unionists were being carried out more or less efficiently by volunteers.

(iv) *Road Transport and Railways*

The field in which Government preparations were most complete was that of road transport. This was both because its vital importance had been fully recognized, and because it was comparatively easy to organize a Haulage Committee and a supply of lorries for a particular area in advance, whereas a supply of dock labour or engine drivers must necessarily be largely improvised. When the railway system is deprived of trade union labour it must necessarily be greatly hampered, however many and willing the volunteers, but comparatively little skill and experience is needed to drive a lorry. The 'Action' telegrams which went out on Sunday night to the road commissioners were passed on to all road officers and chairmen of Haulage Committees, and within a very few hours an organization was in being which functioned with remarkable smoothness. It was the Government's confidence in its arrangements for using road transport that enabled Churchill to decline so confidently the offer made by the TUC to help in food distribution: 'What Government in the world could enter into partnership with a rival Government, against which it is endeavouring to defend itself and society, and allow that rival Government to sit in judgment on every train that runs and every lorry on the road?' he asked.

The function of road transport, as conceived by the Government, was to move food from one area to another; to supplement the railways in moving essential goods from the docks; and, with the aid of dispatch riders, to provide a network of communication over the country. In rural districts the system worked almost without friction. The Eastern Division of England comprised Cambridgeshire, Bedfordshire, Huntingdonshire, Norfolk and Suffolk. Its headquarters were in Cambridge, where a school had been set up for the training of volunteer drivers. These drivers, however, were never called on because there was an abundance of volunteers; and for the same reason there was never any need to invoke the regulations for requisitioning transport. Flour came from Ipswich and all other food from London, and little attempt was made by strikers to interfere with vehicles. There were no dock troubles in this area, and the ordinary postal service worked so well (in sharp distinction to London and other parts of the country) that it was not found necessary to organize a local system of dispatch riders.

The TUC organization in much of this area was very rudimentary. Lowestoft, for instance, reported to Eccleston Square on Friday: 'The spirit of the men is not good. A good deal of drinking is going on in the club, and when the money is spent it is felt that many men will return to work. The chairman of the Strike Committee resigned last evening and went back to work.' A similar report came from Yarmouth, but in Norwich enthusiasm was intense, and many non-unionists came out on strike.

The problems facing the Haulage Committees and the Road Commissioner showed clearly, by contrast, in the North-Western Division, which included the industrial area of south Lancashire, as well as important docks, and such rural counties as Cumberland and Westmorland. Here the postal service broke down almost completely, and a service of dispatch riders had to be organized, covering the whole division from Caernarvon to Carlisle. The dispatch riders left Liverpool headquarters twice a day, in the morning and evening, and provided three main services to Carlisle, Stockport and Caernarvon, as well as several branch lines. They carried important letters and verbal messages, and acted as distributors for the Government's *British Gazette*. They met with little interference from strikers except in a few industrial districts; even there the interference was generally not organized, but individual. A youthful dispatch rider in the neighbouring North-East Division, reputed to be one of the roughest in the country, met very little of the stone-throwing and savage picketing which caused the dispatch riders to be sent out in groups. In the mining town of Consett, which was a strike centre, his group parked their motor-bicycles by the roadside for safety, and walked apprehensively into the town to deliver their circulars and letters. Things were so peaceful that on another visit, two days later, they drove straight into the town.

The speed with which the Liverpool Docks began to function was exceptional. The docks at Preston stayed closed until Saturday, and there was considerable interference with the unloading of foodstuffs and petrol. An emergency meeting was held, attended by the local Haulage Committee and the Civil Commissioner and Road Commissioner. Voluntary labour was organized, police protection obtained, and the docks were opened. In Manchester there was more difficulty in obtaining volunteers, and the pickets were more militant. The docks here remained closed almost until the end of the strike.

The Government lorries bore labels saying 'Food Only', 'Petrol', or 'Food Supplies'. One of these lorry drivers (not a volunteer), operating in the Brighton municipal scheme for road transport, gives a vivid picture of some unusual aspects of the work:

> All the vehicles were liberally plastered with labels, ESSENTIAL FOOD ONLY. Also, all drivers were issued with an imposing-looking document, well splashed with official seals and signatures, calling on everybody, and particularly the police, to give every aid to the bearer.
> The boys would have been less than human if they hadn't made the most of such a document. Imagine the unholy joy of leading a convoy through some small town

en route, finding the police station, drawing all the lot of them up in a line outside, and telling the sergeant: 'We're going up the road to get a meal and a wash. Put a couple of men on to look after the lorries while we're gone – thanks.'

The police did a certain amount of escorting convoys, but it rarely worked out. They would escort us part of the way, then left us to go on. The problem seemed to be that they worked within that area, and the handing over from area to area was a flop. However, they did a good job in giving us a clear run-in to the actual docks or wharf gate.

This same working-class driver stumbled on one of the strike's unexpected amenities, when he was leading a convoy near Southampton, and was directed by an arrow to a large private house:

Very posh entrance hall. It seemed all wrong, but we chanced it. Probably none of us had had our clothes off for the best part of a week and even washing had been a bit sketchy. In we went, and were ushered into a large lounge and billiards-room by a very prim and proper Girl Guides' mistress. Tea and coffee were thrust upon us gratis and our needs gone into. Did we want a bed, a bath, our socks mended, letters written, or what have you? Most of us finally settled for a thorough wash and a feed. Eggs and bacon about 3*d*. Ham and eggs and fixings about 5*d*. All served in the best Ritz manner by relays of *very* clean Girl Guides or some similar organization.

The labels attached to lorries, whether by Government or local intention, were often inaccurate. The TUC received reports from all over the country that 'Petrol' or 'Essential Foods' labels were often used for lorries containing barbed wire, coal, bedding and other supplies. 'Please advise as to procedure to be adopted in holding up lorries on the high road marked "Food Supplies", as several cases have come to our notice of lorries being so marked and carrying other matter,' says a typical Strike Committee report. As the strike developed the volume of these reports swelled into a chorus.

D

'People are often found masquerading as loaves of bread,' one of the strike sheets remarked dryly. There was little the General Council could do about such complaints. Its offer to help in the distribution of food had been rejected, but it was not prepared to give positive orders for inspection of all lorries.

This was one of the strike's crucial issues. Were Government lorries to be stopped or not? Cramp of the NUR gave instructions that no traffic whatsoever was to be allowed, by road or rail. But what did this mean? The General Council never made up its mind whether this instruction should be interpreted as implying rigid picketing or as mere abstention by union men from help in working traffic. The vital decision was generally left to local Strike Committees. Some were militant, others slack. The attempt to operate a permit system is discussed later; here it may be noted that in those places where Strike Committees tried to take complete control of all transport they often imposed the condition, not only that the goods carried must be essentials like food and petrol, but that the vehicles must be driven by trade unionists. Edinburgh and District Strike Committee reported:

> At Longcroft the road picket is so effective that the football park is full of vehicles of all descriptions, impounded until a permit and a union driver are produced.

There can be no doubt that had this severe picketing prevailed throughout the country the conflict would at once have sharpened. No doubt the General Council was anxious to avoid this: but it does seem also that it did not realize the effectiveness of the Government's road transport arrangements. It was upon this system that the country's supplies— and therefore the defeat of the strike – mainly depended, and it was never within measurable distance of breaking down. The requisitioning powers were hardly ever used, and in some places the number of volunteers, and the amount of transport available, was a positive embarrassment.

Lord Winterton, Civil Commissioner for the South Midlands Division, whose headquarters were in the abandoned Reading Jail, found that at the end of the strike he
had 10,000 volunteer workers whose services he could not
use.

A failure of the road transport system would have been a
serious matter, for the breakdown of the railway system was
at first almost complete. The General Council had originally planned to use the trains for distributing food and
essential goods, but Bromley raised the objection that 'we
shall be working certain trains for milk and other foods, etc.,
but if the OMS tries to work troops or material, naturally
my people will feel that we are doing damage by working
food, and thereby setting them free to work troops'. The
three railway unions decided that no movement of traffic of
any kind should be made by railwaymen during the strike.
When this decision had been communicated to the General
Council, it obligingly said that the matter was 'left entirely
to the unions concerned'. Cramp then sent out, in association with ASLEF and the RCA, the telegram already mentioned, saying that 'no trains of any kind must be worked by
our members' and that 'all traffic by road or rail must be
stopped'.

The completeness of the railwaymen's response was
achieved in face of reminders from the railway companies
that 'your means of living and your personal interests are
involved' (GWR), and that 'the company desire to impress
upon the staff that if they leave work in the manner indicated they will be breaking their contract of service'
(LNER). It was an unexpected blow to the companies when
many members of the RCA with such responsible jobs as
that of station-master joined the strike. They were forced to
rely almost wholly on voluntary labour. If plans had really
been made for training OMS volunteers, their results were
not apparent.

The completeness of the walk-out can be shown by the

official LMS figures, which closely resemble those of the other companies:

		Normal	*At work*
Engine Drivers	.	15,062	207
Firemen	. .	14,143	62
Guards	. .	9,979	153
Signalmen	.	12,015	853
Shunters	. .	7,671	82

At the beginning of the strike 41 per cent of the LMS salaried staff were on strike, and 85 per cent of the wages staff. On this and other lines the railway service, as an effective means of passenger or goods transport, hardly existed for the first four days of the strike. The stream of information to the contrary that was poured out by Government propagandists, broadcast by the BBC, and published by the *British Gazette*, may have served the purpose of maintaining public morale, but it bore little relation to the truth. When the *British Gazette*, for instance, said on the fifth day of the strike that 'the underground railways are now giving a regular and ample service', the truth was that sixty trains ran out of 315. When it said on the same day that 'nearly 3,000 trains ran yesterday', it omitted to mention that this was less than 10 per cent of the normal running.

The figures issued by the railway companies themselves show the extent of the breakdown. Passenger trains run by the LMS Railway were 3·8 per cent of normal on the first day of the strike, and had increased to 12·2 per cent by the end of it. The figures for the other railways were:

Southern Railway 5·1% on first day 19·1% by end of strike
LNER   .   3·5% ,, ,, ,,   12·8% ,, ,, ,, ,,
GWR   .   3·7% ,, ,, ,,   19·2% ,, ,, ,, ,,

These figures need no emphasis. And it must be remembered that they are for passenger trains. The comparable figures for goods trains were far behind them – at the end of the strike the GWR goods service was 8·4 per cent of normal, the LMS 3 per cent and the LNER 2·2 per cent. When the strike ended railway sidings were still choked with loaded goods trains left there on the night of 3rd May.

In saying that the railway services were chaotic, and functioned with only a small fraction of their normal efficiency, one is attacking a much-cherished myth. No aspect of the strike took a deeper hold on the middle-class imagination than that of the volunteers driving trains successfully, or acting as firemen, shunters and signalmen. Photographs of grimy men standing on the footplate, waving happily and triumphantly at the end of a journey, appeared in newspapers and periodicals; signalmen in Fair Isle jerseys and plus-fours, volunteers turning a locomotive, checking points, cleaning the Flying Scotsman – such pictures supported a myth which is deeply rooted in the national consciousness. The very finest opportunity given by the strike for fulfilling childhood dreams of adventure came in this chance of working on the railway. One is not denigrating the enthusiasm of the volunteers in saying that their activities were in most cases ineffective. The actual driving of a railway train, like the driving of a car, is not difficult: but to distinguish the correct signal, to discern the proper line, to keep up steam on a gradient, requires a degree of skill and experience which very few of these volunteers possessed. It is extraordinary, not that there were some minor accidents and misadventures, but that so many trains reached their destinations without mishap.

The Strike Committee bulletins found that the railway services offered opportunities for easy irony. 'We understand that luncheon cars are to be put on trains running between Westminster and Blackfriars,' said the *Westminster Worker*, and the Bristol Central Strike Committee bulletin broke into verse:

> Early in the morning, per broadcast from London,
> See the little puff-puffs all in a row.
> D'Arcy on the engine, pulled a little lever,
> Expansion of the boiler – UP WE GO!

A trade union view of a railway journey during the strike is offered by this report of a local business man's journey from Hull to Selby in Yorkshire:

> The train was manned by the usual volunteer personnel in sweaters and plus-fours, and all went well, though necessarily very tardily, until Staddlethorpe Junction was reached. Here the line divides into two branches, one leading to Selby and the other to Saltmarshe and Goole. The train was pulled up and the amateur driver was solemnly assured by signalmen of a similar type that the junction points were set in the direction of Selby. A fresh start was made, but in course of time the business man looked through his window and was alarmed by the unfamiliar scenery. The train was again pulled up when it was found that it had in fact reached Saltmarshe. With a fine disregard for all Board of Trade regulations prohibiting this mode of procedure for trains conveying passengers, it was propelled backwards to Staddlethorpe Junction for resumption of the journey.

Such stoppages were frequent. One amateur engine driver, whose experience had been confined to driving ore trucks along a two-mile narrow gauge railway to a mine, successfully managed the driving of a fish train to Grimsby and a milk train to Paddington. He ascribed his success to the fact that when visibility was poor he always halted the train, got out of the cab and walked up the line to the distant signal to make sure that it was not against him.

The railways attracted social figures of some note. The Honourable Mrs Beaumont led several other society women in undertaking stable duty at Paddington station; Lord Monkswell acted as signalman at Marylebone, the Honourable Lionel Guest successfully drove a train from Liverpool Street to Yarmouth. The prospect of work on the footplate induced that characteristic strike euphoria noted elsewhere. An Indian Army officer home on leave went along to the LMS at Euston, and told them that he knew a great deal about trains, had been keen on them all his life, and had recently made a number of footplate trips on Indian railways. He was greeted with open arms, and lodged in a hostel at the Camden Running Shed, where he met the other footplate men. 'They were mostly volunteers like myself, and a few regular drivers and cleaners,' he says. 'I do not remember any regular firemen. The drivers were elderly men with no sympathy for the strike, but they had no wish to be seen working near their homes. The restaurant car staff had not struck, and some were employed at the hostel to feed us all. The company looked after us very well, providing free food, drink and tobacco and trade union rates.'

This officer was at first detailed as one of two volunteer firemen accompanying a regular driver on a daily express to Birmingham and back. This driver was tolerant and helpful, and although they met black looks and shaken fists on some overbridges, friendly waves were more numerous. Next he fired on the Shrewsbury run for an ex-driver who had been dismissed some years before for his part in a mailbag robbery, and boasted about being on the job again in a way that led to a free fight with other drivers in the Camden Shed. At last the day came when he was taken out on test, and then given an engine of his own:

> I was given an old 'Imperator' class engine, my fireman a young cleaner from Liverpool. We had difficulty in raising steam, and I did not feel too happy. We were late out of Euston, and failed on the bank before reaching Camden. We got off again, however, and eventually reached Bletchley. Here I took my engine to the shed, and told the loco superintendent that it was a dud, asking for a replacement. He replied that he was sorry, but he had no runner available. On the return journey I was forced to make frequent stops to regain steam pressure, and helped the fireman in shovelling coal. The trouble proved to be due to leaking boiler-tubes.

Travelling in the trains was not comfortable. In many places railway strikers gathered in groups and threw stones. Windows were broken and people were hit, although few of them were seriously injured. A young bank clerk and his

mother had a mildly adventurous journey from Newcastle
to Morpeth, sixteen miles away, where they were spending
a summer holiday:

> The train arrived very late – a small engine and one
> carriage – and to our surprise we saw that many windows
> were broken, and were asked not to board the carriage
> until the glass had been swept from the seats. We were
> told that we should have to run the gauntlet of the strikers,
> who had posted themselves on a pit heap near Annitsford
> station. The heap where the stone-throwers were stationed
> was immediately to the north of the station, and an old
> workman conceived the idea that if we stood above the
> windows, any glass would only fall at our feet. Accord-
> ingly two of us stood on the seat and held on to the lug-
> gage rack, while the workman lay down full length and
> placed his coat over his head. The carriage was duly raked
> from end to end, but we took no harm from it. Arrived at
> Morpeth, there was not a window left on that side of the
> carriage.

The most interesting thing about these activities is their
essentially trivial nature. There were few serious attempts at
sabotage. The most important was the derailment of the
volunteer-manned Flying Scotsman, at Cramlington near
Newcastle, on the seventh day of the strike. Here one rail
was lifted out of its chairs, with the effect of derailing the
engine and one of the coaches. No passengers were killed,
but several were taken to hospital for treatment. A volunteer patrol approaching the scene was stoned by men and
youths, and afterwards various tools used by platelayers
were found near by. Even this piece of sabotage was poorly
planned. Had the strikers wished to do so they could
probably have made sure that no trains at all ran in some
parts of England, for in the unglamorous jobs concerned
with repairs and maintenance the Government organization
was particularly weak. 'I volunteered initially as a plate-
layer on the railway,' one man says. 'We spent one day in
a dreary fen between March and Ely, shovelling granite
chips between the metals. By the end of the day we were so

blistered that there was no question of turning up again next day.' One of the pleasant things about volunteering was that if you didn't like the job you were doing, you could leave it and do something else.

In some parts of Scotland and northern England indignation against the volunteers was strong, but it was not often carried to the point of violence. A clerk trainee at Hylton station, in Durham, was normally allowed to keep his motor-bicycle in a shed in the goods yard. He had volunteered for service as a dispatch rider, and when one day he returned to the station with his machine was greeted with angry murmurs from the strikers. A striking signalman stood by the locked door of the wicket gate through which the bicycle had to be taken. Without a word he unlocked the gate and held it open for the volunteer to pass through.

The prestige of the British railway system suffered a body blow during the General Strike, in the sense that its dependence on skilled workers in a time of emergency was clearly shown. It proved possible to unload ships at the docks without the help of dockers, and to keep the power stations going without the help of the trade unionists who should have worked there, but the railway companies failed in their attempt to run an efficient railway system without skilled railwaymen.

V

SPECIALS, POLICE AND ARMY

From the first moment that a strike was threatened, those members of the Cabinet who saw a Bolshevik revolutionary in every striker were eager to enrol the largest possible

* D

number of special constables. On Wednesday, 5th May, Sir William Joynson-Hicks announced in the House of Commons that 7,900 old special constables had enrolled and 3,000 new ones. This, however, as he emphasized on the wireless that night, was by no means enough, and he made an appeal 'to London alone' to provide several thousands more, adding that 1,400 or more had been promised from the Stock Exchange, and that he expected proportionate responses from the Baltic, Corn Exchange, Lloyds, and other big markets. Reservists and territorials would be welcomed. On Friday a message from him, read on the wireless that night, called for:

> A strong, and indeed an enormous force of special constables, particularly throughout London. I want to get another 50,000 special constables by Monday morning.

On Monday an announcement appeared in the Government's *British Gazette*, saying that volunteers were coming in splendidly, but that the Home Secretary was still 'a few thousands short'. He asked for 'men in such numbers that we may have mobile forces of young and vigorous special constables available in any London area where trouble is anticipated'. These special constables would, it was said, 'release the regular police for perhaps sterner work'.

It will be noticed that this appeal was confined to London. This is not because disturbances in London were worse than in other cities. In Glasgow, Edinburgh, Leeds, Manchester, Newcastle and Birmingham there were more or less serious riots. The Government's concern was for London because it felt, and rightly, that the example of London was vital to the rest of the country. The appeal for special constables in London was a recognition that, in a sense, the struggle was fought out in London, as it could be nowhere else.

The newly enrolled specials were sworn in, issued with a warrant and an armband, and received sketchy instruction in police duties. This instruction had its comic side. One of them writes:

The first day was rather dreary, hanging around the station yard and being instructed in the correct handling of a truncheon. I was fortunate in being given the regulation weapon, because after the first day the issue consisted of chair-legs with a cord threaded through a hole in the foot. The correct way to wear the truncheon was down the trousers with the loop of the strap handle hung just below the uniform tunic. The drill was to place the thumb in the loop, withdraw the truncheon, and with a quick flip of the wrist swing it round so that the strap passed round the back of the hand with the handle falling automatically into the palm of the fist.

I soon discovered that although truncheon drill might be excellent for a young policeman in uniform, it was useless for one dressed in grey flannels and a hacking coat. I found it difficult to sit down with the truncheon inserted down my trouser leg, and I could never find the loop of the strap with any certainty when groping for it under the laps of a longish coat. I therefore stuffed the truncheon into the hare-pocket of my jacket.

The dullness of this young special's life was diversified by the arrival of six hefty oarsmen from Jesus College. They enlivened the routine by putting on policemen's helmets and trying to break the chair-leg truncheons on them. Other London specials were given lectures by police officers. They were told how to deal with burglars and car accidents, and how to carry out a beat. It was made clear to them that for the most part they were relieving the regular police on such duties, and that the police themselves would deal with strikers. Some of them were sent to act as guards on the buses, or on lorries coming into and leaving London. The majority, however, remained based on their parent police stations throughout the strike.

In general, the strikers regarded the specials as fair game for attack. A special in Birkenhead notes 'the extreme dislike of special constables, in particular those who were foolish enough to wear plus-fours'. Stones were often thrown at them in the streets, and it was always impossible to obtain witnesses of such assaults. The same special praises the efficiency of the regular police, and their skill in checking what might have been serious riots in a very early stage.

To most of the specials, as to the undergraduates working on the docks, railways and power stations, the strike was a lark, an agreeable change from everyday work. The spirit in which they entered fights, brawls and riots was one of joyful inquiry. Most of them accepted the idea that the police were there to maintain order, and that their own function was anything that those in authority cared to make it. They would not flinch from fighting, but in the meantime they were out to enjoy themselves.

This spirit is evident in the letter of an Indian army colonel, who put on old clothes and joined up as a special at Harrow Road police station. One day he was told to report to Paddington railway station to act as guard on a lorry delivering eggs to several dairies in north London. Two undergraduates were allotted to the lorry as porters, and a young clerk as driver:

> I sat beside the driver, and in the course of conversation asked if he had done much driving before. He replied that he hadn't. I didn't feel at all happy about the erratic course he was steering, and it was not long before my fears were realized. Suddenly we swerved across to the wrong side of the road, and collided with a Rolls-Royce, ripping off one of its wheels. The driver of the Rolls was naturally angry, but our driver, in spite of the evidence of his incompetence, resented the aspersions cast on his ability. A fight was impending, and a crowd of idle strikers gathered round, and began to take sides in the dispute.
>
> We had been instructed what to do in the case of accidents, but hadn't been told how to handle hostile crowds. I descended from my perch, flourished my truncheon, and said, 'Stand back there'. This appeal had little effect, and I began to wonder what my next move should be. I became fully conscious of my lack of training, and that what I had

learnt in command of a regiment was of little use here. An ugly situation was impending, when a regular police sergeant appeared. As if by magic he took control of the situation. He told the lorry driver to pull up to one side and then buzz off, and proceeded to pacify the driver of the Rolls.

We delivered eggs to various dairies, all of us giving a hand in the unloading, and at one place got a tip of sixpence each When our last load was delivered the dairy proprietor suggested that we should go to the local and have one on him. We agreed. I removed my armlet, and tucked my truncheon up my sleeve. We had one on him, and then he had one on us. This was followed by one on each other, and we soon became very merry indeed At last it was time to go. As soon as we started the driver said, 'Now I'll show you how to drive,' and show us he did. We came roaring down Haverstock Hill and on into Tottenham Court Road, travelling very fast indeed. Police on point duty signalled us to stop. He took no notice. Pedestrians jumped for the kerbs and islands, and finally we turned into Oxford Street on two wheels. We slowed to a reasonable pace. The driver turned to me. 'Well,' he said, 'can I drive?'

Life was not always so gay. Another patrol, composed of Roehampton polo players mounted on their ponies, and armed with cut-down polo sticks instead of truncheons, lost their way on a Whitechapel beat. They were unwise enough to ask a young strike picket to direct them to a main road. He guided them into a cul-de-sac, where upper windows were suddenly flung open and the contents of chamber-pots and other receptacles showered down on their heads.

Another special, based on Vauxhall, encountered trouble almost every night, and found the trouble-makers elusive.

The road was deserted, no trams or traffic, and the only pedestrians in sight were three youths who were stopped by a police sergeant. They said they had been to the cinema, and were advised to get to their own houses quickly.

We were led at the double to a mean street running down from the main road towards the river. At the bottom was a howling mob throwing brickbats and other missiles. We were told to charge. As we broke into a run we were chilled to hear the most horrible screams coming from above us. At the open windows were women, smashing the necks of beer bottles on the window-sills and then hurling them down. The danger from this fusillade was negligible, but the noise those women made was frightening.

The charge down the street took only a few seconds, but arrived at the bottom there was nothing with which to do battle. The mob disappeared into boltholes, while the women continued the assault from above. As the street formed a T-junction with another similar street, we ran along this until we came to a passage leading back to the main road. Down this came the three youths who had been accosted earlier by the police sergeant. They hesitated, but it was too late. My party, with blood-curdling yells and swinging truncheons, were on them. Before I could prevent it three innocents were laid on the ground.

This special's group (he was made a sergeant) was sometimes involved in hand-to-hand fighting, in which their opponents used knives as well as the more usual bricks and stones. They learned the wisdom of the police injunction never to stand against the wall of a house, when one of them had his helmet forced over his face and his nose smashed by a window-box dropped on to his head. The police sergeant with them gave instructions to break open the door:

The interior was, to me, the most astonishing experience of the strike. The walls of the room were unpapered and mottled with damp and dirt, the stairs uncarpeted. What one saw was not just poverty but a complete neglect of any creature comforts. Upstairs we found a woman and three children in one bed, with another couple lying on an ottoman in the corner. Filth and stench were everywhere, but more astonishing were the holes knocked in the dividing walls. Crawling through these we were able to go through four houses before emerging at a front door again. The whole place was a warren. The regulars told us that it was extremely difficult to arrest a man in these tenement buildings, and that they would certainly not risk going in alone.

This man also noted the contempt and hatred felt by the strikers for the specials. They thought, with some justification, that the specials were ready and eager to use their truncheons; and although most of them had no love for the police uniform, they felt a kind of moral indignation at the fact that men out of uniform were allowed to discipline them. This special was among the minority whose feelings were changed by what he saw:

It was not difficult to understand the strikers' attitude towards us. After a few days I found much of my sympathy was with the men rather than with the employers or the Government. For one thing I had never realized the appalling poverty which existed then in the Wandsworth, Nine Elms and Vauxhall districts – and probably elsewhere in London was just as bad. The squalor of those living conditions could not have been endured by anyone earning sufficient wages to get out of it. I know now that had I been aware of all the facts which led to the General Strike I should not have joined up as a special constable, though I still cannot imagine myself lining up on the other side.

The regular police, for the most part, regarded their newfound comrades with the good-humoured tolerance often felt by the professional for the amateur. In general they took the strike phlegmatically, behaving with restraint often under considerable provocation. In certain parts of London – Vauxhall, the Elephant and Castle, Hammersmith, Poplar, Bermondsey – there was trouble every night, but it was hardly ever organized or widespread. Here is a report of incidents at Putney and Hammersmith on the second day of the strike, which is typical of many in its nature. The report was made to the TUC Intelligence Committee, and allowance should be made for that fact in judging the remarks about 'Fascists', and the statement that 'no trade unionists were implicated':

At Putney two buses were stopped on the bridge and the magnetos removed. There was a *mêlée* in which local people and Fascists took part. But no trade unionists were implicated.

At Hammersmith buses were stopped near the station and parts removed by strikers. Later, at 8.30 pm, the occupants of buses began to jeer at the crowd. Some of the crowd boarded buses and roughly handled the drivers and conductors. One conductor was injured. Local Fascists, it is said, threw stones from a building near by. The police later drew their batons and we are informed that forty-three people were arrested, only one of whom was a trade unionist, and he was released because a mistake had been made.

Dozens of such incidents occurred in London during the course of the strike. They seemed alarming, even terrifying, to those involved in them, yet their importance was slight. They were the rumblings before a storm that never broke, damped as it was continually by the insistence of trade union leaders that the strikers must offer no provocation. There was a good deal of provocation, in the form of stone- and brick-throwing, but it remained, almost without exception throughout the country, sporadic and unorganized. It would be tedious to describe the incidents in detail, because they so closely resemble each other. At Canning Town and Poplar there were riots and baton charges, in the Old Kent Road an unruly crowd was dispersed with some resultant injuries, there were determined and for a time successful efforts to stop vehicles from using the Blackwall Tunnel. Outside London there was a fairly serious riot by some thousands of strikers in Leeds, attempts to march on factories in Nottingham, a certain amount of looting in Edinburgh. Punishment for those arrested was swift and severe when they came up in magistrates' courts. One man who struck a police officer was sentenced to six months' imprisonment, and terms of imprisonment ranging from seven days to six months were imposed at Old Street for offences including assaults on the police, stone-throwing and interference with food lorries. The Parsee Communist MP for North Battersea, Shapurji Saklatvala, was arrested for a speech made on May Day, and sentenced to two months' imprisonment.

These incidents occurred during the first forty-eight hours of the strike. During the following days the situation did not change materially. There was severe rioting in the east end of Glasgow throughout Thursday, because of a rumour that student volunteers for the tramways had been housed overnight at the depots. There were many baton charges, both in the morning and after nightfall, and at one time more than a hundred police were fighting the strikers. They made sixty-six arrests, and cleared the area by midnight. On the same night police in Edinburgh made repeated baton charges to clear High Street and Canongate, and made twenty-two arrests. In Hull City Square mounted and foot police charged a large crowd of strikers who were trying to stop volunteers from enrolling at City Hall. In Middlesbrough attempts were made to hold up a passenger train, and the station-master was hit about the head. Here also there were police charges with drawn batons, but only a few arrests.

Various local factors affected the extent and nature of the disturbances. In many areas the relations between the police and the Strike Committee were friendly; and when, in addition, the local council was on good terms with the strikers, disturbances were few. Much depended upon the individuals concerned. The conduct of the chief constable of Monmouthshire was severely criticized even by Government supporters; on the other hand, the chief constable of Lincoln behaved with great fairness, and here the trade unions provided all the special constables. At Ilkeston the Strike Committee reported that the police assisted rather than interfered with them, and at Swindon the police allowed the Strike Committee to handle the situation when the mayor tried to put two tramcars on to the streets.

There is a certain amount of evidence that some of the police sympathized with the idea behind the strike – although not, of course, with its manifestation in the form of rioting. Most of the strikers regarded the police as men doing a job, the specials as interlopers. The secretary of the Nine Elms Strike Committee addressed a complaint about the activities of the specials to the TUC on the fifth day of the strike:

> I am instructed to write to you concerning the action of the police in this neighbourhood. Realizing that close on 10,000 members sign on here daily, it must obviously mean that between 10 am and midday the Wandsworth Road gets congested with people. On more than one occasion during this congestion baton charges have taken place, but what aggravates the men most is the sudden arrival of irresponsible youths called specials in motorcars, who jump out and commence clashing about with their batons without using any discretion whatever. Several of our members have been batoned in this manner and a few have been arrested.

The dislike felt for the specials was based partly on the feeling that they were members of an enemy class, partly because of the fact that they were given the status of police without wearing uniforms: but beyond these two emotional reasons for dislike was the good practical one that they often behaved with an irresponsible violence unknown to the regular police. This was particularly noticeable when the specials came from another town or district. The young countrymen who asked Lord Winterton to send them as special constables to Glasgow so that they 'could have a crack at them dirty Bolshies on the Clyde' might well have felt sympathy for the strikers in their own locality. As one Government supporter innocently put it: 'It was thought that a special constable, recruited from a given village, might feel some compunction about summarily arresting his best friend for seditious talk on the village green.' Specials were, wherever possible, employed in areas away from their homes.

There was a certain amount of friction between chief constables and civil commissioners in relation to the disregard of police boundaries inevitable during the strike. British police organization is highly localized, and some resentment was felt at the idea of convoys of lorries, with regular police and specials guarding them, passing from one area to another. Indeed the Home Office positively refused permission for the police from Winterton's South Midlands Division to cross the Metropolitan Police boundary, so that from the time his lorries reached the London area they went without protection, and in some cases were turned back. Winterton complained to the Chief Civil Commissioner, Mitchell-Thomson, and threatened to resign. Protection was given to the lorries shortly afterwards.

The Army played only a small part in the strike. Naval ratings were used in considerable numbers at the docks and power stations; the RAF provided, among other things, a shuttle service for urgent documents; but the Army's role, with one or two exceptions of which the most notable was the London Docks convoy described in a later chapter, was passive. This is not because the Army was disloyal – the pipe dreams of Cook about fraternization were quite wide of the mark, and so were the rumours of mutiny among the Welsh Guards and naval units at Chatham. Army units were moved into, or near to, all the big industrial districts, and if a revolutionary situation had arisen no doubt they would have been used to deal with it; but the police and specials were able to handle all the outbreaks of violence that occurred, without army assistance. By deliberate Government policy, the Army remained in the background. They trained for the possible violence to come, as one young artilleryman remembers:

My unit was the 8th Field Battery, 13 Brigade RA, and our weapons then were a relic of World War I. When the General Strike started we were given single horse mounts, and issued with specially made wooden staves. They were shaped and sized much like the conventional cavalry sword, and similar to the batons carried by the few remaining mounted police of today.

Thus armed, we careered round Woolwich Common in all manner of weird formations, while swarms of soldiers on foot simulated angry strikers. The drill was that we should break up the crowds of real strikers if and when the situation got out of hand, at the same time administering gentle taps on the head with our staves. On one occasion we trotted along Blackheath, down through Greenwich and on to Deptford, where there was supposed to be some trouble with overturned vehicles. I cannot recall any instance when we struck terror into the hearts of the strikers. They did, in fact, make some loud and ribald remarks about our wooden swords.

Soldiers who had recently returned home from abroad were sometimes told to get into plain clothes, go down to a particular area, mix with the strikers and report on the situation. One lieutenant was sent down to Gravesend and Tilbury, and told to give his CO a daily report on 'what these chaps are saying and thinking'. He spent the strike dressed as a workman, in the pubs, parks and playgrounds. His opinion of the speakers at open-air meetings was low. 'Never have I heard such confused rubbish. I devoted some space in my reports to the urgent need for adequate counter-propaganda.' This army agent found no trouble in Gravesend, but at Tilbury broken glass had been strewn on the ground in many places, and there was considerable unrest. 'The CO thought it would do no harm to have two companies of Loyals in the docks. They went in swiftly, silently and by night. The Royal Navy had taken over the Gravesend–Tilbury ferry from the LMS and there was considerable resultant damage to wharves and piers, for they were unused to the tricky local current.'

Another regular soldier, this one a sergeant stationed at Chatham, was sent down to Tilbury to 'report any evidence that came my way of sedition and subversion'. He was given suitable clothing and documents, and had a daily rendezvous with a motor cyclist who received his reports. This sergeant was, on the whole, sympathetic to the strikers. He 'heard a great deal of wild talk that shocked me, but ran into nothing significant of the kind I was told to look for. By the third day I still felt that there was justice in the cause of the strike, but that the strike must nevertheless be brought to an end. This was also the feeling of the great majority of the men with whom I mixed, and I reported in that sense.'

Probably these reports should not be regarded as typical, in the sense that the Army had men everywhere reporting on the situation; but there can be no doubt that a number of agents all over the country were mixing with the strikers, and that the Government was ready for the revolutionary situation that never came.

VI

THE POLITICIANS TALK

The political position at the beginning of the strike was a curious one. Baldwin, having done, as he felt, his utmost, was content to sit back and let things work themselves out; or at least, that is the impression he gave to some of his colleagues. He attended few of the meetings of the Cabinet Committee held each day at the Home Office to deal with the crisis. These meetings were presided over by Joynson-Hicks, 'frock-coated, eloquent, determined to rise to a historic occasion', as the Secretary for Air, Sir Samuel Hoare, noted. Baldwin, Hoare thought, seemed singularly detached from the committee's decisions. It is possible, of course, that the Prime Minister's private secretaries are right in saying that, having made all possible preparations, he felt that there was nothing further to be done. Had he not been assured by Sir Alfred Mond that 'all sane public opinion will stand behind the Prime Minister if he lays down his conditions and compels their acceptance'? To lay down conditions was not Baldwin's way, but his evident lack of concern to negotiate a settlement had a similar effect. This masterly inactivity took on, at least in the eyes of those opposed to him, the air of an ultimatum demanding unconditional surrender.

Other ministers were less temperate. 'The best and kindest thing now is to strike quickly and hard,' Neville Chamberlain told his diary, and Churchill, Birkenhead and Joynson-Hicks, although perhaps not much concerned to do the kindest thing, were in agreement about those quick, hard strokes. There was certainly no tendency to compromise; there was, rather, a refusal to negotiate. We have seen how brusquely Churchill rejected Henderson's attempt to open conversations on Monday evening, and this attitude remained unchanged during the strike. Baldwin implicitly, and some of his chief ministers openly, demanded surrender.

That the leaders of the Parliamentary Labour Party would have been happy to make such a surrender, if it had been suitably cloaked as a compromise, cannot be doubted. Success for the trade unions, Snowden thought, was hopeless from the start. He may have been right, but his view that there was little or no enthusiasm for the strike among the workers was surely based chiefly on his own feelings. Clynes, who had said in April that the strike would be 'a national disaster', avoided speech-making himself, and advised against the holding of mass meetings. The attitudes of MacDonald and Thomas have already been made clear. Henderson, although he played an active part in the strike, had no faith in it. What these men believed and thought in their parliamentary capacities, however, was comparatively unimportant. The centre of power in the Labour movement moved during the strike to the TUC headquarters in Eccleston Square, and what was being said in the House of Commons bore little relation to what was going on in the country.

Thus on Monday the first concern of Parliament was to arrange for the carrying on of business, and the Minister of Transport, Colonel Ashley, assured members that he had made arrangements for cars to transport them to and from their homes. Baldwin then announced the existence of the state of emergency, and followed it with a speech which may be called masterly in its apparently impartial presentation of the owners' viewpoint. Did their suggestions imply a big drop in wages? he asked, and answered that, although that did appear to be the case, one had to remember the reduction in the cost of living. He referred to the *Daily Mail* affair in remarks about 'acts perhaps not so great in themselves, but great in their possible consequences and certainly in their signification'. In a peroration that impressed listeners on both sides of the House by its sincerity, he said that everything he cared for was being smashed to bits at the moment, but 'before long the angel of peace, with healing in his wings, will be among us again, and when he comes let us be there to meet him'.

Thomas and MacDonald followed with two splendid pieces of shadow boxing. 'I feel in my bones that a last effort ought to be made. I still plead. The die may be cast. The fight may come,' said Thomas. It was important even then, he added, that we should not lose our heads, and that there should be no bitterness. MacDonald emphasized his respect for the constitution and his desire to see fair play and justice, loftily adding that 'with the discussion of general strikes and Bolshevism and all that kind of thing, I have nothing to do at all'.

The pacific tone of these speeches was a little disturbed by Churchill, who said that the cost of the subsidy had 'ruined and shattered the finances of two successive years', and gave a solemn warning that parliamentary institutions must triumph. Churchill ended by saying that the Government was not refusing to negotiate. 'Anyone can approach the Government who has authority, and can parley with them, and it is our duty to parley with them.' It was an hour or two after this that Churchill rejected Henderson's attempt to parley. Obviously, wherever the Government thought authority lay, it was not with the Labour leaders. Not one of them, during the debate on this vital evening, had supported the strike, even in the sense of considering its success as a possibility. Among political leaders only Lloyd George expressed this view, saying that he thought that the strike was a mistake, but that he believed the Government would be forced by circumstances to negotiate. It is significant that this speech of Lloyd George drew Churchill's heaviest fire, and that Duff Cooper, one of the Conservatives most strongly opposed to the strike, noted in his diary that he had 'never heard Lloyd George worse'.

On Tuesday the House occupied itself with budget resolutions, but on Wednesday Joynson-Hicks moved the acceptance of the emergency regulations which gave the Government, among other things, the right of arrest without warrant and the power to take possession of land, buildings and other undertakings during the emergency. During the course of a fairly acrimonious debate, in which Labour back-benchers cried 'Mussolini' to Joynson-Hicks, and Lord Hugh Cecil said that the attempt to suppress the *Daily Mail* showed a 'revolutionary mind' at work, a long argument developed between Thomas and MacDonald on one side, and Baldwin on the other, about just exactly what had happened on that Sunday evening when negotiations were called off. Had there been a formula, had Thomas accepted it, had they been within minutes of a settlement? Baldwin, who had been in the chair at a meeting of Conservative members in a committee room at the beginning of Thomas's speech, came in and said that it really all showed the importance of that *Daily Mail* episode, and how deplorable it was that a strike should have been declared. MacDonald, fervent in the cause of truth, supported Thomas, and a furious argument developed about the exact meaning and nature of the formula, while frustrated back-benchers demanded to know what the formula was, and Lord Hugh Cecil reasonably suggested that if a formula existed that was agreeable to both sides, it should surely be produced. After some unsuccessful amendments to the regulations moved by the Clydesiders, Baldwin and Thomas returned to the argument, defending their virtue with the fury generally attributed to assaulted virgins. They had asked for a meeting at six-thirty on Sunday, Thomas said, but had not got it until nine o'clock. Baldwin retorted that Thomas had said he wanted some dinner. Chamberlain and Steel-Maitland chimed in to say that Thomas had said he was not empowered to act on behalf of the miners. Thomas reproached them with making public matters discussed in confidence. He was extremely skilful in such arguments, and upon the whole gained a points victory over his opponents. These hours of discussion had little relevance to anything that was going on outside, in the world where the General Strike was being fought, but it may be that they gave Thomas some satisfaction.

From the beginning the Government stressed that in their view the issue was not an ordinary industrial one, but that the strike was a threat to constitutional government as such. It put the country 'nearer to civil war than we have been for centuries past', Baldwin said. Churchill embellished the theme by saying that the strike would 'inevitably lead to the erection of some Soviet of trade unions', and Sir Robert Horne added that 'a junta of men may, without consultation with their constituents, decide to bring the country to a standstill'. These Government spokesmen now received support from an unexpected ally.

The Liberal Party had from the first condemned the strike unequivocally; and although, at a meeting of its Shadow Cabinet on Tuesday, it was agreed that the Government must bear some part of the blame, the Asquithian Liberals were not inclined to stress the Government's deficiencies, in view of what they felt to be the disgraceful attitude of the TUC. On Tuesday Asquith wrote in his diary:

> We are plunged into the cataract of the strike and already London presents an abnormal aspect. I cannot think that it will last long; it is very unpopular and they are short of funds for anything like a severe struggle.

Asquith, however, was in the House of Lords; and the

speeches made by Lloyd George in the Commons on Monday and Wednesday did not at all conform to Asquithian Liberal feeling. Certainly he condemned the strike; but he appeared to condemn the action of the Government much more strongly, regarding their action in breaking off negotiations as 'precipitate, unwarrantable and mischievous'. In a parliamentary sense Lloyd George appeared to the Government a more formidable antagonist than Thomas and MacDonald. Members of the Cabinet had an uneasy feeling that Lloyd George would manage to use the strike in some way to his personal advantage. Whereas Asquith and Grey supported the Government's demand that the strike notices should be withdrawn unconditionally and agreed that the strike was a threat to constitutional government, Lloyd George insisted that the people involved had no intention of threatening the constitution and expressed himself in favour of a negotiated settlement. On 10th May, when the Liberal Shadow Cabinet met again, Lloyd George absented himself, sending a letter to the chief whip in which he said that the party had been committed to a point of view with which he disagreed. Within a few weeks of the strike's end, this disagreement had led to the final split in the Liberal Party. Lloyd George had been excommunicated by the Asquithians, and Asquith himself, unprepared for the struggles that lay ahead, had resigned from the leadership.

All this has its relevance to Sir John Simon's speech in the House of Commons on Thursday night. He had been Home Secretary in Asquith's War Cabinet, a position from which he resigned because he disapproved of conscription; and although he had not since then held ministerial office, he was one of the most important figures in the Liberal Party. More than that, he was one of the most eminent lawyers of his day, a man whose opinion would be respected by all parties. His temperament was cautious, even conservative. Such a man does not make a speech which he knows to be important, without weighing carefully in advance the effect of his words.

It seems likely that what he said was decided in advance with other Liberal leaders and that it was meant, at least partly, as a blow at Lloyd George.

Simon rose on Thursday night just after eleven o'clock. He apologized for speaking at such a late hour, but excused his lateness by the importance of what he had to say. The General Strike, he declared, was not like other strikes, as members on both sides had too simply thought. It was, in fact, not a strike at all.

A strike, properly understood, is perfectly lawful. The right to strike is the right of workmen in combination, by pre-arrangement, to give notice to employers to terminate their engagements, and to withhold their labour when these notices have expired. . . . It is an essential part of the rights of the British wage-earner that he should have the right to strike, and that it never ought to be taken away from him . . . (but) the decision of the Council of the Trade Union Executives, to call out everybody, regardless of the contracts which these workmen had made, was not a lawful act at all.

Every worker who was bound by contract had broken the law, Simon said, and although, he added (with what a Labour member afterwards stigmatized as true Liberal hypocrisy), he had 'not the slightest desire to blame or praise', those workers should understand that they were taking part in an altogether illegal proceeding. He was 'speaking not in the least in the language of threat', Simon went on, but every railwayman who was on strike in disregard of his contract was personally liable to be sued in the county court for damages, and every trade union leader was 'liable in damages to the uttermost farthing of his personal possessions'. Still avoiding the language of threat, Simon went on to say that any trade unionist who ignored the strike order would not lose his union benefits, as he might have feared, since the order itself was unlawful; moreover, he suggested, trade union funds, which in 1906 had been granted legal immunity, would not be immune from the consequences of an illegal act.

Simon's speech came at the end of a day spent in debating the emergency regulations asked for and obtained by Joynson-Hicks, in spite of the gallant rearguard action fought by Labour back-benchers. There was a phrase in one clause about the police right to arrest a person of 'known character'; and when George Buchanan pointed out that Lloyd George might be a 'known character' if near a land-lord, or that Lady Astor might be one if near a brewery, the Prince of Wales and the Duke of York, who were in the gallery, roared with laughter.

That was all good fun: but Simon's attack was serious, de-liberate and meant to do damage. One might have expected that it would have received an immediate answer; but when on Friday Sir Henry Slesser, who had been Solicitor-General in the 1924 Labour Government, approached MacDonald and said that he thought Simon should be answered, Mac-Donald told him not to speak. On Monday Slesser, who was convinced that Simon's interpretation of the law was wrong, rose to reply in defiance of MacDonald's prohibition. He was greeted with prolonged cheers from the Labour benches. Slesser maintained that the General Strike was not rendered illegal merely because there were individual breaches of con-tract, and expressed doubts whether any employer could prove that this strike was a conspiracy against the State.

On the following day Simon replied, and in doing so made considerable use of an interlocutory judgment which had been given by Mr Justice Astbury in the Chancery Division that morning. It will be remembered that Havelock Wil-son's National Sailors' and Firemen's Union had voted against the strike. The Tower Hill and Mersey branches of this union had passed a resolution supporting the strike deci-sion, and calling on members of the union to come out. Wilson thereupon went to the courts and asked for an in-junction against these branches, on the grounds first that a two-thirds majority of all members ashore was required for a strike call, and second that the strike was contrary to law.

On 6th May Astbury granted Havelock Wilson an *ex parte* application, and on 11th May gave judgment. He pointed out that the union members were ignoring the two-thirds rule, but it was his observations on the strike's legality that were quoted by Simon:

> In my opinion (Astbury said) the so-called General Strike called by the TUC is illegal and contrary to law, and those persons inciting or taking part in it are not protected by the Trade Disputes Act of 1906. No trade dispute has been alleged or shown to exist in any of the unions affected, except in the miners' case, and no trade dispute does or can exist between the TUC on the one hand and the Government and the nation on the other. The orders of the Trades Union Council above referred to are therefore unlawful, and the defendants are at law acting illegally in obeying them and can be restrained by their own union from doing so.

Simon buttressed his reply to Slesser with this judgment, and extended his remarks about the strike by saying that any strike which put pressure upon the community as a whole must be illegal.

Was Astbury's a good judgment? Was Simon right? These questions were argued after the strike was over, and the balance of legal opinion was unfavourable to them. It was pointed out that Astbury's judgment was arrived at without citing a single authority, in a case where the defendants were not represented by counsel and no arguments were heard; and although Simon was supported in the *Law Quarterly Review* by Sir Frederick Pollock, his view was challenged by the editor of the periodical, A. L. Goodhart. After a lengthy analysis of Simon's arguments, Goodhart pointed out that the purpose of a sympathetic strike must always be to bring pressure to bear upon some third party, and expressed the opinion that 'the coercion of the Government was merely incidental' to a strike which was genuinely in furtherance of a trade dispute.

All this was after the event and could not cancel the effect

of speeches and judgment. About the nature and depth of
that effect there is a sharp division of viewpoint. At the time
Duff Cooper thought Simon's 'a most important and impressive speech', which might lead to him supplanting Lloyd
George as leader of the Liberals in the House of Commons.
Other Conservative members had no doubt about its importance. It should be made known as widely as possible,
one of them said, because then 'the present state of affairs
would begin to see its end within twenty-four hours'. The
cautious attitude of the Attorney-General, Sir Douglas
Hogg, was somewhat resented. After the strike Simon's
speeches were often referred to as a decisive blow, that terri-
fied the wavering trade union leaders, put into their minds
the idea that they might all be arrested, and thereby
hastened the end of the strike. 'This speech', according to
Sir Osbert Sitwell, 'completed the discomfiture of the strike
leaders. . . . From this moment on the strike leaders, in their
blue serge suits, with their moustaches and bowler-hats,
found that they had come perilously to resemble rebels. . . .
Everywhere Sir John's declaration produced in the people of
this country, tolerant and law-abiding by nature, an immediate response. "Good gracious," they exclaimed primly,
"what I'm doing isn't respectable", and many of them
longed in consequence to return quietly to work.' Astbury,
for his part, often claimed that his judgment had saved the
nation.

This has a plausible sound; but in fact, according to those
most closely in touch with them, the trade union leaders remained unshaken by Simon's remarks. Slesser, who talked to
all of them at the time, maintains this, and says also that
Astbury's judgment had even less effect than Simon's speech.
'It has the distinction of being irreconcilable with all other
judgments ever pronounced on the Trade Disputes Act,'
Slesser notes acidly, and adds that the trade union leaders
concerned had the position explained to them, and were not
at all moved by the speech or the judgment.

It is no doubt true that some people longed to return to work, but there is no evidence to show that Simon's speech induced them to do so. Whether MacDonald's reluctance that Simon should be answered sprang from a feeling that his speech would be better ignored, or from a hope that it might have precisely the effect that Sitwell ascribes to it, is a matter of opinion; as is the question whether Simon was animated chiefly by the wish to pass on his legal knowledge, by his belief that the General Strike was morally wrong, or by his dislike for Lloyd George.

VII

WHAT HAPPENED AT NEWCASTLE?

In the afternoon before Simon made his speech, the House had been surprised, and the Conservative majority in it disturbed, by an interpolation from Martin Connolly, Labour MP for Newcastle East. The position in Newcastle, Connolly told MPs, was 'that the OMS has entirely broken down, that the authorities have approached the trade unions and asked them to take over the vital services, and that the trade unions have consented to do so on condition that all extra police, all troops, and all OMS services shall be withdrawn. This has been done, and the city is going on all right.'

The meaning of Connolly's last phrase obviously varied according to one's political opinion, and an hour later the Attorney-General took an opportunity of assuring Conservatives that he had spoken to the chief constable at Newcastle, and that there was absolutely no truth in the statement. Connolly repeated that the OMS had broken down, and that the city was being run by the trade unions.

On the following Monday the question was raised again. Sir Harry Barnston, Comptroller of the Household, said that the organization in Newcastle was working quite satisfactorily. Connolly then read a statement issued by the Newcastle Trades Council, saying that Sir Kingsley Wood, Civil Commissioner for the North-East, had appealed to the trade unions for help. 'He admitted that he had lost control of the situation, and asked the Transport Union to co-operate in maintaining supplies. The position was so desperate that provided the unions would come to his help he was prepared to ask the Government to withdraw the troops and marines.' Sir Harry replied that all these statements were absolutely untrue, and said he was surprised that Connolly was not ashamed to repeat them.

What really happened at Newcastle? There are two answers, one based on official statements and local newspaper reports; the other that given by the account of the proceedings of the Northumberland and Durham General Council and Joint Strike Committee. This document, presented to the council within a few days of the strike's end, is of unique interest, because it is the only detailed account made public of a Strike Committee's workings. It illuminates many of the difficulties encountered by trade unionists during the strike, in particular the problems raised by the imprecise or contradictory instructions that sometimes came from London; and what it has to say about control of the city must be weighed against the sparse official reports.

On the evening of Monday, 3rd May, an informal meeting took place at the Newcastle offices of the National Union of Distributive and Allied Workers, and on the following day another meeting was held, attended by representatives of twelve trade unions, plus the Gateshead Labour Party and Newcastle Trades Council. Will Lawther and R. Page Arnot were also present. Lawther was a militant member of the Labour Party's left wing, and a member of the National Executive. He acted as unofficial representative of the

Durham Miners' Association, which was so lethargic that it did not set up a Strike Committee of any sort. Page Arnot was a Communist intellectual, and a director of the Labour Research Department. The committee chairman was James White of the TGWU and the secretary Charles Flynn of NUDAW. A General Council and a Strike Committee were appointed, with various sub-committees. Their first problem came immediately, in the shape of a complaint that miners' clubs were sending in cars to collect beer, while transport workers were out on strike.

On the very first day of the strike the Strike Committee had to abandon its sub-committees. In the words of the report:

> Sub-committees must necessarily proceed from a body whose own movements have attained some degree of simple co-ordination, whose members know one another, and whose machinery has been tried and tested. The Strike Committee was not in this position.

All activities were therefore concentrated into the Strike Committee's own hands, and it dealt with each problem as it came up. A local strike bulletin was taken over, and the committee decided to issue a publication as soon as a permit was granted by the Typographical Association. On the second day of the strike the committee began to assess the situation:

> It became clear that the stoppage had not been fully effective as ordered on Monday midnight; and that the operation of the General Strike had only been getting under way in the course of Tuesday. For example: some obstruction had prevented the printers at Sunderland from coming out till Wednesday; a scratch meeting of the RCA in one locality had resulted in a vote against coming out on strike, a vote which was subsequently to be over-whelmingly reversed at a later meeting.

There was also a considerable amount of transport still at work, because the various unions here, as elsewhere, made

E

different interpretations of the General Council's instructions to continue to supply food, health and sanitary services.

The two main problems that confronted the committee were those concerning permits and those relating to negotiations initiated by Sir Kingsley Wood. Applications for permits of all kinds poured into each individual union's district office. Moreover:

> The abuse of permits was beginning to reach gigantic proportions in the course of Wednesday afternoon. Unscrupulous contractors or employers were conveying any and every sort of goods under the aegis of 'Food Only' or 'Housing Materials Only'.

On Wednesday evening all permits for the transport of building materials were withdrawn, and no new ones were issued. It proved impossible, however, for the committee to get a permit from the Typographical Association for the printing of an official strike bulletin.

> The dispatch sent off to the TUC General Council on Friday afternoon emphasized the necessity, as every telephonic communication had emphasized it up till then, of having in the Newcastle district a paper which would give accurate information, up-to-date information and local information to meet the extremely virulent poison that was being poured out from the blackleg sheets.

The committee received 'sympathetic replies from Mr Citrine and others for four successive days', but never got a permit. The strikers had to rely here on unofficial news sheets like the *Northern Light*, *Workers' Chronicle* and *Workers' Searchlight*. Although the official paper, the *British Worker*, first appeared on 5th May, copies did not reach Newcastle until 11th May.

On Wednesday the OMS were brought to the Newcastle quayside to unload food supplies. The trade unionists working there under permit stopped work, partly because of this and partly because they resented the presence of two destroyers and a submarine, which were moored beside the food ship. Their stoppage prompted the intervention of Sir Kingsley Wood, who interviewed members of the Strike Committee, and then visited its headquarters, Burt Hall. On Thursday the Strike Committee representatives met Sir Kingsley, General Sir Kerr Montgomery (previously head of the OMS in the region and now Food Officer) and the Road Commissioner, R. S. Moon. The visit to Burt Hall was mentioned in local newspapers.

According to the Strike Committee minutes, Sir Kingsley Wood said that the outside labour imported on to the quay was there without his knowledge or authority. The committee asked that only food cargoes should be unloaded, and also said that 'it was impossible for us to agree that our men should be forced to work under the shadow of guns'. Wood said that the boats were kept there to deal with possible riots or attacks on power stations, 'but appeared to indicate that a suggestion from him to the commanders of the vessels might have the desired effect'. With regard to the unloading, Wood and Montgomery suggested a system of dual control, with two officers appointed to deal with any trouble, one from the Government and the other from the committee. Montgomery offered to see that any chauffeur whose normal work was not to drive the lorries should be put off the quays.

The Strike Committee's reaction was to refuse this dual control and to withdraw all permits. It should be added that, in a statement made in the House of Commons after the strike had ended, Sir Kingsley Wood denied that any form of dual control had been offered. After the Strike Committee decided to withdraw trade union labour, he said, 'voluntary labour took the place of the men who refused to work, and from that day to the end of the strike the whole of the work of the food supplies in that district was carried out by voluntary labour under police protection'.

The decision to withdraw all permits sharply affected the Co-operative Societies. In considering this point the committee's report suggests that one key move towards victory in the strike would have been the provisioning of strikers by the Co-operatives. They ask why this had been ruled out by the TUC, and conclude that the reasons were lack of preparedness, and the fact that the CWS directors had, in the spring, issued a note refusing credits in advance, thus ranging themselves in working-class opinion on the side of the Government and against the unions. The feelings in Newcastle upon this point were reproduced in other parts of the country. Really effective picketing, such as the Strike Committee here envisaged and in part carried out, involved the strikers themselves going hungry. The Co-operative Societies (to whom the Strike Committee here finally gave permits for bread and milk deliveries) were hamstrung while private traders, who received full Government support, were comparatively little affected.

In spite of this the Strike Committee considered that on Friday 'the success of the General Strike appeared completely assured', since the Government organization was unable to cope with the task imposed on it. The likely sequel, the committee told the Intelligence Department of the TUC, was an attempt to break down picketing by force, 'and this forecast proved to be right . . . the actions of the police culminated during the week-end in many baton charges and in the arrest of many prominent persons'.

Not surprisingly all this contrasts very sharply with the views of the local press. The *North Mail and Newcastle Chronicle*, with its companion evening and Sunday papers, appeared in printed form throughout the strike, and went from strength to strength. Over 500,000 papers were printed at the week-end, and the Newcastle Aero Club flew a number to London every day in their little crimson machines, making a steady 90 mph to Northolt. The *Newcastle Daily Journal* also appeared every day, with the news in typographic facsimile, often rather difficult to read. The papers agree with the committee that pickets effectively stopped buses and trams, and at one point held up food lorries on the quays, and they found 'an uneasy atmosphere' in the city; but they go no further.

They give prominence to Sir Kingsley Wood's statement that Connolly's remarks in the House of Commons were entirely false, and that 'to say he had promised to ask the Government to withdraw troops was absurd, as no troops had been drafted to this district'. (Connolly's statement presumably refers, inaccurately, to the discussion about the destroyers.) But what the newspapers emphasize is the peacefulness and normality of the city. At the week-end, the *Daily Journal* remarked on the busyness of the shopping centre which presented almost its customary appearance. 'There was no appreciable shortage of foodstuffs, and prices seemed much as usual.' Specials were on point duty for the first time, creating good-humoured comment. The cinemas were open, and so were theatres. Six hundred Newcastle students had offered to run the tramcars. Post was arriving in the city by air. At a meeting of the British Women's Temperance Association, Lady Kaye of York moved a resolution congratulating the Duchess of York on the birth of a daughter, and a delegate suggested that they should make the baby an honorary 'Little White Ribboner'. The suggestion was not acted upon.

At the week-end there were many disturbances, in spite of the lord mayor's plea for tolerance. (On the second day of the strike the Newcastle City Council carried a resolution urging the Prime Minister to secure a resumption of negotiations.) The police made several baton charges on a crowd of some thousands in Bigg Market. Arrests were made liberally, and the trade unionists said that the police behaved brutally. The arrests which caused most attention were those of Will Lawther and of Henry Bolton, a local JP and Labour leader. The circumstances of these arrests certainly bear the marks of deliberate planning. On Sunday the police, who were accompanying a food lorry, saw Lawther and Bolton outside a pub, and asked them to help in food distribution. Lawther, by the police story, asked if they had a permit from the

Chopwell, Blaydon and Ryton Council of Action, and suggested that the food should be handed over to him for distribution. After some further argument both men were arrested. When the case was heard Lawther and Bolton were accused of establishing a 'reign of terror' in the district. They denied this, and denied also much of the police story, saying that this particular distributor was breaking an agreement made with them that he should not deliver goods on Sundays. They were fined £50 with the alternative of two months' imprisonment, and chose to go to prison. The trial was marked by a great demonstration in support of the accused men. Several thousand people marched to Gateshead County Police Court and sang the Red Flag. They were dispersed only after a number of baton charges and many arrests.

The happenings at Newcastle, in one of the strongest Labour areas, are instructive in any consideration of the strike's course. Some of the things that happened there were duplicated in many places where the Labour movement was strong, and the Strike Committee attempted to face the fact that only by obtaining complete control of transport could the strike be won. The confusion about permits; the difficulty in obtaining control of transport without practically declaring war upon authority; the more or less abortive attempts to provide an information service which should counteract the flood of Government propaganda: all these things were common to the experiences of Strike Committees in Crewe and Coventry, Wolverhampton and Wellingborough, as well as in big cities like Newcastle. Common, too, was the problem of maintaining successful communications with Eccleston Square for towns more than fifty miles from London. There were decisions to be made, there were interpretations of decisions which seemed clearly wrong for a particular time and place; and for the most part the local Strike Committees tried hard not to take any step that was out of line with the general plan. In Newcastle the Strike

Committee 'felt themselves bound to carry out the TUC decisions to the letter, no matter how many misgivings they might have'.

Beyond this there is apparent in the Newcastle report the kind of unjustified optimism that is a vital element in militant movements, and yet is also a dangerous and heady tonic. Accepting this report at its face value, what does it amount to? The strikers had checked the free flow of food, but that was a success which must have most effect upon their own supporters. They had stopped public transport. They had organized, very quickly, a plan of operations. These were real achievements, but they gave no cause for optimism. There does not seem to be any evidence to justify Connolly's claim that the Government had lost control of the situation, or that its organization broke down in any serious sense. To say that on Friday the success of the General Strike 'appeared completely assured' was mere self-deception.

Such self-deception was not confined to Newcastle. Ellen Wilkinson's exultant statement that at Crewe the strikers were running the town, so that no food entered or left without their permission, and every worker on light or gas operated under their permit, implied a recognition by the authorities of the trade unions' strength, but was in no other sense a victory. For the strikers to co-operate with the authorities in running a town, as happened in Crewe, might give the local Strike Committee a temporary feeling of power, but could in the end only assist the Government by easing an awkward situation. There was some point in the questions asked of Raymond Postgate afterwards at a meeting in Paris. Why were not more policemen killed? his Paris audience asked. And was it not proof of treachery when the General Council issued orders to strikers to play games and cultivate their gardens, rather than to go into the streets and fight the police? These questions reveal, obviously, a fundamental misunderstanding of the situation, in the sense that very few of the strikers wanted to go into the streets and fight the police: but they do also expose the uncertain intentions and half-hearted actions of those conducting the strike from Eccleston Square.

VIII
CONFUSION AT ECCLESTON SQUARE

At 4 am on 3rd May, on the eve of the strike, Beatrice Webb noted in her diary that 'the General Council of the TUC has certainly succeeded in giving an epic quality to their slow and reserved but decisive attitude towards the miners' dispute'. 'But', she observed on the following day, 'when all is said and done we personally are against the use of the General Strike in order to compel the employers of a particular industry to yield to the men's demands, however well justified their claims may be.' Her argument was very much that used by Government spokesmen in the House of Commons. If the strike succeeded 'it would mean that a militant minority were starving the majority into submission to their will, and would be the end of democracy, industrial as well as political'. She thought, however, that the strike would fail; and then the effects might be salutary, leaving both workers and the governing class in a better frame of mind. The governing class would 'compel the coal-owners to reorganize or clear out'. That, at least, was one of her thoughts: but on the same day she remarked that the strike would afford a justification of victimization on a considerable scale, and that its failure would be 'one of the most significant landmarks in the history of the British working class', marking the death gasp of 'the pernicious doctrine of "workers' control"'.

Her view of the General Council showed similar fluctuations. 'If it had not been for a few ambitious spirits like Bevin, egged on by middle-class theorists, there would never have been a General Council endowed with powers to call out the whole movement,' she said at one time – ignoring, one may feel, her own quality as a middle-class theorist. A few days later she felt more sympathy for the General Council. After all, they meant so well. They had been badly treated by the miners, and although they had been 'equally impossible' in their own treatment of the Parliamentary Labour Party, one had to forgive them in the end. 'They are so genuinely kindly in their outlook; they would gladly shake hands with anyone at any time, whether it be a Tory Prime Minister, a Russian emissary or their own employers.' But then again, news came that made her feel doubtful. 'All the intellectuals who watched the GC and Miners' Executive during these days . . . made one observation: those fifty or sixty men who were directing the GC were living a thoroughly unwholesome life – smoking, drinking, eating wrong meals at wrong times, rushing about in motor-cars, getting little or no sleep and talking aimlessly with one another.' How could men living so unhealthily be expected to make rational decisions?

The vacillatory feelings of Mrs Webb are interesting because – oddly enough – they so closely resemble those felt by many members of the General Council itself. They too were upon the whole against the use of the strike weapon. 'Pure fatalism,' Cramp had whispered when the Conference of Executives was taking the vote to strike. 'We can't win.' Why did they accept without protest the idea of a strike which so many of them felt could not be won? An onlooker at the conference said that he had never felt before at any meeting 'that the persons concerned were being carried away by the feeling that they had to do it, that the rank and file would expect it, that another Black Friday would be intolerable'.

Like Beatrice Webb, also, many members of the General

*E

Council had ambivalent feelings about the strike. They intended no betrayal of the workers who looked to them for leadership: yet every militant step tugged them in the direction of 'the pernicious doctrine of "workers' control"', every step in the direction of what seemed to them reasonable compromise worked to the advantage of a Government that was determined on complete victory. The strike was prosecuted with most determination by the few ambitious men like Bevin and Citrine, who felt confident of their own ability to deal with any left-wing revolt once victory had been won: least enthusiastically by men like the right-wing chairman, Arthur Pugh, of whom Hamilton Fyfe, editor of the *Daily Herald*, wrote that 'he might have made a fortune as a chartered accountant'. The words were meant for praise, but the qualities that make a good chartered accountant, valuable as they doubtless are, are hardly those to be looked for in the leader of a national strike. Of such an honest right-winger as Pugh perhaps nothing more was to be expected but that he should provide (to quote Fyfe again) 'a steady brain . . . vastly useful in this vast crisis'. But the left-wing trade union leaders played what seems in retrospect a strikingly timid part. They were outnumbered, but they occupied important positions. One of them, Purcell, was chairman of the Strike Organization Committee; George Hicks, John Bromley, Ben Tillett and A. B. Swales were leading figures on various committees. After the strike was over some of them spoke brave words to the effect that it had been a class struggle, yet during the nine days there is no suggestion that opinion in the General Council was seriously divided at any time. These men must surely have been opposed to many of the things done, or left undone: but they were too much overawed by the strike's implications, or too nearly overwhelmed by the personalities of Bevin and Thomas, to speak their minds effectively.

One prime concern felt by the General Council was to remain respectable in public eyes. It was rather an embarrassment for them to learn that there had been widespread demonstrations in support of the strike in the Soviet Union, that collections were being taken in all industrial centres, that many Russian workers had voted to contribute part of their wages towards a strike donation, and that all British ships in Russian ports had been held up. This embarrassment was increased by the offer of the All-Russian Trade Union Council to contribute 2 million roubles towards strike funds. Their reaction was immediate. As the *British Worker* put it: 'The council has informed the Russian trade unions, in a courteous communication, that they are unable to accept the offer and the cheque has been returned.' It is unlikely that the Russians expected very much from the strike. The Conservative MP, Robert Boothby, who was at that time on an unofficial mission in Moscow, was given an interview by Karl Radek, who advised him to return home because 'it is more interesting now there than here'. Radek added: 'But make no mistake, this is not a revolutionary movement. It is simply a wage dispute.'

Reactions to the strike on the part of the trade union movement elsewhere in Europe were enthusiastic. The International Transport Federation became the organizing centre of a trade union boycott on all transport to Britain. The International Miners' Federation placed an embargo on the transport of coal. There were many cash contributions, including one of 5,000 dollars from the International Federation of Trade Unions and another of 10,000 dollars from collections made at mass meetings in Germany. Elsewhere the Indian trade unions decided to prevent the bunkering of British ships, as did the Mexican Federation of Labour. In the United States the Amalgamated Clothing Workers sent a contribution of 10,000 dollars, although the AFL merely declared its sympathy for the miners. Messages of congratulation and solidarity came from trade union movements all over the world. They made, no doubt, heartening reading, although their practical effect was slight.

The emotional reactions of the General Council, already mentioned, had a practical effect upon every decision it made. The various committees were deluged with the detailed work involved in the sudden organization of a great strike for which they were unprepared, and the activities of the Strike Organization Committee, which made the vital hour-to-hour decisions, were coloured by Bevin's desire to keep power within his own hands. The Government had made elaborate preparations to give each area a large measure of autonomy; the General Council strove desperately to maintain the greatest possible degree of centralization. Where autonomous powers were given, they were to individual unions and not to Strike Committees. A little of the confusion caused by this centralization has been noted: one has to imagine it multiplied three or four hundred times to get some idea of the flood of inquiries that poured into Eccleston Square. Perhaps it was right in theory that no policy decisions should be made without reference to the General Council, but in practice this continual reference back wasted time and caused irritation in both large and small matters. Typical of the large matters was Newcastle's complaint about running a local paper; typical of the small ones was the annoyance caused to the ILP staff, who offered their services to the TUC at the beginning of the strike, to be told after three days had passed that their office boy would be useful as a messenger.

Bevin's principal achievement was to organize, within hours rather than days, a system of communications which, although sparse in many parts of the country, never actually broke down. This may seem meagre praise; yet to cover the country with a network of dispatch riders, and to organize their reception in towns and districts, was a considerable administrative feat. The General Council was aware of what was going on in every part of the country, and there were no blind spots of great importance.

One of the few major policy decisions made was that relating to permits. At the beginning of the strike permits were issued by national and local strike bodies. The Government's decision to ignore the TUC and the widespread abuse of permits by commercial firms caused a change of policy. On 6th May an announcement under Bevin's name was made in the *British Worker* that no permits were to be issued by any individual trade union or Trades Council. A Joint Transport Committee was to be set up in every district, and 'all existing permits must be reviewed by the Transport Committee at once'. It was also announced that a National Committee operating from Unity House (telegraphic address: Beware, Eusroad) would deal with the release of foodstuffs.

This announcement provoked a sharp reaction. The Government immediately accused the TUC of trying to blackmail the nation by holding up food supplies. 'An organized attempt is being made to starve the people and to wreck the State,' said the *British Gazette*. It also caused confusion in London, where many applications were made to the National Committee for local London permits, which were being handled by the London Transport Committee. In other places the confusion was increased by the fact that the Co-operative Society had not been mentioned in relation to permits. Since the feeding of the strikers depended largely on the Co-ops this was a maladroit omission, and in some cases was ignored. In others it gave rise to much heart-searching before the local Strike Committee and the local Co-op came to some kind of compromise.

The situation in Birmingham indicates the kind of position that arose. Here the Emergency Strike Committee decided at once that permits should be issued only to trade union labour for the unloading and distribution of goods and food-stuffs, and a local magistrate was appointed Permits Officer. But this decision involved the committee in a cat's cradle of complicated interpretation. Cadbury's had been given a permit to move cocoa and chocolate, but this was withdrawn when it was learned that some of their staff were acting as blacklegs in the electrical department. Some permits were held up for a week while others, for similar goods, were granted at once because they were for corporation use. Attempts to favour the local Co-operative Society caused more problems. On Friday an assumption of power to grant long-distance permits was made when the Co-op was allowed to move twelve tons of soap from Birmingham to Manchester. At last, uncertain of the extent to which it should assume responsibility, the Birmingham Strike Committee sent a deputation to London. They were told that the National Committee of Transport thought that the Government should be responsible for the movement of food in bulk, and that no permits at all should be issued for this purpose.

The CWS resented the attitude of the General Council. They went so far as to send out a circular to societies on the subject, pointing out the difficult position that had been created by the fact that the Co-ops had been refused exceptional treatment. A good deal of freedom was allowed to local societies, and some of them actively supported the strike by giving credit to members, while an equal or larger number refused such facilities.

These arguments over permits had about them a certain unreality. While local committees were trying to decide whether or not the Co-ops should be given permits to move coal or soap, the Government was moving foodstuffs and other supplies in quantities that made the General Council's decisions seem almost irrelevant. The issue of permits envisaged a situation that never arose, in which the General Council (and through them local Strike Committees) should have a control over transport which, except in one or two areas, they never obtained.

These were two of the three important policy decisions made by the General Council during the nine days. The third was the decision taken on 7th May to call out on 11th May the engineering and shipyard workers. But there were other decisions that it flinched from making, which had more effect upon the fate of the strike than anything which the council positively decided to do. It took no action regarding the postal and telegraph workers; and it never seriously faced the problem of how the workers who had come out on strike were to occupy their time.

The Union of Post Office Workers was comparatively weak, and although its representatives voted in favour of the strike at the Conference of Executives, the obedience of members to a strike call was thought to be doubtful. The effect of leaving them at work was to place this means of communication firmly in the hands of the Government, an action of which it naturally took full advantage. It was not until 11th May that the General Council took steps to counteract the Government's use of its powers. On this day instructions marked 'Secret' were sent out to dispatch riders in a letter signed by H. H. Elvin of the General Purposes Committee:

> I have found that a large number of telegrams sent by dispatch riders *en route* have never reached this office. . . . There is no doubt that the telephonic messages are being tapped. It is essential, therefore, that the following code should be used. All that will be necessary will be to give the name of the driver, the route number, the town and the necessary code words.

There followed the code words, which had been devised by somebody with a sense of humour. The code word for police was 'beauty', for baton charges 'beautify', for troops in control of police 'beautiful', and for troops firing on crowds 'beautifully'. Other matters for which provision was made in code were the wavering and return to work of engineers, railwaymen, transport workers and printers, the arrest of Strike Committees, and shortage of food. It is unlikely that these code telephone messages would have resisted penetration by the Government for more than a day or two, but the instructions show clearly the unfavourable position of the General Council in relation to post and telephone. Whether they would have been better placed had the post office workers been called out, and the Government compelled to use volunteers for the switchboards, is a matter of opinion. Such a move would have helped to destroy the prevailing good temper of the strike. It would also have involved a devolution of authority by the General Council to local Strike Committees. It would be hard to say which of these twin results the General Council would have considered the more undesirable.

Its determination that the strike should remain as far as possible pacific was responsible for the evasion of another decision: how were the strikers to occupy their time? The question, to be sure, received a kind of answer in the first issue of the *British Worker*:

> The General Council suggests that in all districts where large numbers of workers are idle sports should be organized and entertainments arranged
> This will both keep a number of people busy and provide amusement for many more.

This instruction was faithfully obeyed. Local Strike Committees arranged football matches, sports, concerts and other entertainments. American newspaper correspondents, who had come over to report on a revolutionary situation, found strikers playing football matches against the police. 'The chief activity of the police was to improve their standard of football in competition with the strikers' teams,' Ellen Wilkinson said. At Plymouth the chief constable's wife kicked off, in a match which the strikers won by two goals to one. At Lewes the police and strikers arranged a public billiards match. At Peterborough the mayor and chief constable gave use of the sports grounds at reduced prices or free of charge to committees who were organizing concerts and games of tennis, bowls and football. Cardiff Strike Committee advised the men: 'Keep smiling. Refuse to be provoked. Get into your garden. Look after the wife and kiddies. If you have not got a garden, get into the country, the parks and the playgrounds.' All over the country local Strike Committees organized 'Sport and Entertainment' sections, which did their best – and often that best was very good – to keep idle men amused.

All this was a tribute to the good humour of strikers and the ingenuity of entertainment committees: but it was not the way to win a strike. The greatest enemy of men on strike is lack of money, but closely after it follows boredom: and boredom is only temporarily alleviated by watching a football match or going to a concert. In spite of these pious injunctions, men did stand about idly talking, and it was noticeable that this tendency grew during the strike. Idleness carried its concomitants of purposeless violence among some groups of strikers, and among others an inclination to go back to work. The best tonic for men on strike, and particularly men engaged in a great sympathetic strike like this one, is action, or preparation for action: but against this the General Council set its face from the start. It insisted that picketing should be peaceful, and firmly refused requests made by many Strike Committees that they should be allowed to form Workers' Defence Groups. A few such groups were formed, but this was in defiance of orders from Eccleston Square. What would have happened to these men, who were bored and fretful within a week, had the strike continued for the month or more that was originally prophesied as its likely term? There can be no other conclusion than that many of them would have gone back to work, because the strike offered them no emotionally valid reasons for enthusiasm.

One must not be unjust to the General Council. Many of its mistakes (like that of permitting individual unions to issue strike notices) were the forgivable result of unpreparedness. Lacking administrative machinery it sought to improvise an administration; lacking the reality of power the council's leaders bravely wore its mask. But it must be said of these leaders also that no sympathetic strike, with one or two exceptions, could be won in the way they conducted this one. They were not rash but feebly timid; they hoped for the collaboration of their opponents and never wholly trusted the mass of their supporters; they feared the consequences of complete victory more than those of a negotiated defeat.

IX

SOLIDARITY IN THE COUNTRY

'Trades Union Congress officials were astonished by the completeness of labour's response to its call. All its calculations were too pessimistic,' wrote the London correspondent of the *New York World*. He added: 'On the other hand no man could have foreseen or thought possible the speed and efficiency of the Government's counter measures.' The steadfastness and optimism of the strikers may be attributed partly to their ignorance of the Government's moves. Nevertheless the spontaneous growth of working-class organizations to handle the problems that arose, and the enthusiasm and ingenuity with which they were met, was altogether remarkable.

Many stories testify to the spontaneity of working-class reaction, but only a few of them can be recounted. A young man named Leslie Paul walked with a friend to the office of the Lewisham Labour Party on the Monday before the strike. They were astonished to find that the office was closed. They got little more help from the secretary of the local Trades Council, who was embarrassed and surprised by their offer to help with his strike plans. He would be along, he said, first thing after dinner to get things going, 'though, however, comrades, I don't quite know what we can do'. On Monday afternoon, while they kicked their heels at Labour Party headquarters, they found the man they were looking for in the shape of a fitter named James, who was the Trades Council chairman. 'Well, what do you young bastards want?' he asked. When Paul told him, with some vigour, he grinned. 'Steady, mate,' he said. 'One —— thing at a time.' With James's help Paul and his friend concocted a bulletin which Paul typed out on a wax stencil. The bulletin told what they knew of the strike call and asked the Lewisham workers for a 100 per cent response. It was delivered by bicycle to each trade union branch secretary.

That was a beginning. Within a day or two an organization had sprung into being. 'Quite soon, and almost without thinking what we were doing, we would have created a machine, if things had gone our way, capable of administering the borough,' Paul says. The Council of Action, as it was called, organized rosters of messengers from the strikers who came to the offices. They parked their cycles, motor-bicycles and cars outside, and waited for jobs to be given them. James handled all trade union affairs, organized mass picketing where necessary, and rushed groups of men to any factory where workers were trickling back or had not come out. When building workers on housing sites, who had been told to stay at work, left their jobs in protest, James went to the site, talked to them, and induced them to go back. A woman member planned soup kitchens and relief parcels of food. A finance secretary was in charge of raising money. A headquarters guard was organized, after an attack by the local Fascists. Paul was in charge of propaganda. He distributed the *British Worker*, produced a local daily bulletin, and held several open-air meetings every night of the strike. Large collections were taken at these meetings, and as the strike went on they obtained some middle-class support.

One of the problems that faced the Lewisham Council of

Action was that of the unconscious blackleg, who regarded the strike as a holiday from his ordinary work during which he could take up another temporary job. Another was that of the informer. At Lewisham the Council of Action was joined by an informer or Government agent, named Johnstone, who was the local secretary of the Unemployed Workers' Committee Movement. The council refused to accept his services, but ran into trouble with another perfectly sincere local trade unionist, who was no sooner on the platform than he provoked the police by daring them to arrest him, which they willingly did. For the most part, however, the General Strike was for Paul and his friends a happy time, and one which convinced them of the great capacity for extempore organization inherent in the working class.

This impression is confirmed by what happened elsewhere. Local Trades Councils set up organizations everywhere to deal with the strike. In most cases they had no paid officials, and some had no premises of their own. Nevertheless they constructed organizations which acted jointly with trade union branches, and sometimes with the Co-ops. In some cases the joint organization was called a Council of Action (a name frowned upon by the General Council), in others a Strike Committee or Emergency Committee. Sometimes union branches refused to co-operate, sometimes the unions maintained a Strike Committee of their own, but generally the union representatives worked harmoniously with the Trades Council.

These committees were everywhere the backbone of the strike resistance. They met once or twice every day, and covered almost every conceivable aspect of the strike. There were Publicity and Entertainment committees, committees to handle permits and picketing, distress, food, sport and transport. Their effectiveness varied from district to district, but the overall picture is one of triumph over local and sectional difficulties. In many cases these committees evolved almost at once the kind of devolution of authority that was essential if the strike was to continue for some weeks. At Merthyr Tydfil there was a Central Strike Committee, with sub-committees dealing with food, finance, communications, sports and entertainments, permits and intelligence; then, further, there were four District Strike Committees, each with four local sub-committees. Such a system could be used only where the Labour movement was strong: but there is a great deal of evidence that in many places the workers were very willing to assume the responsibilities of power.

A certain intoxication often went with this assumption of power, well exemplified in the arrogance of a sheet metal worker who was on the committee at Ashton, outside Manchester:

> Employers of labour were coming, cap in hand, begging for permission to do certain things, or, to be more correct, to allow their workers to return to perform certain customary operations. 'Please can I move a quantity of coal from such and such a place' or 'Please can my transport workers move certain foodstuffs in this or that direction'. Most of them turned empty away after a most humiliating experience, for one and all were put through a stern questioning just to make them realize that we and not they were the salt of the earth.

The secretary of the Strike Committee at Ynysybwl, near Pontypridd, gives rather more sympathetic glimpses of the way in which power was exercised. Here the committee ran a canteen and supplied strikers with food when they had filled up a questionnaire giving details of the numbers in their family. The number of strike families using the canteen grew quickly from 200 to 900.

> On the fifth day, while the committee sat, a knock came on the door, and I found our youngest daughter there, about twelve years of age, with a small tin jug in her hand. She said: 'Mum wants you to let her have some soup. She is washing and can't make dinner today.'
>
> I told her: 'Tell your mother to fill in the form and come tomorrow.'
>
> Naturally I felt some compunction. When I got home

that evening I had 'tongue pie', highly peppered. My wife did not apply afterwards. It so happened that on that day for the first time we were five quotas short for those registered. Had I supplied our daughter, and those who had gone short come to know, there would have been strong representations to the committee.

Going home one day I found my wife with dark bruises on her face and arms. She said that while putting clothes on the backyard line she had fallen. By discreet questioning of the children (we had five) I found that the mother had neglected feeding herself so that the kiddies should have more.

There were two transport applications which, although unusual in themselves, reflect the kind of problems met by the committees:

One was from a local operator. It will be remembered that no transport should be allowed. This kind gentleman offered the committee a hundred free tickets, which would allow persons authorized by the committee to attend District Council Federation meetings outside the village. His letter received a direct negative.

The other application was from the local vicar, and caused a little searching of hearts. The vicar wanted permission to engage a brake to convey a number of the youngest of his flock to confirmation at a neighbouring church. He naturally stressed that the children would be grievously disappointed if the ban was adhered to. Some of the committee members were moved by this, but in the end the application was turned down.

Some of the moves made by the Councils of Action more or less directly contravened the General Council's instructions. The most important of these was the formation of Workers' Defence Corps or some other form of workers' police. The Minority Movement had urged the formation of such a corps after the July crisis, but the sub-committee set up by the General Council to consider it reported that the idea was both unwise and impracticable. In a few places the Councils of Action organized such a force, to prepare for a possible sharpening of the struggle. At Chatham and Col-chester the force took the form of special pickets for meetings; at Methil, in East Fife, a corps of some hundreds was organized and used for regular patrol work. Sowerby Bridge, in Yorkshire, reported 'a few men appointed to assist in maintaining peace in the streets and highways – a huge success'. The men were not armed with rifles or revolvers, and acted more as workers' police than as military formations.

The weaknesses of the Councils of Action and Strike Committees were those of the Labour movement as a whole. Where local organization was weak comparatively little was done. The strong Councils of Action in some areas tried to counteract this by acting as a link between the General Council and small towns and villages, but this did not work very satisfactorily. In Hampshire and the Isle of Wight all attempt to undertake organized work was abandoned, because the numbers available were quite inadequate to cover the area.

Yet upon the whole the picture throughout the country was one of sudden improvisations carried through successfully; of local organizations growing throughout the strike in power and militancy; and of a quite remarkable solidarity among the workers in all but the weakest districts.

X

AMUSEMENT AS USUAL

The strike's effect upon the economic life of the country was not paralleled by any comparable effect upon public amusements. At first indeed the public was hesitant. The attendance at the opening of the Royal Academy on the Monday before the strike was the poorest ever known. Visitors wandered through the rooms like unwilling victims, pausing only to contemplate gloomily Ambrose McEvoy's portrait of Ramsay MacDonald and Glyn Philpot's of Stanley Baldwin. Edgar Wallace's *The Ringer* opened at Wyndham's, but there was some doubt about how long this, or any other, theatre would stay open, since it was expected that central London would be deserted in the evenings. A man who found his barber's empty was told by the attendant that everybody was afraid of revolution. Doubts were expressed whether racing, cricket or any other form of sport could or should go on.

Only in one respect were these gloomy expectations fulfilled. The first two days' racing at Chester, on Tuesday and Wednesday, were carried through, and it was estimated that the crowd on Wednesday was only 20 per cent smaller than usual; but because of transport troubles there were not sufficient runners to make racing possible on the third day, and the stewards of the Jockey Club and of the National Hunt Committee decided that racing should be abandoned during the emergency.

In other sports the situation was different. The football season had finished just before the strike, with Huddersfield at the top of the First Division, but two international matches against Belgium and France were postponed. The continuation of cricket was decided after an approach had been made to the Prime Minister in person. The matter was brought before the Cabinet by Baldwin, and it decided that cricket should continue, 'as it involved no expense or strain on any resources of the country in the present crisis, and would be the means of promoting good feeling between all sport-loving classes'. The MCC issued a statement saying that:

> They recommend the counties to carry on their programme as well as circumstances permit, although, owing to transport difficulties, some matches may have to be reduced to two days or even abandoned. . . . They suggest to cricketers that they should be guided by a sense of public duty rather than by affection for their counties, but

they strongly recommend that the best possible elevens should be put into the field against the Australians, as on these occasions cricketers may, out of courtesy to our guests, legitimately obtain leave from their public duties.

Thus magisterially encouraged, county cricket continued undisturbed. The Australians pursued a triumphant way, making 532 runs in a day against Essex at Leyton, and on Saturday making 301 runs for 6 wickets against Surrey at the Oval. Twenty thousand people came to watch them, and the crowds at most matches were as large as usual.

The tennis tournament at Hurlingham also continued, and at Harrogate O. G. M. Turnbull and J. D. P. Wheatley won both their singles in the Davis Cup against Poland. Sportsmen generally seem to have felt that their duty was to sport, although there were a few exceptions like Lionel Tennyson, who acted as a police inspector, and the rising lawn tennis star Bunny Austin, who drove a bus.

In the theatre an alarmist note was struck. Sir Lewis Casson writes:

> When the strike was declared my wife, Dame Sybil Thorndike, and I were playing *Saint Joan* at the Lyceum, under the management of Bronson Albery and myself. An emergency meeting of all West End managers took place the next morning, at which Sir Alfred Butt (manager of the Palace Theatre and a Conservative MP) proposed that all theatres should at once close down. He received little support, and it was decided almost unanimously that the theatres should carry on as long as possible. With considerable difficulties in getting the members of our company home after the show, we finished the first week.

Casson was one of the comparatively few theatrical people who took an interest in the strike, apart from its direct effect on him. Although he thought that the General Council had been manœuvred into calling the strike, he felt it his duty to support them, and an Tuesday morning reported at Eccleston Square with his car. He was given the job of driver to Smith and Cook, and took them to various meetings and consultations. It was an open car, and the police knew Smith and Cook well by sight, but any prejudice they may have felt against the miners' leaders did not affect their customary courtesy.

On Wednesday night the taxi-cab drivers joined the strike, an action which was thought likely to affect theatre audiences. Eight theatres closed down for the duration. Most of those that stayed open did extremely good business. A visitor to the Empire, where Fred and Adele Astaire were playing in *Lady, Be Good*, could get only standing room at the back of the stalls. At the Court Theatre *The Farmer's Wife* moved towards its thousandth performance, and at Drury Lane *Rose Marie* was in its second year. Both continued to attract large audiences every night, and so did *The Ringer*. Musical shows, among them *No, No, Nanette* at the Palace, were packed out. Emboldened by this, the Royal Opera House went ahead with its plans to open the season during the strike. On Monday, 10th May, *The Marriage of Figaro* was presented at Covent Garden with great success. Every seat was sold, and some of those in the gallery had been waiting all day for admission. Men in silk hats, and women wearing tiaras and necklaces, emerged from limousines which blocked the narrow streets round Covent Garden. It was all quite as usual, at least until the time came to go home; and even then most people seemed to have cars. The audience gave five minutes' continuous applause to the German conductor Bruno Walter.

In the provinces also cinemas were full, and many theatres played to capacity. A girl living in Edinburgh noted in a letter to a friend: 'I walked to the Lyceum Theatre, saw and muchly enjoyed *She Stoops to Conquer*, and walked quietly back again along the salubrious neighbourhood of Fountainbridge between 10.30 and 11, all being as peaceful as you can imagine.'

Perhaps one should include under the heading of amusements the activities of some schoolchildren during the strike.

School attendances, the wireless said, were remarkably well maintained, and there is no reason to doubt that this was true. For those who lived more than a few minutes' walk from home, however, the strike offered exceptional opportunities for free travel. That, at least, is the way in which one enterprising eleven-year-old schoolboy remembers it:

'My preparatory school was at Swiss Cottage, my home a penny fare away on the Metropolitan Railway, and it was on the return journey in the afternoons that I made the most of the absence of trams and buses. I used to wait in a doorway until a racing car – preferably a Bentley, but this was rare – came roaring down the Finchley Road. The driver seldom failed to pull up when he saw the small boy in shorts and cap standing on the kerb, clutching school books in one hand and signalling hopefully with the other.

The great art in the ensuing negotiations was not to be trapped into stating one's destination. 'Are you going in the direction of Harrow, sir?' was, I found, a useful gambit which led me on many pleasant journeys of exploration. I remember one afternoon when, with a feeling of freedom such as I have seldom recaptured since, I drove in luxury past the corner of the street where we lived, *en route* to visit an entirely imaginary aunt in Ealing.

Such experiences were fairly common, but not all schoolboy recollections of the strike were so pleasant. For working-class boys in the north, particularly, it marked the beginning of a period of hardship and parental bitterness, the reasons for which were only vaguely understood. Another boy, living in the small Devonshire seaside town of Dawlish, remembers his fear on walking through the old part of the town and seeing the men standing about and talking, with an air of sullen anger. There was something in the air, he thought; and since nobody had explained to him that the something was a strike, he was frightened by it. Boys at boarding schools were little affected by the strike, although they were given news of it, which had for the most part, naturally, a strong bias in favour of the Government.

XI

FREEDOM OF THE PRESS

At the six o'clock press conference on the first day of the strike J. C. C. Davidson announced that the Government was printing a newspaper which would be called the *British Gazette*. The paper, he said, would cost a penny, would contain authoritative news, and would be in fact a Government publication. Almost all other questions put to him about the paper were answered by the words, 'You will see tomorrow', but he did add that the paper would be run by experts. In view of this remark it seems strange that the anonymous editor of the paper should have been Winston Churchill.

The reason for Churchill's appointment as editor of an official Government paper, a task for which he was by temperament peculiarly unsuited, is a matter for speculation. It may be that his colleagues remembered that he was the only member of the Cabinet with practical journalistic experience, even though that experience was more than twenty years old; or it may have been felt, as was less kindly suggested, that his immense energy should be directed into a channel in which it would not disrupt the Government's already prepared organization. 'Don't forget the cleverest thing I ever did,' Baldwin said long afterwards to his biographer, G. M. Young. 'I put Winston in a corner and told him to edit the *British Gazette*.' If a diversion was intended it was singularly unsuccessful, for within a day or two the *British Gazette* had become an object of furious controversy, which continued until the end of the strike. It was not long before the Government appointed Davidson as Executive Officer, to watch over the exuberant editor, to use a blue pencil on copy that he might have passed, and to persuade him that he was making no concessions to Bolshevism by printing reports of football matches between police and strikers. Churchill found the experience delightful; it seemed to him, he rather oddly said, a combination of a first-class battleship and a first-class general election.[1]

The decision to publish an official newspaper was taken only after a meeting on 3rd May between Churchill and representatives of the Newspaper Proprietors' Association. At this meeting several possibilities were canvassed: continued independent production by newspapers, a combination to produce one single strike edition, and Government support for either of these plans. No formal decision was taken, but the idea of a single strike edition was ruled out. Some speakers in the discussion were doubtful about the chances of obtaining skilled men to produce newspapers of any kind, and it was the expression of this doubt that finally moved the Government to produce its own newspaper.

It was necessary to find a plant in which the paper could be printed. The *Daily Mail* and *Daily Express* offices were inspected and turned down, because they were situated in narrow, easily blockaded positions, and J. S. Elias, managing director of Odhams, refused the use of their plant. At this point H. A. Gwynne, editor of the *Morning Post*, got into touch with Davidson, offered to produce 100,000 copies of a four-page daily bulletin with Government co-operation, and suggested that if any difficulty arose some large newspaper office (such as the *Morning Post*) should be commandeered. This suggestion, or invitation, was acted upon; the take-over was confirmed by a Cabinet minute, and Sir Malcolm Fraser was put in charge as direct representative of the Government. Production of the first issue of the *British Gazette* began, with the help of all but one of the machine-room overseers, and of the composing-room staff. At five o'clock on the morning of 4th May, however, a staff representative who

[1] In a recent television interview, Davidson has claimed that he was in fact the editor of the *British Gazette*.

had been sent to the London Society of Compositors for instructions returned with the information that they were forbidden to touch the work. Only five of the fourteen columns for the first issue of the paper had been set.

At this point, as often before and after, Lord Beaverbrook came to the help of the Government, by lending to them what was afterwards described as 'the one man without whom the situation could not have been saved'. This was Sydney Long, night superintendent of the *Daily Express*. Long set most of the other nine columns of this first issue with his own hands. Two other experienced technicians came with Long from the *Daily Express*, and the chief stereotyper of the *Daily Mail* helped in the foundry a little later. In the machine-room a few *Morning Post* technicians, including the works manager and the machine-room overseer, were joined by several members of the editorial staff, who had to be initiated into the work. The initiation was not carried out without some trouble. A mould was broken in the foundry, and it took nearly two hours to clear away the splashed metal so that the autoplate would work again. It was midnight on 4th May before the last plate had been locked on the cylinder. Early on the following morning 230,000 copies of the *British Gazette* had been produced, and most of them had been distributed. The first supplies were sent by aeroplane to the provinces, and the rest were sent out in London by car and van.

The production of a newspaper with so few experienced hands, and at such short notice, was a remarkable achievement; and the strain of production was increased, rather than lessened, by subsequent issues. Work on the paper had to begin at ten o'clock in the morning, because there was only one man operating the linotype. Members of the editorial staff acted as copyholders in the reading-room, pulled proofs and did half a dozen other jobs in turn. Some of them worked, with snatches of sleep and rest, for seventy-two hours at a time, and few of these key men left the building to go home during the strike. Their amateur assistants were divided into three gangs; numbered among them were undergraduates, clerks, artists, stockbrokers, medical students, doctors, music professors and coffee planters. Arrangements had to be made to feed them, to provide accommodation for those who wished to stay in the *Morning Post* building and to take others home. The building itself was protected by a small army of police and special constables, and admission to it could only be gained with a pass. 'It took on', said its anonymous historian, with a touch of over-emphasis, 'the aspect of a beleaguered fastness.' In fact, very little attempt was made to interfere with the production or distribution of the paper, and the special constables' zeal found no more effective outlet than in denying Lord Birkenhead admission because he lacked a pass.

The first issue of the *British Gazette* was dated 5th May, the last (No. 8) 13th May. At the end of the strike the paper had reached a circulation of well over 2 million copies, certainly the quickest circulation increase in history. An offer by Churchill to carry on for a few days after the end of the strike on 12th May was rejected, and the organization so quickly devised was as quickly dismantled. On 14th May an 'emergency edition' of the *Morning Post* appeared.

The *British Gazette* was a large four-page sheet, which displayed the notice 'Published by His Majesty's Stationery Office' on its masthead. Its make-up bore many marks of amateurishness. In the first issue pep talks and exhortations to enlist for one or another form of voluntary service were blended with Zoo Notes, half a column about ice hockey in Canada, and a story about the testing of water pipes. In this first issue, also, the two middle pages were blank, nominally so that the paper could conveniently be pasted up on walls but in fact because of setting difficulties, and in several of the later issues the same news items appeared on two successive days. Thus the 3 am edition of 11th May and the issue of 12th May carried exactly the same material on the middle pages, only pages one and four providing fresh news.

From the first the *British Gazette* made no pretence of impartiality. It was natural that a Government paper should be optimistic about the outcome of the strike, but there is a point at which unrestrained optimism becomes untruth, and this point was often passed. When the paper said on 5th May that the strike 'was by no means so complete as its promoters hoped' it may merely have been misinformed; when it added that 'there were far more trains running than was the case on the first day of the railway strike in 1919' this must have been written with the knowledge that the railway services had been practically extinguished. When, on the following day, under the heading 'Why Walk to Work?' it said that the LGOC had 200 buses on the streets, the actual official figure was 86. When it said that there was a 'full service to-day' on the Central London line and that other services were 'still improving', the facts were that 8 trains out of 29 were running on the Central London and that a total of 43 out of 315 were in operation over the whole underground service.

These small falsifications were generally ineffective in London, since people saw the realities of the situation for themselves. The attitude adopted by the *British Gazette* towards the strike and strikers, however, seriously threatened the prospect of future industrial peace. From the first the editorial attitude was that the strike threatened the constitution, and was an attempt to set up an alternative form of government. The protests and denials made by the General Council of the TUC against these statements were ignored. 'His Majesty's Government . . . will use all the resources at their disposal and whatever measures may be necessary to secure in a decisive manner the authority of Parliamentary Government,' said an editorial on 6th May, in a statement which went beyond anything said by Baldwin. In the following issue, under the heading 'Official', it was said that any man who remained at work or returned to work would be protected by the State from 'subsequent reprisals', and on Saturday, 8th May, the following announcement was featured on the front page:

> All ranks of the Armed Forces of the Crown are hereby notified that any action which they may find it necessary to take in an honest endeavour to aid the Civil Power will receive, both now and afterwards, the full support of His Majesty's Government.

This order was regarded by the General Council and the Labour Party as an incitement to violence, and the manner of its display was certainly provocative. The king, whose influence throughout the strike was consistently exerted on the side of moderation, wrote through Lord Stamfordham to the War Office: 'His Majesty cannot help thinking that this is an unfortunate announcement.'

This issue contained an instance of the paper's highly selective attitude towards news. A statement by Asquith, expressing his complete opposition to the strike, was given a double column heading on the front page. A statement issued by the Archbishop of Canterbury and other leaders of the Church in England, appealing for a negotiated settlement, was omitted altogether. The storm of parliamentary protest caused by this action was headed by Lloyd George. In a powerful speech he attacked the suppression of a document 'given with a real desire to save the State from disaster, and given by men who, it is hardly necessary to say, the last thing they desire is to upset the law, the constitution and the well-being of this country'. Churchill's reply was conciliatory but evasive. Type, he said, could only be set very slowly by amateurs; no doubt a number of pieces which should have gone in had been omitted. If importance was attached to this one –

'A statement by the Head of the Established Church!' interjected Hugh Dalton.

But Churchill was not to be moved by sarcasm. He

F

promised to put in the statement, but refused to say exactly
when it would appear. It was inserted, inconspicuously on
the back page, on the last day of the strike.

This was not the only parliamentary attack made upon
the *British Gazette*. It was under fire from the day of its publication, when Commander Kenworthy asked under what
powers or regulations publication was made, and was told
that 'the Government are acting under the authority applicable to every Government from time to time'. It was attacked for printing biased news and unfair statements, and
for showing continual partiality in the selection of news
items. To this Churchill replied: 'I cannot undertake to be
impartial as between the fire brigade and the fire.' He was
stung, however, by Lloyd George's contemptuous remark
that the *British Gazette* was 'a first-class indiscretion, clothed
in the tawdry garb of third-rate journalism'. The duty of
those responsible for the paper, he angrily retorted, was not
to publish a lot of defeatist trash. That was no doubt true:
but the manner in which the *Gazette* selected and presented
news often disquieted the Government's more moderate
supporters. 'The *Gazette* was often read with derision,' wrote
the London correspondent of the *New York Times*. 'Certain
ministerial dabblings in journalism did not produce the
desired result.'

There was, in fact, little need for a Government newspaper; the Newspaper Proprietors' Association had been too
pessimistic about the capacity for improvisation shown by
the skeleton staffs remaining at work. Almost every London
newspaper produced some kind of edition, with the help of
volunteer labour. For the first day or two these papers often
consisted of a single sheet in facsimile typewriting, sometimes with the headings written in, but by the fifth day of
the strike, at the week-end, they had settled into regular
forms. The *Daily Graphic* and *Daily Mirror* were presenting a
four-page sheet with two picture pages on front and back;
the *Daily Telegraph* was a neat quarto size four-page sheet,

packed with news (and rumours) in rather small type; the *Daily Mail*, *Daily Express* and *Evening News* all produced some kind of paper every day. In addition to these the continental *Daily Mail*, printed and published in Paris, was brought over to England by aeroplane in large quantities, and was often selling in south coast towns by nine o'clock in the morning, and only a little later in London. There were also many news sheets, which generally gave only news contained in the wireless bulletins, and a number of local papers such as the *Brixton Free Press* and the *Streatham News*, which produced papers of quite respectable size.

Outside London the situation was easier. The *Scotsman*, which was printed by non-union labour, remained unaffected by the strike, and many other provincial papers rallied after the shock of the first forty-eight hours. The *Yorkshire Post*, for instance, produced a strike edition of almost normal size, and distributed it by the firm's own vans, helped by a fleet of private cars headed by a large silver racing car whose driver was said to wear a mask, and to drive straight through the barriers erected by strikers outside some towns. A young freelance journalist with some experience of jobbing printing, who offered his services to the paper, thought of the strike simply as fun. The presses were kept running by foremen and managers, the caseroom work was undertaken by the reporters with the aid of a few volunteers, and a million copies of the paper were produced every night. Pickets hung about the entrance, but made no attempt to interfere with the paper's distribution. 'After the night's work was over I used to curl up on some paper bales and sleep. It was too much trouble to walk home, and I felt disinclined to waste day time in bed when I could be out and about seeing the fun. Undoubtedly it *was* fun for young people. All we were conscious of was a change from normal routine, a sense that life had suddenly become an adventure, and a feeling that great events were actually touching our own lives.'

Two or three factors made possible this substantial defeat of the attempt to stifle the press. The first was the pride felt by many newspaper workers in their particular paper. In most cases they came out on strike, but they often did so unwillingly, and the conflict of loyalties was very real. A small minority of technicians ignored the strike call and remained at work, and they were supplemented by members of the editorial staff, who often were not trade unionists and felt no sympathy for the miners' cause. With this nucleus of skilled and semi-skilled workers some kind of newspaper could be produced, and here another factor operated, for to unskilled and volunteer workers the production of a newspaper had something romantic about it; like driving a train or a bus, it was the fulfilment of a childish dream. And one must add yet another consideration: that many of those who helped in the production of newspapers had some sympathy for the strikers, but felt that it was morally wrong and practically unwise to attempt to deprive the country of news.

The journalistic triumph of the strike was undoubtedly the production of *The Times*. Although neither the editor, Geoffrey Dawson, nor the manager, W. Lints Smith, was in England when the strike began, preparations were made for the recruitment of the paper's old pensioners in case the whole trade union staff came out, and for the production of a multigraph newspaper. Although the members of the three maintenance chapels afterwards assured the chairman that 'they had entered the dispute with feelings of sadness', they seemed to feel that they had no choice about coming out on strike. 'There was no general recognition that in maintaining what they regarded as loyal obedience to their unions they were also violating contracts solemnly made and scrupulously observed on the other side,' wrote Geoffrey Dawson in a record of events compiled after the strike's end. The issue of 4th May was the last to be produced by trade union labour. The strikers, coming out of Printing House Square in the early hours of Tuesday morning, found that they had no means of getting home. At the suggestion of the chairman, Major Astor, they were transported in the cars which had been ordered specially to avert strike transport problems.

The next issue of *The Times*, No. 44,263, is something of a collector's item. It was a single sheet, measuring thirteen inches by eight, printed on front and back. The front page gave a variety of strike news; the back contained an account of parliamentary proceedings, financial and sporting news, and the broadcasting programme. The issue was printed on the six multigraph machines which had been installed, together with their operators, on the afternoon of Monday, 3rd May. The total number printed, when the machines were stopped at eight o'clock on the morning of 5th May, was no more than 48,000: but this was the only regular London newspaper issued from its own office on the first day of the strike.

On Wednesday afternoon an attempt was made to set the office on fire. A stream of petrol was poured into the machine-room through the inadequately closed port for unloading supplies of paper from the street. The petrol was lighted, and a great blaze of flame went up. One man happened to be at work on the machines, and he gave the alarm. The machine-room floor was concrete, and by the time fire engines arrived the fire was under control. After this attempt at arson a system of passes was instituted, patrol watches were set throughout the day and night, and police and special constables guarded the exterior of the building.

A large number of enthusiastic volunteers, many of them of high social position, also descended on Printing House Square. Other papers received similar assistance – Lady Louis Mountbatten acted as a telephone operator in the *Daily Express* and a galaxy of society women sold the *Sunday Express* in the streets – but *The Times*, as might have been expected, was chiefly favoured. Among those who drove lorries for the paper were the Duchess of Westminster and the Duchess of Sutherland, Viscountess Massereene and Ferrard, and the daughter of the Marchioness of Londonderry, Lady Maureen Stanley. The roll of masculine helpers was even more impressive. To quote *The Times*'s own narrative of the strike:

> *The Times* became the very centre of the fashion. A strong contingent of the Chairman's friends in the House of Commons came down at once, and continued to come night after night. . . . Members of half the clubs in London offered their services. Undergraduates began to appear from the universities. . . . The list of volunteer motor-drivers included directors not only of *The Times* itself but of great banks and public companies. A Governor-elect put in some strenuous shifts as a packer in the intervals of packing his own boxes for the Antipodes.

The enrolment of these packers, drivers and handymen and women did not solve the basic problems of newspaper production. 'If *The Times* was to appear in anything like its usual form – its columns composed by linotype or monotype, its pages duly cast and printed, its presses supplied with the necessary power – then skilled volunteers and craftsmen must somehow be found for half a dozen different processes.' Found they were. A married couple, able to use the linotype, were brought from their Southampton home to London; the Monotype Corporation and one or two other firms lent skilled men; a search through the provinces yielded a few skilled volunteers. The editorial staff supplied hand-setters and proof-readers. The work of the foundry-men and machine-minders was done largely by amateurs, including two descendants of the original John Walter, under the supervision of a few ex-printers and engineers with general knowledge of the work. The army of enthusiastic amateurs watched over by a few sceptical professionals produced the issue of 6th May – no more than a four-page sheet, but recognizably an issue of *The Times*, produced on its own rotary presses. More than 78,000 copies of it were printed. From this point onward the paper went from strength to strength. On Saturday, 8th May, the number of copies printed was 166,700; on Monday it had risen to 250,000, and on the last day of the strike, 12th May, 342,000 copies were printed and distributed. On this day, also, an afternoon edition of *The Times* was published for the first time in its history, with the leading article rapidly rewritten, and the complete official statement about the end of the strike.

The four-page paper produced during this period was, in tone and substance, a model of its kind. Misprints were few, and some of those few, like the addition of a question mark after the 'Lab.' that followed J. H. Thomas's name, may even be thought felicitous. Almost the only questionable feature was the retention of a full page of advertisements: one is hardly convinced by the argument offered in favour of the publication of the record of births, marriages and deaths, that these were 'carefully selected for their value as news'. The other three pages, however, were admirably written and conspicuously fair. Parliamentary debates were reported fully upon both sides, with no such adjectival emphasis as that of the *British Gazette* ('Mr George Lansbury, a wild Socialist, passionate and shouting'). Space was found for important letters. The Archbishop of Canterbury's appeal was given the prominence it warranted. Statements issued by the Government and the TUC were given equal emphasis. Academic manifestoes in support of the strikers' case were printed, with their subsequent rebuttals. With all this, *The Times* never concealed its own belief that the strike must be opposed and defeated.

Performing, as they felt, a public service, the directors of *The Times* were naturally concerned when a quarter of their stock of newsprint was commandeered by the *British Gazette*. Dawson, who had now returned, went to see the Prime Minister, and on 7th May wrote an indignant letter saying that 'the broad effect of this action is to threaten the suppression of *The Times*, and presumably also of every other newspaper'. He added that if the Government's real purpose was to commandeer the paper used for the TUC's *British Worker*, that would seem to him an equally disastrous policy. The letter was passed by Baldwin to Churchill, and answered by him in a way which shows that he meant to make the most of his editorial opportunities. After saying that the requisitioning order, which had been made on all papers, was essential, he added:

> The *British Gazette* printed 836,000 copies last night. I hope to print over a million on Monday, and over a million and a quarter on Tuesday. It is devouring paper at a terrible rate. But remember this is the one means which at present exists of holding together, in direct contact with the Executive Government and Parliament, the whole loyal mass of citizens throughout the nation. . . .
>
> I do not at all agree with your idea that the TUC have as much right as the Government to publish their side of the case and to exhort their followers to continued action. It is a very much more difficult task to feed the nation than it is to wreck it.

In fact, the *British Gazette*, after a few days, was palpably overprinting. To quote *The Times*'s account:

> It was a familiar complaint that two copies, one folded inside the other, were thrust into houses where none had been ordered. . . . Its output was palpably far larger than the public demand or the means of effective distribution, and London was soon littered with large bundles of *Gazettes* that, so far from being read, were never even untied. If there was ever the prospect of a real famine of newsprint, which was very doubtful, this was certainly the way to bring it about.

Effective distribution of *The Times* was not achieved without some trouble. The London representative of the *New York Times* saw 'a lively scene' going on under his windows when the second issue came off the presses. 'I reached the window in time to see several bundles of the paper hurled into the slippery street by the strikers as fast as they were brought out from the presses. The assistant foreign editor, Mr Peterson, objected strenuously and got into a furious fist fight with three or four strikers sending smashing blows to his face and body. They finally knocked him into the mud, but not before he got home with some savage blows.'

After this incident a body known as the 'shock troops' was employed to load the cars and see them away from Printing House Square. Members of the Sporting Department, known to the pickets as the jazz band because of their Fair Isle sweaters, acted as patrol leaders. They included well-known football players, cricketers and golfers, and a number of MPs, including Duff Cooper. Their tactics were vigorous and effective, but they were not often needed. 'When the moment came and we sallied forth to fight we found there was practically no opposition at all,' Duff Cooper wrote. Once the cars were away from Printing House Square they drove to destinations carefully plotted in advance. In one or two instances aeroplanes were used, and towards the end of the strike trains were brought into the scheme, but the backbone of distribution was the motor-cars with their volunteer drivers. Thanks to them, *The Times* was on sale in the south and east Midlands a little earlier than usual, and in Manchester, Liverpool and the north only a little later. After the end of the strike one subscriber wrote from Bournemouth:

> Every day throughout the strike, *The Times* was on my breakfast table at 8.15 – the same time that it reaches me in normal times in London – 100 miles nearer your office. What an organization!

*   *   *   *

On the afternoon of Tuesday, 4th May, Hamilton Fyfe, editor of the *Daily Herald*, the night editor, William Mellor, and the general manager, Robert Williams, met the TUC General Council's Press and Publicity Committee to discuss the production of a newspaper which would present the trade union case. Publication of the *Daily Herald* itself was stopped because the compositors on other papers would not agree that the *Herald* men should remain at work. It was

*F

decided that an eight-page evening paper called the *British Worker* should be produced, about the size of the *Star*. Difficulties were raised by the printing union, and it needed an order from the General Council before the men required for production of the paper would go to work.

Just before the first issue was ready for machining the offices were raided by the police. A large crowd had gathered outside the *Daily Herald* offices in Tudor Street. Mounted police moved them back, and then a number of plain-clothes men entered the building and ordered that the machines should not be started. They had a warrant giving them power to search the building, and to seize all copies of the *Daily Herald* for 4th May. It soon became clear, however, that they were less interested in the past *Daily Herald* than in the future *British Worker*. The detective inspector in charge asked that a dozen copies of the paper should be specially run off for the City Commissioner. This was done, and the inspector took them away, leaving some of his men in the building. A member of the staff hurried down to the TUC headquarters in Eccleston Square, and Ben Turner, Citrine, and J. W. Bowen of the Post Office Workers came down to represent the General Council at Tudor Street, while Pugh and E. L. Poulton of the Boot and Shoe Union went to the House of Commons to inform Ramsay MacDonald and Arthur Henderson of the situation. These precautions proved unnecessary. After about an hour and a half permission to print was received, and the first issue was on the streets just before midnight on 5th May. From that time onwards the *British Worker* functioned smoothly until the last issue (Number 11) appeared on 17th May. The workers on the paper were all trade unionists and experienced men, so that none of the technical difficulties encountered by other papers troubled them. The first issue was of 320,000 copies, and this figure quickly rose to half a million. After the first two eight-page issues, the Government's move in commandeering paper forced a reduction to half size, and the *British Worker* remained a four-page paper until the end of the strike.

The paper received much praise for the neatness of its make-up and for the moderation of its opinions. *The Times* called it 'on the whole a straightforward and moderating influence', the Conservative *Northern Whig* said that it was 'in make-up easily the best strike effort in newspapers', and the *New York Times* praised its 'measured statements of the trade union position, its scrupulously fair presentation of facts and its appeals for calmness and order'. In spite of this praise the *British Worker* was, it must be said, an extremely dull paper. In the tone of its encouragement to the workers, its uncritical affirmations that everything everywhere was going on splendidly, its reiterated emphasis on the need for complete trust in and obedience to the General Council, it resembled a public school pep talk more than a strike news sheet. No general news was given in the paper, and the only relief from the unrelenting stream of announcements by the General Council, and affirmations of strike solidarity in different areas, were occasional poems by 'Tomfool' (Eleanor Farjeon) and comic notes by 'Gadfly' (C. L. Everard) of the *Daily Herald*.

The most interesting aspect of the paper was the effort made by the General Council to counter in its columns the *British Gazette*'s assertion that the strike had a political end, which could only be gained by unconstitutional means. On the front page of the first issue appeared a 'Message to All Workers':

> The General Council of the Trades Union Congress wishes to emphasize the fact that this is an industrial dispute. It expects every member taking part to be exemplary in his conduct and not to give any opportunity for police interference. The outbreak of any disturbances would be very damaging to the prospects of a successful termination to the dispute.

In this the Council was asking for something impossible.

When blackleg drivers of lorries are determined to go on, and pickets are determined to stop them, how can disturbances be avoided? Day after day, however, the General Council desperately disputed statements that they were a lawless lot and asserted, with perfect truth, their extreme respectableness.

From the first the General Council exercised a firm control over the *British Worker*. This was reasonable enough, since the paper was published under its authority, but the way in which this control operated greatly restricted the paper's appeal. A group of censors from the Press and Publicity Committee, Poulton, Bowen and Arthur Henderson's son Will, shared Hamilton Fyfe's table with him, and looked at every line of type. Their chief purpose was to keep out of the paper 'anything which might cause uncontrollable irritation and violence'; and it may be agreed that they were successful. It was by the decision of the General Council that general news was excluded, in spite of a strong protest by Hamilton Fyfe, who said that 'even our own people buy the *British Gazette*', and asked that at least he should be allowed to include details of the cricket scores. The General Council's reply shows a monolithic complacency. The *British Worker*, its committee said, was a strike bulletin and not a newspaper. 'It also considers that the anxiety of the people generally to get hold of the *British Worker* needs no stimulus from the inclusion of cricket scores or any other matter of that kind. . . . It is the view of the committee that the whole contents of the journal should be such as to convince the public that the General Council is in strong control of the strike situation and that everything which occurs is according to plan.'

An effort was made through the paper to control the information published by local Strike Committees. A circular sent out on 4th May instructed officers of local organizations to 'confine their statements on the situation to the material supplied by the committee and to add nothing in the way of comment or interpretation'. Distribution of the *British*

Worker was very patchy. Many large towns did not see copies until the strike had been in force for a week, and had to rely for news upon the BBC and pro-Government publications. It was obvious that the solution of this problem was for the TUC to use its control over the printing unions to produce editions of the paper in other places. Separate editions were planned for publication in Leicester, Manchester, Cardiff, Liverpool, Glasgow, Newcastle and elsewhere, but difficulties were placed in the way of their production partly by the printing unions and partly by the General Council itself, which feared that rash statements might be inserted in these separate editions.

The multifold troubles involved in them is indicated by what happened in the cases of the Manchester and Glasgow editions. Fenner Brockway, secretary of the ILP, was asked to go up to Manchester and take charge of the local edition to be published there. Brockway was handed the copy and it was emphasized, both to him and to the local Strike Committee, that only material in the *British Worker* was to be used, with a different date-line. 'No alterations permitted,' said the telegram to Manchester. When Brockway reached Manchester he found the local Executive of the Typographical Association very friendly, but the Co-operative Printing Society refused to print the paper because the TUC had stopped all their other printing work. Another local Co-operative organization agreed to take on the job after Brockway had driven fifty miles to Southport to see the manager, but the Manchester edition was not produced until shortly before the end of the strike.

On Sunday, 9th May, arguments were still going on about the Glasgow edition, which had been set up with material not included in the original *British Worker*. On Sunday Poulton telephoned to the man handling the paper in Glasgow, and offered to make an arrangement by which a blank page would be left on the London copy of the paper so that a page of Scottish news could be included. 'We have a report lying on my desk now, saying that your people are wanting to extend the strike in all kinds of ways,' Poulton said. 'Will you see that all that stuff is kept out and nothing provocative put in.' The Glasgow edition, again, appeared too late to be of much use.

In Leicester there was trouble because the local Typographical Association proved unco-operative. The Leicester branch said that members of the association had had no opportunity of voting for or against a general strike, and that it was therefore unconstitutional. 'We do not see how smashing up the printing industry will help the miners, and call on members to honour their agreements with their masters,' they said. This was on 11th May, the last full day of the strike.

After all this one feels some sympathy for the plaintive note sent on the same day by the Publicity Committee to the Epsom Strike Committee, in reply to their letter of thanks for supplies of the *British Worker* and other literature. 'I shall have pleasure in laying this before my committee as it is practically the only letter we have received showing thanks for the work we are doing here.' The way of the co-ordinator is hard: but sympathy cannot conceal the fact that the editions of the *British Worker* outside London appeared too late. Apart from local duplicated strike sheets the *British Gazette* and the other papers which supported the Government had things all their own way.

The absence of the *British Worker* gave the strike sheets a vitally important part to play in keeping strikers in good heart. Upon the whole they performed this task admirably, and their duplicated or cyclostyled productions often had a liveliness and ingenuity altogether absent from the *British Worker*. The General Council attempted, without very much success, to discourage local printed bulletins; at times indeed it almost seems that they were anxious to restrict all public pronouncements to those that emanated from Eccleston Square. A letter to Councillor Armstrong, who was responsible for a bulletin in Leeds, emphasized that 'the policy of the General Council, as applied through its Publicity Committee, is to restrict all printing through the publication of this, the official strike bulletin'. When the Bradford and District Trades Council triumphantly sent a copy of their *Bradford Worker* to London, they received a sharp note stressing that they were violating instructions. Preston Strike Committee, who had succeeded in producing a printed *Strike News* with the help of volunteer labour from the Typographical Association, received an order to cease publication, which was not obeyed. No doubt the General Council feared that the Typographical Association might react unfavourably to the idea of a printed bulletin, as they did in Leicester: but they were persistently worried also by the possibility that provocative material would get into these local sheets and they thought (rightly) that local bulletins would generally be in the hands of left-wingers.

The way in which material for these strike sheets was gathered is indicated by one of the little group responsible for the publication of the duplicated *Sheffield Forward*:

> We had the *British Gazette* and the local newspaper (the *Sheffield Telegraph*, which produced a skeleton edition with the help of apprentices), and made comments on matters appearing therein; a radio set had been installed and the news bulletins were received and commented on; various people brought in news of local events, and we had telephone conversations with representatives in neighbouring areas – Barnsley, Rotherham and Chesterfield for the miners, Doncaster for the railwaymen, etc. There were many rumours of collapses in various places, and our main task was to check these and counter them by publishing denials 'from our correspondent on the spot', so to speak. The paper was foolscap size, sometimes more than one sheet, and there was never any difficulty about selling it on the street.

Mr Stephenson, the editor of the stencilled *Northern Light*, which covered the strongly Labour Durham colliery area, remembers that they used to move to a new headquarters every night to produce the paper. The *Northern Light* was one of the most militant strike bulletins, and its distributors were often arrested. A touch of generosity, which would have been unthinkable in most countries, entered into relations between police and strikers here in Durham. When Stephenson was fined £2 with the option of fourteen days' imprisonment, he chose to go to prison, but asked the police not to call at his home on the day he was due to go inside. They agreed, and he met them at the railway station. When Stephenson asked how they knew that he would keep his word, the constable was surprised. 'Funny thing, nobody ever thought of that.'

The number of copies of these local bulletins issued varied greatly. In some cases only a few hundreds were produced; in others as many as 10,000 were issued daily, by the use of two machines and several stencils. Their form was equally varied: it ranged from direct reproduction of material from the *British Worker* and other propaganda material sent out by the TUC, to bulletins with a designed heading, one or more cartoons, several jokes and a considerable amount of local material. These were undoubtedly the most popular, as well as the most valuable, bulletins. News of what was happening in their own district brought home to people the realities of the strike with a directness that could never be possessed by the '100 per cent solid in all areas' kind of message conveyed from London.

The Communist Party made preparations to print a special strike paper called the *Workers' Daily* at a small press of theirs in the Borough. The editorial staff for the paper consisted of the Marxist literary critic, T. A. Jackson, and Leo Condon of the Tass Agency. On the night of Saturday, 1st May, the press was raided by the police, who dropped the cylinders of the presses and removed the distributor bars of the linotypes, thus effectively immobilizing them. The first number of the *Workers' Daily* lay on the bed of the printing machine, and was never pressed to paper. The contents are not known, but no doubt closely resembled those of the typewritten *Workers' Bulletin* and the *Sunday Worker*, which adopted a line of extreme intransigence throughout the strike. The Government was unable to find the place of issue of the *Workers' Bulletin*, but Marjorie Pollitt was arrested on a charge of being concerned in its publication. The Communist Party publications, however, had a small circulation and probably influenced events less than the local strike bulletins.

One major defect of these publications, and to a lesser extent of the *British Worker*, is obvious. They were read only by those already convinced of the justice of the strikers' case. A paper which, while supporting the strikers, gave general news as well, might have been read by waverers. The paper projected by Lloyd George, which was to appear on behalf of the three Liberal newspapers published in London (the *Daily News*, the *Westminster Gazette* and the *Star*), might have performed this function: but the *Daily News* withdrew its agreement to such a joint production and the paper never appeared.

To sum up: the General Council's attempt to stop the production of newspapers was overwhelmingly defeated. The Government was able to print and effectively distribute its own newspaper: an indifferent production, it is true, intemperate in tone and dishonestly selective in its choice of material; but a paper that, particularly outside London, was influential in forming opinion, because no effective counter to it existed. Nor was the production of other newspapers stopped – except, significantly, of those Liberal newspapers which were in favour of a negotiated settlement, and which maintained that (to quote from the unpublished leading article written for the projected joint Liberal paper) 'on pretexts which in a calmer time would not for a moment be considered, the Government declared war'. All the national newspapers which were most powerfully opposed to the strike managed to appear in some form; and many provincial papers appeared as well. To counter them the TUC had only the *British Worker*, which altogether failed to reach some parts of the country, and local strike bulletins.

Can one say, then, that the General Council would have been better advised not to call out the printing trade? The effect of leaving all journals free to publish would at least have been to permit a ready flow of information upon both sides. Had local branches of printing unions been left to decide for themselves whether to withdraw their labour from work on individual papers, the conditions created might have favoured the strikers. But in the end one comes back to two points: the General Council's unpreparedness and its unwillingness to act boldly. The only thing that could seriously have helped the strikers, in a propaganda sense, was the selective closing down of newspapers hostile to their cause: but the General Council had neither the will to impose such restrictions nor the capacity to enforce them.

XII

IMPARTIALITY ON THE BBC

On the night of Saturday, 1st May, Beatrice Webb was in-furiated by a message broadcast on the wireless. 'Before giving the weather forecast and news bulletin', the announcer said, 'there is a message from the Prime Minister.' Then came the message, repeated two or three times 'in a sten-torian voice, each time with louder and more pompous emphasis: "Be steady, be steady" – pause – "Remember that peace on earth comes to men of goodwill".' Had Bald-win spoken himself, she thought, the message might have been effective, but 'in the emissary's melodramatic shout it sounded not a little absurd'.

The British Broadcasting Company was in an anomalous position, in the sense that it was supported by Government funds, without being a Government agency. During the strike the question of the company's relationship to the Government of the day was sharply posed, and the strike became, in one aspect, a struggle on the part of the company's managing director, John Reith, to preserve its independence.

Reith had become general manager of the newly formed British Broadcasting Company in December 1922. The company was still at Savoy Hill, and broadcasting still in its infancy, when the strike crisis came. Reith did not welcome the crisis, but as he said afterwards, 'I admit to welcoming the opportunities which crises bring'. This tough, prickly and immensely forceful introvert realized, perhaps unconsciously, the power which had been suddenly placed in his hands, and fought with much determination to retain it.

Baldwin had already agreed that the BBC should remain independent, and asked Reith to explain his views to the Cabinet Committee. On Thursday Reith met the committee and Joynson-Hicks, the chairman, told them of Baldwin's views. Churchill immediately objected, saying that it would be monstrous not to use such an instrument as the BBC to the best possible advantage. Joynson-Hicks replied that if anybody felt strongly about the matter, it should be discussed at a full Cabinet, and the point was dropped. Churchill's desire to commandeer the broadcasting medium during the crisis was circumvented, perhaps, by the increasing application of his energies to the *British Gazette*, and Reith was left in rather uncertain control.

Arrangements were made to broadcast news bulletins five times a day during the strike, the first at ten in the morning, the last at nine-thirty at night. The first of these bulletins, at

ten o'clock on the morning of Tuesday, 4th May, stated the
position of the company. The BBC, the announcer said, had
no opinions of its own and would give only objective news.
It would do its best to maintain a position of fairness and
asked for fair play from both sides. Reith's own sympathies
were certainly not particularly with the coal-owners. Four
years earlier he had written to Clynes, feeling that in the
Labour Party there was most chance of finding the essence
of his own beliefs about a practical application of Christian
principle to national and international affairs. But although,
like many other liberals, he might have supported the
miners against the coal-owners, he was certainly not prepared to support the strikers against the Government.

The attempt to maintain impartiality was genuine. The
BBC broadcast messages from the General Council, as well
as messages from Downing Street; it quoted the speeches of
trade union leaders, in Parliament and out of it; it referred
to the *British Worker* as well as to the *British Gazette*; a clear
distinction was made between news from the press agencies
and announcements issued from the Chief Civil Commissioner's office. This could hardly have been achieved by the
company under the direction of a less determined man than
Reith; yet, as he said himself, it did not amount to impartiality, nor was complete impartiality possible in the
circumstances. By broadcasting the various Government
appeals for volunteers the BBC was materially helping the
Government; no similar appeal could be made by the
General Council, even had the BBC been willing to broadcast it. The company broadcast also the Government's appeal to owners of private cars to give lifts, and the various
Government announcements encouraging men to stay at
work or return to it.

The company's own organization for gathering news was
at this time rudimentary, and it relied largely on what it
was told. Inaccurate reports of returns to work were frequently broadcast. Typical examples are the reports on

Friday, 7th May, of enginemen and firemen returning to work at Oxford, of the strike's breakdown at Salisbury, and of the discharge of six food ships at Immingham, near Grimsby. All of these reports were corrected by the unions in the areas, and the *British Worker* sometimes published such corrections, but although the BBC were informed of them they were not broadcast.

The chief problem that faced Reith during the strike was the question of broadcasting the Archbishop of Canterbury's appeal, which is discussed in a later chapter: but other broadcast messages also raised difficulties. The most important of these was Baldwin's own message on Saturday night, which by its reasonable and even sympathetic tone allayed the disquiet felt by many people over the bellicosity of the *British Gazette*. 'I wish to make it as clear as I can that the Government is not fighting to lower the standard of living of the miners or of any other section of the workers,' he said. 'That suggestion is being spread abroad. It is not true.' He expressed his own sympathy with the miners, and ended with an extremely effective peroration, in characteristically homespun style:

> I am a man of peace. I am longing and working and praying for peace, but I will not surrender the safety and the security of the British constitution. You placed me in power eighteen months ago by the largest majority accorded to any party for many, many years. Have I done anything to forfeit that confidence? Cannot you trust me to ensure a square deal to secure even justice between man and man?

This broadcast was delivered from Reith's house, because he thought that there would be a big crowd at Savoy Hill. Baldwin handed the manuscript to Reith when he arrived, with a request that he should say what he thought of it. The opening phrases of the final paragraph were written by Reith himself, and Baldwin added the last three sentences. Then he struck a match right in front of the microphone, lit his pipe, and began to speak. That striking of the match was an excellent piece of public relations, whether or not deliberately devised.

On Sunday night Lord Grey spoke, to give the Asquithian Liberal viewpoint, and Reith went to collect him from 11 Downing Street. There he met Churchill, who asked if he was connected with the BBC. Reith said that he was the managing director. 'Are you Mr Reith?' Churchill said, and went on to express his indignation about some of the news items broadcast. He regarded references to any official collaboration with the TUC (such as that by which power was maintained at London Hospital) as practically giving comfort to the enemy. The argument between them was conducted politely, with Grey supporting Reith. Then Churchill came out to the car with them. He had heard, he said, that Reith had been badly wounded in the war. 'In the head, wasn't it?' Reith said it was, but that his present attitude was not traceable to the wound.

On Tuesday, 11th May, Ramsay MacDonald telephoned to ask if he might broadcast, and sent along a draft of his speech, with an offer to make any reasonable alterations. It can hardly be doubted that the speech was moderate in tone, but in spite of Reith's strong recommendation it was not broadcast. Ever present in the minds of Baldwin and his advisers was the fear that the terrible Churchill might try to insist upon some drastic step, and they were prepared to go a good deal further in the way of placating him than merely keeping Ramsay MacDonald off the air. Davidson told Reith that MacDonald's message could not go out, because 'it would set Churchill off again'. There was a limit, after all, to the BBC's autonomy and to Reith's independence.

The influence exerted by the BBC during the strike was immense. 'The sensation of a general strike, which stops the press, as witnessed from a cottage in the country, centres round the headphones of the wireless set,' Beatrice Webb noted in her diary. What she wrote of herself was true of perhaps a quarter of the population. 'I still have amongst my junk,' an old age pensioner writes, 'the little home-made crystal set, which worked lovely with the iron bedstead for aerial and the gas stove for earth, and which told me and my wife (each with one earphone to the ear) what was really happening.' *What was really happening:* it is a revealing phrase. The news broadcast by the BBC was accepted in many places where the *British Gazette* was regarded with distrust or derision. In thousands of country districts the wireless set was almost the only means of obtaining news, and even in towns the main features of the latest news bulletins were posted up outside shops or sold in the street. 'A *Sussex Gazette* was published and we procured a copy, but we get most of our news from the wireless,' a woman at Eastbourne noted in her diary. 'Those who, like ourselves, do not possess a wireless set, gather in little groups outside the radio shops and hear the latest news and also quite a Bradshaw of the trains.'

Upon the whole the BBC performed its difficult task well and conscientiously. It became, inevitably, a Government information agency; but the inaccuracies in its news bulletins were the result of misinformation and not of deliberate distortion on the part of the company's officials. In the one case where the BBC suppressed an important item of news – the Archbishop of Canterbury's appeal on behalf of the churches – the decision, although nominally Reith's own, may be said to have been made under duress.

XIII

THE APPEAL OF THE CHURCHMEN

Nothing else that happened during the strike showed so clearly the sympathy felt for the miners than the appeal for a negotiated settlement issued by the Archbishop of Canterbury on behalf of the Christian churches. Randall Davidson, the Archbishop, could not be suspected of Labour sympathies, and the appeal was therefore all the more remarkable. It is impossible to say what effect it might have had upon events, had it been given the publicity that was warranted by an appeal made on behalf of the established churches by the leader of the Church in England.

Davidson discussed the possibility of a strike very fully in advance, both with Baldwin and with Hugh Cecil, and gave them the impression that he fully supported the Government's attitude. On the first day of the strike he listened to Asquith's speech in the House of Lords, and afterwards noted approvingly that he was 'excellent – very strong about the iniquity of the strike'. On the following day Davidson spoke himself, to the same effect. The strike was, he said:

> So intolerable that every effort is needed, is justifiably called for and ought to be supported, which the Government may make to bring that condition of things speedily to an end.

How did it come about that within forty-eight hours of making this speech the Archbishop sponsored the appeal for conciliation that so profoundly disconcerted the Government? In fact, the archbishop's attitude had not changed. Neither he, nor many other liberal-minded people, understood the Government's determination to force a complete and utter victory over the General Council. A compromise settlement would have been a humiliation to them, and conciliatory moves of any sort seemed to them little short of treachery. It is not likely that Baldwin himself adopted this point of view, but behind his appeals for personal trust were the demands of Churchill, Birkenhead, Chamberlain and Joynson-Hicks for unconditional surrender.

On 6th May the Bishops of London and Southwark, with a strong group of Nonconformists, came to Lambeth and issued an appeal, which was broadcast, asking for prayers and saying that they were anxiously considering ways in which Christian opinion could be brought to bear on the problem of the strike. On the following day Davidson saw a number of churchmen. They included the Bishops of Ripon and Southwark, Dr Burroughs and Dr Garbett, and representatives of many other branches of the Church, as well as the coal-owner, Lord Londonderry. After much discussion, they agreed upon an appeal for the resumption of negotiations, based upon three points: renewal of the Government subsidy 'for a short definite period'; withdrawal by the mine-owners of the suggested new wage scales; and cancellation of the General Strike. Agreement on these three points was to be made 'simultaneously and concurrently'.

Davidson then went to the House of Commons. First he saw MacDonald who thumped the table in his enthusiasm, and said that the idea was 'inspired' – but, he suggested, it would be more tactful if the third point about the cancellation of the strike was put first. Davidson agreed to this, and went to see Baldwin. The Cabinet was sitting, and he could make contact only through a secretary, who went to and fro. Baldwin approved of everything except the words 'simultaneously and concurrently'. The withdrawal of the strike, he said, really must precede the beginning of negotiations. He further said that he would not prevent the appeal being broadcast. His phrasing here was careful and deliberate.

After receiving and reading the appeal, Reith got in touch with J. C. C. Davidson, who has already been seen acting in various capacities during the strike. Davidson told Reith that the statement should not be broadcast and that Baldwin, no matter what he might have said, hoped it would not be. The threat of Churchill was raised: to broadcast such a statement, Davidson said, would provide him and others with an excellent excuse for taking over the BBC. Reith was much disturbed. He telephoned Randall Davidson and told him that to broadcast the appeal would 'run counter to his tacit arrangement with the Government about such things'. When the Archbishop asked whether the Prime Minister had objected, Reith replied, with literal accuracy, that he was acting on his own responsibility. So he was. But he was acting also under the threat that the BBC might lose its independence.

The appeal was published on 8th May in the *British Worker* and in *The Times* but not, as has already been mentioned, in the *British Gazette*. Randall Davidson was both surprised and distressed. On the following morning he wrote to Reith, pointing out that:

> The position is that yesterday morning the authorities of the churches in England, not sitting formally but carrying the imprimatur of the two archbishops, several bishops, the leaders of the Free Churches, and all, in short, who could be got together to represent what may be called official Church opinion in this country, agreed upon a statement which they desired me to put forth in their names. Cardinal Bourne has expressed his full concurrence in it. ... Are we to understand that if the churches desire to put something forth their grave utterance must be subject to the approval of its wording by the Broadcasting Committee?

Reith saw the Archbishop that afternoon. Davidson noted his visitor's evident distress, but Reith repeated what he had already said, that Birkenhead and Churchill were eager to take over the BBC. The Archbishop seems not to have pressed his point further, and the statement was finally broadcast as an item in the news bulletin at 1 pm on 11th May, four days after it had been issued.

The Archbishop was making an address on Sunday night at St Martin-in-the-Fields which was being broadcast. He offered to submit his notes, but Reith refused to look at them. However, Lane-Fox, the Minister of Mines, had no such fine scruple. He approached Davidson to ask what the Archbishop was likely to say on Sunday night, and received an assurance that in the sermon he would not think of trying to deal with the economic question. In fact he did plead for 'not only a reasonable but a generous settlement', without going into details. On this Sunday the Roman Catholic Archbishop of Westminster, Cardinal Bourne, who had said that he was in agreement with the appeal, expressed himself in very different terms at High Mass in Westminster Cathedral.

'There is no moral justification for a general strike of this character,' he said. 'It is therefore a sin against the obedience which we owe to God. . . . All are bound to uphold and assist the Government, which is the lawfully constituted authority of the country and represents therefore in its own appointed sphere the authority of God himself.'

Need it be said that the *British Gazette* gave considerable prominence to this statement?

The Archbishop's appeal divided clerical opinion as sharply as any action during his career. Many members of the Church were indignant, and wrote to tell him so; probably the majority supported him. Some Conservative MPs, also, were extremely angry, and told the Archbishop to his face that the Church would suffer discredit as a result of his action. In several parts of the country small groups formed to advocate a settlement on the lines of the appeal. At Oxford an Archbishop's Committee met in the house of A. D. Lindsay, Master of Balliol. A group of Cambridge dons wrote a letter to *The Times* supporting it. It is possible –

one would put it no higher – that, had it been fully publicized, the appeal of the churchmen might have caused a decisive change of informed opinion, in favour of a compromise settlement. The Government, by taking such steps to suppress the appeal as lay in its power, made sure that no change of opinion took place.

XIV
THE MEDIATOR RETURNS

After his work as chairman of the Coal Commission was finished, Sir Herbert Samuel went to northern Italy, to work on that book which was to clear his own mind of confusion and help others to arrive at some body of belief. When the strike threatened he sent a telegram to the Prime Minister asking whether his services might be of use. He received a polite negative by way of reply. Nevertheless when the threat became reality he felt bound to return. He reached Dover on Thursday, 6th May, and, as the result of a telegram sent to the Postmaster-General, Mitchell-Thomson, found the famous racing motorist Major Segrave waiting for him at the port. After a call on Samuel's sister at Folkestone they roared up the empty roads in Segrave's Sunbeam, reaching the Reform Club in Pall Mall from Folkestone in seventy minutes.

Comfortably settled there Samuel was confronted by a problem: what could he do that might be useful? He called together his colleagues of the Royal Commission, but their response to his idea of making some informal intervention was not encouraging. A telephone call to J. H. Thomas, however, brought a different reaction. Thomas, like Samuel, was a believer in the prime virtue of negotiation. Negotiation indeed was Thomas's element; he negotiated as others play chess or bridge. At their first meeting in the Reform Club, Thomas said that he would put Samuel in touch with the Negotiating Committee of the TUC.

Having progressed so far, Samuel saw Baldwin, Lane-Fox and Steel-Maitland. He was firmly told by them that abandonment of the strike must precede any other negotiations. Steel-Maitland went so far as to write a letter emphasizing that the Government could not possibly agree to 'procure the end of the General Strike by a process of bargaining':

> I am sure that the Government will take the view that, while they are bound most carefully and most sympathetically to consider the terms of any arrangement which a public man of your responsibility and experience may propose, it is imperative to make it plain that any discussion which you think proper to initiate is not clothed in even a vestige of official character.

That was plain enough: but it should not be thought that the Government was opposed to such discussions. It had everything to gain by receiving the TUC's suggestions for ending the strike, as they were filtered through Samuel, while remaining on its own side completely uncommitted. The negotiations were all on one side. Samuel's suggestions, as he made clear from the start, carried only the weight of his own personality and influence.

On Friday, Saturday, Sunday and Monday Samuel met the TUC Negotiating Committee. They met in the Bryanston Square house of Thomas's friend, the mining magnate Sir Abe Bailey. There, in Bailey's drawing-room, looked down upon by a number of brownish old masters, the unofficial Samuel met secretly with the trade unionists and tried to work out a basis of settlement. Smith and Cook were not invited to attend these meetings, although they heard of them on Saturday, and of the Parliamentary Labour leaders only Thomas was present. According to Clynes he, Thomas, Snowden, Henderson and MacDonald moved about behind the scenes, trying to negotiate a settlement, but if such movements took place they had no tangible result. The essence of any negotiation was secrecy, for the Labour movement was in no mood to hear talk of a settlement, except upon equal terms. When MacDonald gave an interview to reporters in which he said that he was keeping in continual touch with the Government side and was 'hourly in conference regarding settlement of the strike', the *British Worker*'s censors forbade its publication, and the General Council sent MacDonald a sharp rebuke. What truth there was in MacDonald's story cannot now be known, but it seems unlikely that he was in direct touch with any member of the Cabinet.

The discussions in Bryanston Square went on and on. Samuel soon saw that, if his own area of negotiation was a narrow one, the TUC leaders were eager to find a way of ending the strike which would not be interpreted by their followers as surrender. Samuel drafted a memorandum for discussion, in which it was proposed that no wage cuts should be made without some assurances that 'the measures of reorganization proposed by the committee will be effectively adopted'. A Mines National Board with an independent chairman should be set up to seek a final settlement. The board would prepare a simplified wage agreement which should not affect the wages of the lower-paid men, and it would fix 'reasonable figures, below which the wage of no class of labour should be reduced in any circumstances'. These were the commission's old proposals revamped. 'All the proposals', as Samuel says, 'were within the framework of the commission's recommendations.' They provided a basis for argument, and by the week-end both Samuel and the Negotiating Committee were beginning to see a way clear – without having yet consulted the miners.

It has been said that Thomas was a great negotiator: and on Saturday he attended a luncheon party at Wimborne House in Arlington Street, which had also been designed to seek an end of the strike. The hosts were Lord Wimborne, at one time Lord-Lieutenant of Ireland, and his wife: the oddly assorted guests were the coal-owners Lord Londonderry and Lord Gainford, Lord Reading, Osbert Sitwell, J. A. Spender, Mrs Snowden (deputizing for her husband, who was not well) – and Thomas. The conversation at luncheon, according to Osbert Sitwell, who was perhaps not inclined to minimize the importance of the occasion, quickly became 'so important in its matter, so vehement in its manner', that 'the footmen . . . had to be told almost at once to leave the dining-room, and only to return when summoned'. The luncheon, Sitwell thought, showed Thomas that Lord Reading at least – unlike his fellow Liberal Simon – did not think of all Labour leaders as potential rebels; and the trade union leader light-heartedly committed himself to the view that the miners were now inclined to accept the Samuel Commission report. Here Thomas was misleading his listeners, either deliberately or in his natural exuberance, for as the miners' leaders showed in the next forty-eight hours, they had not in any way changed their minds about the report.

One member of the luncheon party reported the trend of the conversation to Tom Jones, Deputy Secretary to the Cabinet, through whom it was certain to reach the Prime Minister. Lord Reading and Lord Wimborne hurried off to the House of Commons with a new formula, which they presented to Churchill and Birkenhead. Its reception was not encouraging, but the Wimborne House group did not despair. They felt – and in this they were perfectly right – that nobody was more anxious to see the end of the strike than Jimmy Thomas.

XV
THE FOOD CONVOYS

The Government's decision to make a show of force in moving meat, flour and other supplies from London Docks up to the Hyde Park depot was taken on Thursday. It was a concession to the Churchillian group, who had been pressing for some dramatic move of this sort: but some such move was urgently necessary, because of the stranglehold exerted by the strikers on the London Docks. No more than forty men out of 14,000 were available for work, and the narrow streets round the wharves were packed with strikers. When the Food Officer for London, Horace Woodhouse, urged individual traders to send in their trucks, they replied that it was useless to do so, because the pickets would throw the drivers into the river. Those lorries that tried to get through were stopped by crowds filling the streets, and police attempts to support the lorries resulted in fights, in which local conditions put the police at a disadvantage.

The Government operation to raise the siege of the docks was in two parts. They had first to get volunteers on to the docks to unload the waiting ships and fill lorries; and also to get the lorries through the crowd of dockers, if possible without incident. The volunteers were transported down the river by boat, and in darkness. One of them, a Cambridge undergraduate, remembers that in his group about fifty volunteers were brought up from Cambridge in cars on Friday afternoon. Their leader was Lord Burghley, of Magdalene College. They went first to the Hyde Park depot and then, with some hundreds of other volunteers, were taken in lorries, escorted by police cars, to Westminster Pier.

At the pier we climbed into barges – down below – and were towed by tugs manned by naval ratings down the

Volunteers in the forecourt of the Foreign Office on 3rd May

Steam lorry and trailer with load of City workers at the Bank

A bus with volunteer driver and police escort
A bus, immobilized by strikers, being towed away

Office girls on the back of a lorry outside the Bakers' Arms, Leyton
Rations for sailors at Neasden Power Station being unloaded from lorry

Stanley Baldwin about to enter the back door of 10 Downing Street

Winston Churchill greeting a small child outside 10 Downing Street

etrol wagon escorted by mounted police along St George's Road, Southwark

Mounted police clearing the road after a riot at the Elephant and Castle

The food convoy on 9th May in East India Dock Road

The food convoy on 9th May passing through Poplar

Ramsay Macdonald (*front, next to driver*), Ben Tillett (*standing in back*) and Arthur Henderson leaving Eccleston Square for Downing Street

Herbert Smith, A. J. Cook and W. P. Richardson arriving at a conference in Downing Street

Police v. Strikers. The teams in the football match at Plymouth

The first tram after the strike leaves New Cross under police escort on 14th M

river. I remember looking up from the bowels of the barge and seeing rows of policemen's helmets looking down at us as we passed under Waterloo and other bridges.

After an hour or so, and in darkness, we arrived at the King George V Dock, and disembarked. We were led to an old P and O liner, *Bendigo*, lying alongside, and more or less left to ourselves to find cabins to dump ourselves and our kitbags, etc. There were a few stewards about but I think there had been little warning of our arrival, and that evening and next morning there was precious little to eat – though that was put right during the next forty-eight hours.

Moore-Brabazon, the Special Commissioner, watched with interest as the barge swung round and just got straight in time to go under the bridge. The orders for police guards on the bridge had come from him. In the morning the volunteers, most of them undergraduates or unemployed men, began to unload the ships. Their presence was a complete surprise to the strike pickets, who had a twenty-four hour guard on the dock gates. The unloading was more enthusiastic than efficient:

Early in the morning we were taken by naval motor launches to Rank's big flour mill up in the Victoria Dock – and from about 7.30 am until midday we were engaged in filling up a lorry convoy with great sacks of flour which we found on the top floor of the mill. These sacks were trundled across the floor to a special chute down which we joyously tipped them. I'm afraid a great many were damaged through our inexperience, and I fancy the Rank officials who were directing us must have felt pretty depressed.

Another volunteer doing different work offers a more optimistic view.

We had a varied experience of unloading frozen meat and grain, and it was no easy job working in the hold and stacking the meat so that it could be taken up by crane to the shore, but we did not lose many carcasses, although an

G

occasional one would splash in the dock through being insecurely packed on the crane. Unloading the grain was very unpleasant without a proper respirator, as the dust was very thick.

The volunteers were well protected. The gates and buildings were guarded by a battalion of the Grenadier Guards, who were fully armed and had mounted Lewis guns at various strong points. There were also hundreds of naval ratings, mostly from Chatham, who took over the cranes. At the East India Docks a mass of strikers outside the gates were intimidated by the sight of bluejackets manning a machine-gun that was directly pointed at them.

The first convoy of 105 lorries moved out of Hyde Park in the cold wet dawn of Saturday morning. The convoy was escorted by twenty armoured cars manned by men of the Royal Tank Corps, and men of the Welsh Guards and Coldstream Guards were on the lorries. The few pickets on duty stared in astonishment, and made no attempt to interfere, as the lorries drew up in parallel lines along the river front, sections of three at a time backing into the chutes at the mills. Later in the morning the strikers massed outside the dock gates, but made no move to interfere with the loading of the lorries. Had they attempted to do so the result cannot be doubted. The representative of the *New York World* reported that:

> The sullen mass of strikers who congregated after dawn were awed by the military and permitted most of the moving on to be done by the mounted police, unarmed as always, but backed this time by enough artillery to kill every living thing in every street in the neighbourhood of the mills.

The volunteers loaded quickly, and the convoy went back before midday. News of it had spread, and cheering crowds gathered in the City to see the lorries and the soldiers returning to Hyde Park. The progression of lorries and armoured cars had an unmistakably triumphal air about it.

'This convoy system was all right,' Moore-Brabazon records, 'but it was not moving enough food into London.' Foodstuffs were normally taken out at the docks and floated up the river in lighters to the wharves, but the strikers refused to let the tugs work. Moore-Brabazon obtained permission from Lord Beatty, who was then First Lord of the Admiralty, for the tugs to fly the white ensign. Under this symbolic protection, 17,000 tons of perishable foodstuffs were delivered to the wharves within forty-eight hours.

The breaking of the docks blockade was of great practical and moral importance. Practical, because the exercise, once performed, was repeated and extended – on the second night the convoy numbered 267 lorries, and after two or three days lorries went to some of the docks without escort; moral, because of its effect on the dockers and on the trade union leaders. Whether the dockers believed what had been said by Cook and others about the troops' kinship with the workers is doubtful, but there can be no doubt that they were shocked by the sight of machine-guns directly trained upon them. The shock was increased by the apparent completeness of their previous victory: after stopping all attempts to get lorries through with perfect ease, they found themselves helpless in the face of organized force. The Government took a chance in making this display of force. What would have happened had the dockers tried to stop the lorries and the troops fired on them is a matter for conjecture; it is possible that such a tragedy might have turned public opinion in favour of the strikers. Policies, however, are justified by their results, and the Government's policy here was triumphantly successful.

XVI
AT THE WEEK-END

The action in the London Docks was not the only indication of the Government's determination to use its resources to break the strike. On Saturday and Sunday there was a marked change in the attitude of the police. It is likely that there were more disturbances, and more violent ones, during the week-end meetings addressed by Labour leaders; certainly they were dealt with more harshly than had been the case during the week. This was especially noticeable in the north and in the Midlands, where the police in many districts made charges to disperse crowds, used their batons freely and made many arrests. People found circulating the multigraphed Communist publication, the *Workers' Bulletin*, were often arrested immediately: exceptions were made occasionally, as in the case of one Oxford undergraduate who was taken to police headquarters, cross-examined for several hours and finally released when his respectable antecedents had been established. This was a lucky one; hundreds of men and women received severe sentences when they came before the magistrates on Monday or Tuesday of the following week. Two hundred people were arrested in Glasgow, and about half of them received sentences of three months' imprisonment. In Hull twenty-five of those arrested received sentences varying from three to nine months. In London the sentences varied from one to three months, for such offences as interfering with the traffic and insulting men on their way to work. Elsewhere the arrests were fewer in number, but sentences were equally severe. Noah Ablett, a member of the Miners' Federation Executive, and a Marxist economist who had considerably influenced Cook, was arrested.

A much more menacing step contemplated by the Government was an Order in Council prohibiting banks from paying out money to any person acting in opposition to the national interest. This was directly aimed at the union funds which, Simon had said in the House of Commons, were liable to seizure. The proposal seriously alarmed the king, who told Baldwin that such a step would be a grave mistake, and added that 'anything done to touch the pockets of those who are now only existing on strike pay might cause exasperation and serious reprisals on the part of the sufferers'.

The feeling that such things were in the air was enough for most of the General Council. There is no doubt that some of them believed that their own arrest was imminent. Purcell, at a week-end meeting, said definitely that the Government had issued warrants for his and Bevin's arrest, as chairman and secretary of the Strike Organization Committee. The most open expression of the General Council's eagerness for peace came, as might have been expected, from Thomas. In a speech at Hammersmith on Sunday afternoon, sandwiched between one of the TUC meetings with Samuel and his private negotiations with Wimborne, Thomas said that he had never been in favour of the principle of a general strike, and that whatever the end the condition of the nation would be worse than before it. He concluded:

> The responsibility is indeed a heavy one. But there will be a graver responsibility on whichever side fails to recognize the moment when an honourable settlement can be arrived at. That moment must be accepted and everyone must work to that end.

In the context of the strike situation, such words were an offer to capitulate. The significance attached to them may be judged by the fact that the BBC used an extract from the speech in its nine o'clock bulletin that night, and that the *British Gazette* subsequently displayed an extract from it in a panel every day.

The difference between things as they appeared to those

at Eccleston Square and to those touring the country was very great. Just after the week-end William Whiteley and R. J. Wilson reported from Wolverhampton and district that they had seen no troops, that not a bus or tram was running and that spirits were high. 'The feeling of the workers is that the General Council and the Labour Party must stand firmly for no reduction in the miners' wages. They declare they are out to win.' From Birmingham the Welsh MP, Morgan Jones, and Mrs Adamson, said that the spirit of the strikers was a revelation, and added that they had attended a demonstration of 20,000 people on Sunday. Kingsley Martin, W. A. Robson and Josiah Wedgwood, in a report on 'the state of public opinion' in the Midlands, gave further encouragement. In Northampton they learned that the Rotary Club had passed a resolution on the lines of the Archbishop's appeal, and that the railwaymen were still 100 per cent out with the exception of the RCA. There were no disturbances. In Coventry they found the NUR and RCA almost 100 per cent out, all tram and bus men out except inspectors, and no transport running except a few independent buses. At Birmingham they noticed the danger of a drift back to work, partly because of the successful operation of a transport service by volunteers. Oswald Mosley, however, reported the city 'astonishingly solid'. Everywhere they went these emissaries were told that it had been a mistake to call out the printing unions, since this gave pro-Government publications almost a free hand with the news.

Similar reports came from most of the week-end speakers who had been sent out from London. The picture of enthusiasm and fervent optimism was marred only by a few dark patches. Margaret Bondfield, a member of the General Council touring the south-west, found that enthusiasm for the strike was confined to the towns. At Exeter she addressed three big meetings and found much sympathy with the miners, and at Plymouth she was told that the General Council need not worry – 'we can carry on as long as they like' – but elsewhere she found failures in organization. At Bridport there was no Strike Committee, at Torquay and Totnes she was reduced to leaving 'cheering notes' for committees who had gone home, and although Taunton, Chard and Yeovil were 'all right', she found in all these places an eagerness for the strike to end. In several places members of the RCA had gone back to work. South-west England was one of the weakest strike areas, and it is possible that Miss Bondfield's reaction was coloured by her own lack of faith in the strike.

In London also packed and enthusiastic meetings were addressed by those speakers who retained their belief in the strike's success. Susan Lawrence, the ardent feminist MP for East Ham, addressed a dozen meetings in the East End on Saturday and Sunday. 'A glorious spirit,' she said to Beatrice Webb. 'Never again will the workers be trodden under foot as they are now – we are living in momentous times – a revolutionary reaction – a terrible time – perhaps – many of us in prison.'

Her listener was not sympathetic. 'There is no earthly use in it all except to get rid of a proletarian distemper,' she replied. 'There will not even be a revolutionary reaction. Thomas and Baldwin will see to that – they will broadcast messages of peace and goodwill every few hours until we are all hypnotized into loving one another!'

XVII

NEGOTIATIONS

With the week-end over the General Council was faced with two possible courses: an attempt to end the strike by negotiation or an all-out move to extend it. Characteristically they did both. The strike order to executives, calling out all engineering and shipbuilding workers unaffected by the strike, was sent out on Friday, the order to be effective from Tuesday midnight. This order was in part the acknowledgment of a fact, since many men in these industries had already come out, and the strike was also beginning to exert pressure on factories and workshops through transport difficulties, shortage of coal and of raw materials. Some had closed down, and many more were working short time. Several organizations, alarmed by the way in which business transactions had been brought to a standstill, were trying to reestablish surreptitiously a transport system for ordinary goods.

The confidential circular sent out by the Manchester Chamber of Commerce to its members is typical of such attempts. It pointed out that there were many more road vehicles available than were required for carrying foodstuffs and essential supplies, and suggested that members should use them through the medium of a private Transport Bureau set up by the chamber. 'The chamber will put demand in touch with supply, and all other arrangements will be made directly between the two parties concerned.' The scheme would have to be operated 'unobtrusively', and a final caution was added. 'All these schemes will have a greater chance of success the less there is said about them. Do not leave this letter about where it may get into wrong hands.'

While preparing for an intensification of the struggle the General Council was eager to end it. Samuel, for his part, had been extremely busy. Apart from his daily conferences with the Negotiating Committee, he had seen his Coal Commission colleagues several times, and had also talked to Evan Williams and other representatives of the mineowners. In a report to Baldwin, written on Tuesday morning but never sent, he said that the Negotiating Committee had received his suggestions 'most cordially', and added:

I have ascertained that my late colleagues on the Royal Commission strongly support the adoption of the

National Board principle as the means of solving the wage difficulty.

The coal-owners also raised no positive objection to Samuel's proposals. The miners refused to accept them. This is hardly surprising since, as has already been said, they were the original proposals revamped. Nevertheless their refusal was a blow to Samuel, who had from the first been misled by the Negotiating Committee on this point. He wrote to Baldwin:

> The Trade Union Committee gave me the definite assurance that the miners' attitude had changed and that if the point was put to them in a reasonable way and in a palatable form a satisfactory answer would be obtained. I was given the impression that the principal difficulty was the intense suspicion of the miners that while wage reductions would be a certainty the reconstruction of the industry would prove in fact dilatory and doubtful.

It is likely that the negotiating hand of Thomas is to be seen in this 'definite assurance' which had no basis in fact, as Samuel discovered when he met the miners on Monday afternoon.

> So far as the Miners' Federation is concerned it is Herbert Smith and not Cook who is the dominating influence and his position is up to the present quite immovable. The TUC were deceiving themselves when they informed me that there was no longer an absolute veto upon any kind of reduction in any circumstances. My clear view is that the veto remains exactly the same now as it was throughout the negotiations.

Samuel added that 'both the miners and the members of the TUC spoke very frankly' during the negotiations. The miners' latent suspicions had been revived by the fact that talks had been held about which they were left in ignorance. They were not told that negotiations were taking place until Sunday morning, when they turned down in a summary manner some earlier proposals of Samuel's, passed on to them by the Negotiating Committee. Herbert Smith now

* G

expressed his opinion of Samuel plainly, saying that he did not like his actions or his attitude. Smith's feelings may be judged from the statements he made later. The miners, he said, had not been treated properly. They had been ignored until Sunday. 'It then came out that there had been meetings with Sir Herbert Samuel . . . the miners had had plenty of Sir Herbert Samuel – we knew him quite well and did not want any more dealings with him.'

At the meeting on Monday Smith's remarks were thought by some members of the General Council to be positively insulting, although Samuel bore them with equanimity. Cook and Richardson, who were also present, spoke more temperately, but Samuel despairingly recognized that their three hours' discussion had been wholly negative. On Monday evening the General Council told the miners that it regarded Samuel's proposals, which had been embodied in a memorandum, as a satisfactory basis for reopening negotiations. They suggested that, since the Miners' Executive rejected the proposals, they should submit constructive suggestions of their own. The miners did not do so. In the sense that the General Council used the words, they had no constructive suggestions to make.

In the meantime Thomas was continuing, with unabated zeal, his separate and secret negotiations with Lord Wimborne. On Sunday evening Wimborne's secretary, Selwyn Davies, drove down to see Thomas at his house at Dulwich, and returned with him to Arlington Street. There Thomas, who professed to have found much encouragement in the friendly tone of Baldwin's Saturday night broadcast, had a long talk with Wimborne. He had not long got home before Selwyn Davies telephoned him again, to arrange another meeting with Wimborne and Reading at eight forty-five on Monday morning. This urgent gestation brought forth the following mouse: if 'some assurance' could be given by a 'person of influence' that the recommendations of the Coal Commission's report would be put into operation without delay, it was 'possible that the TUC might call off the General Strike and indicate that the miners accepted the report unconditionally with all its implications'.

This suggestion (only made possible by Thomas's deliberate misstatement of the miners' position) was read over the telephone to Tom Jones, who undertook to place it before the Prime Minister at once. Baldwin very reasonably said that everything for which Thomas asked had already been conceded in his broadcast, and that since this was so he could not see why the TUC did not call off the strike.

By Sitwell's account negotiations continued on Tuesday in an atmosphere of increased tension. Wimborne and Reading pressed Thomas with 'extreme urgency' to call off the strike on Tuesday night or Wednesday morning. The reason for this urgency, Sitwell says, was that the Government had decided to arrest the trade union leaders on Wednesday. This statement is made on the authority of Lord Wimborne and Lord Reading. Its accuracy is denied by many other people, who were more intimately acquainted with the course of the strike. The story goes on to say that Selwyn Davies went on Tuesday night to Eccleston Square, and at midnight mingled with the crowds which had gathered outside the building. He saw the miners' leaders emerge, looking profoundly dejected. Then Thomas came out and walked away. Davies followed him, and 'when they had reached a spot where there were no passers-by', Thomas spoke to him and asked Davies to tell the Prime Minister, Lord Reading and Lord Wimborne that he had obtained a majority vote and that the General Strike would end at noon on Wednesday.

This romantic story is briskly contradicted by Sir Herbert Samuel. His letter to Baldwin, outlining the failure of the negotiations he had conducted, was written on Tuesday morning. The Negotiating Committee was to see him again at three o'clock in the afternoon. Before that time the trade union leaders sent him a message to say that they were proceeding without the miners, and that the General Strike was to end.

XVIII
THE GENERAL COUNCIL DECIDE

The General Council's decision was made, then, by Tuesday afternoon, in spite of Sitwell's story and in spite of what members of the General Council themselves later said to the contrary. Nevertheless the council's meeting with the miners on Tuesday night was a crucial one. The council's leaders realized that it would be disastrous to split the unity of the Labour movement, and at the meeting on Tuesday night they seem to have had no doubt that they would carry the miners with them in the decision to call off the strike on the basis of the Samuel Memorandum. They meant to enforce unity, if it could be obtained in no other way. The document which they put on the table said that the Samuel Memorandum should be accepted, and the strike brought to an end.

'Is that the unanimous decision of your committee?' Smith asked. Pugh said that it was. 'Is it not possible for us to sit down and see how far we can get? Is it just crossing the t's and dotting the i's?'

'That is it,' Pugh replied. 'That is the final decision, and that is what you have to consider as far as you are concerned, and accept it.'

What guarantee was there, Smith and Cook asked, that the recommendations made by Samuel would ever be carried out? Other members of the council put the same point in a different way: could Samuel deliver the goods? Thomas was offended. 'You may not trust my word,' he said, 'but will you not accept the word of a British gentleman who has been Governor of Palestine?'

There was some discussion, and then Smith said: 'Do you people realize the serious position you are putting yourselves in? Are you going back without any consideration for the men who are going to be victimized in the movement? Are you not going to consider that at all?'

He was told that each union could manage its own business if the miners would accept the Samuel Memorandum. Smith, Cook and Richardson then retired to consult with their Executive. While they were away, just after midnight, the Prime Minister's secretary telephoned to ask if the General Council had any news for him? 'How did PM know we wanted to see him?' Ben Turner asked in his diary. 'Strange and unexplained mystery. Who had told him?' From what we know of Thomas's negotiations there was nothing mysterious about it.

The miners came back after midnight. Their Executive said that the proposals implied a reduction in the wage rates of a large number of mine workers. 'They regret, therefore, whilst having regard to the grave issues involved, that they must reject the proposals.'

From the General Council's point of view this was an intolerable attitude, and it was now that the ambiguity of the miners' agreement to let the General Council handle their case appeared. The General Council thought it had the right to settle the dispute and regarded the Samuel Memorandum as 'a definite test of the sincerity of the declaration of the Miners' Executive'. Smith replied that they had not looked at the matter in that light. 'I would not hand the miners' case over to someone else any more than I would expect the engineer to hand his case over to me. Everyone knows his own craft best.' The difference of interpretation was fatal.

The General Council made one last effort to carry the

miners with it. On Wednesday morning Ramsay Mac-Donald asked if he could come and talk to the miners, as their attitude was a tragic blunder. He was told by Cook: 'We do not want you to come to our meeting.' A deputation from the General Council, however, headed by Bevin and Purcell, saw the miners at their headquarters in Russell Square. Bevin appealed to the miners to make common cause with them, saying that if they did not do so they might get less good terms afterwards, and that the whole Labour movement in the country would be split. He spoke of uneasiness about pensions and superannuation pay. Purcell supported him, and Ben Turner said that men were going back to work at Southampton and in the railway centres. The General Strike was 'on the slippery slope', and the men were drifting back to work. Smith's final words in reply were bitter. He accused the General Council of having been on the Prime Minister's doormat without the miners' knowledge, and said that there was more enthusiasm for the strike amongst the rank and file than in their leaders. The deputation withdrew. Within an hour it was with the Prime Minister.

At the inquest that followed, some months after the end of the strike, George Hicks, acting as chairman, indignantly denied that the miners had been presented with an ultimatum at nine-thirty on Tuesday night. The final decision to call off the strike had not been made, he said, until 'well after midnight'. Citrine went further, and said that the General Council 'definitely and finally made up their minds' about ten minutes before they went to see Baldwin on Wednesday. On the other hand, someone very close to the Prime Minister asserts that a delegation from the General Council, including Pugh and Thomas, came to 10 Downing Street late on Tuesday night, to say that the strike would be called off on Wednesday. There is an overwhelming weight of evidence that the decision had been reached by nine-thirty on Tuesday night, and that the only doubt afterwards was implied in the questions put to the Negotiating Committee about Samuel. Ben Turner's diary records:

> It was definitely put: 'If strike called off would lock-out notices be withdrawn and men resume work at old wages and hours?' The Negotiating Committee said yes, that was their opinion and belief.

XIX
SURRENDER

The trade unionists were coldly received on their arrival at Downing Street. First of all they saw Sir Horace Wilson, who asked them their business. Had they come to negotiate or to declare the strike off? They said the latter, and were then taken into the Cabinet room, where Baldwin and several other ministers awaited them. Baldwin asked Pugh to make a statement; and at the end of Pugh's circular platitudes ('As a result of . . . the possibilities that we see in getting back to negotiations and your assurance, speaking for the general community of citizens as a whole, that no steps should be left unturned to get back to negotiations, we are here today, sir, to say that this General Strike is to be terminated forthwith') the Prime Minister said briskly: 'That is, the General Strike is to be called off forthwith?'

That was what it meant, as Pugh, Thomas and Bevin said at length, stressing in suitably vague terms how much they had been impressed by Baldwin's vague broadcast on Saturday night. Bevin, ever so politely ('I do not know whether I am overstepping the bounds'), raised the question of resuming negotiations with the miners. Baldwin was friendly, receptive, but still vague, vague. ('You know my record. You know the object of my policy, and I think you may trust me to consider what has been said.') Bevin pressed a little, just a little, and was gently rebuked. The proceedings then ended. Nothing had been said about lock-out notices, or about wages and hours. The Samuel Memorandum had not even been mentioned. It is not surprising that Birkenhead, Neville Chamberlain and some of the others listening wore triumphant smiles. No wonder, either, that several members of the General Council looked bewildered and depressed as they left Downing Street. Ben Turner (who had himself remained silent) noted in his diary: 'GC flabbergasted at nothing being settled about miners' lock-out notices. Retired and felt dismayed . . . left at 1.10 disappointed and disgusted. Papers out soon about TUC. Surrender.'

XX

WAS THE STRIKE WEAKENING?

One of the points made afterwards by the General Council was that the strike could not have been greatly prolonged, that it was 'on the slippery slope', and within a few days would have disintegrated. Ben Turner made notes in his diary to this effect:

> During Monday night spoke to Cramp at top of steps about it being desirable strike should not go on above the week out. He declared also it must not go on much longer. Tuesday, Thomas saying ditto. Our reports are weakening. 4,000 trains running, etc. Report Bristol Docks weakened, Southampton strikers weakening, etc. etc. Strike Committee had reports of breaks here and there and the feeling was depressing before decision come to.

In the Monday night discussion John Bromley of ASLEF said, according to Cook, that his men were going back, and trains were running. 'Unless the General Strike is called off now there will be thousands of trains running. The result will be that there will be a debacle. It is no good; we cannot go on any longer.' Bromley summed up: 'We are busted.' And Thomas added weight and apparent logic to the railwaymen's case for going back:

> As I said to Herbert Smith: 'When you talk of not going back, what becomes of your resolution that you will be bound as the others are? What is going to happen on the railways? If the miners go back we can look after all our men on the railways, but with the miners out the railway companies will not care whether the strike is ended now or never, because they will be able then to pick and choose by the very nature of things.'

The mines, Thomas said in an expressive phrase, were blackleg-proof, the railways were not. 'You have to bear in mind the records of the number of trains run each day, and what was happening. . . . The criticism is: Why did we not go on? We could not have gone on.'

The railwaymen's part in the strike was vital. If they went back to work in considerable numbers the strike could have no chance of success. But Bromley's and Thomas's statements were not accurate. There was no considerable move on the part of railwaymen to return to work, in spite of the *British Gazette*'s exhortations and misstatements, and in spite of veiled threats like that made by the LNER: 'The company . . . will give preference for employment to those of their staff who have remained at work or who offer themselves for re-employment without delay.' Here are the figures from the Ministry of Transport files of the locomotive engineers who had returned to work:

Railway	Total Staff	Men available for duty	
		May 5	*May 12*
GWR	6,206	79	104
LMS	14,671	93	273
LNER	11,500	94	127
Southern	7,044	?	238

And here are the figures for signalmen:

Railway	Total Staff	Men available for duty May 5	May 12
GWR . .	4,843	384	584
LMS . .	11,871	901	1,152
Southern . .	2,940	?	534

The percentage of firemen reporting for duty was less than that of the locomotive engineers. Only the white collar staff of the RCA showed a considerable defection during the strike. By 12th May roughly two-thirds of them had reported for duty. These white-collar workers generally lacked sufficient technical skill to be employed as drivers or firemen, and the total increase in the number of railway workers available from 5th May to 12th May was not much more than 1 per cent. This is what the General Council's Intelligence Committee had to say about the railways in its report on the morning of Wednesday, 12th May:

> The Government and its supporters put forward a constantly recurring claim that a considerable number of railway workers are going back to work. . . . The reports coming in to this office do not confirm or explain the Government's claims. In many places, of course, the original response of the RCA though good was not absolutely solid. Moreover it should be remembered that though we are receiving reports from a large number of well-organized industrial centres, the information to hand from rural districts is so slight as to be of no real value at all. . . . It may be that the Government are making big claims on the basis of a staff consisting in the main of supervisory grades, clerks and more or less isolated railwaymen in the rural areas.

This was the best information available to the General Council at the time. It seems that Thomas and Bromley were fabricating a case almost out of whole cloth in their eagerness to see the end of the strike.

The Intelligence Committee's report of Wednesday morning contains other points of interest in relation to the strike's weakening. They reported a slight leakage back to work in several places: over 100 tramwaymen back in Portsmouth, a few men back in Southampton, 1,000 brick and tile workers back at Bridgwater, some weakness in Wolverhampton, Rugby and Reading. There were complaints from many districts that reliable news was lacking. 'As a whole the strike is perfectly solid, but the elements of uncertainty cannot be altogether disregarded,' they say. 'While there are no indications of any important tendency on the part of men on strike to resume work many reports show that the strike is extending and that factories and workshops not directly involved are slowing down or shutting down.' Their conclusion is that 'the situation is one in which we are holding our own. But the Government's organization is improving, and its policy is gradually becoming more aggressive. Every day the intensity of the struggle will increase.'

The accuracy of this report is not particularly relevant to the point made here: that if the strike was in danger of disintegration the General Council did not know it. The Intelligence Committee was its chosen medium for the reception of reports from all over the country, and reliance was naturally placed upon the daily surveys which subsumed the matter of these reports. It was not fear of a breakdown, but fear that the strike might get out of their own hands that primarily moved the most influential members of the General Council. As Thomas said frankly in the House of Commons on 13th May: 'What I dreaded about this strike more than anything else was this: if by any chance it should have got out of the hands of those who would be able to exercise some control, every sane man knows what would have happened.' A few months later Charles Dukes of the General and Municipal Workers (not himself a member of the General Council) spoke to the same effect:

Every day that the strike proceeded the control and the authority of that dispute was passing out of the hands of responsible executives into the hands of men who had no authority, no control, and was wrecking the movement from one end to the other.

'The intensity of the struggle will increase,' the leaders had been told. They preferred surrender to such an intensified struggle, with its implicit threat to their own power.

For a day or two the TUC leaders seem genuinely to have thought that they had negotiated a settlement by which the Government agreed to accept the Samuel Memorandum. The *British Worker* on 13th May featured the General Council's announcement that 'through the magnificent support and solidarity of the Trade Union movement' it had 'obtained assurances that a settlement of the mining problem can be secured which justifies them in bringing the general stoppage to an end'. On the same day a circular was sent out to the unions saying that the strike had been ended 'in order that negotiations could be resumed to secure a settlement in the mining industry, free and unfettered from either strike or lock-out'.

There was no shadow of justification for these statements. The Government had given no assurances; Samuel had emphasized his lack of official standing. The miners, on the other side, had made it clear, in Cook's words, that they were 'no party in any shape or form' to the TUC decision. Yet Thomas told the Parliamentary Labour Party that the Government was bound by the Samuel Memorandum and would carry it out, while George Hicks said that 'the strike had been called off on this binding understanding'. Those who really believed that an understanding existed were soon to be undeceived.

THE STRIKE GOES ON

Strikers all over the country heard the news with a bewilderment that quickly turned to anger. A striker at Sheffield records: 'When the news arrived it could hardly be believed, and the departure from the sheds of the first tramcars was regarded as the action of blacklegs.' Lewis Casson, who had been carrying encouraging messages to Strike Committees in various towns as far north as Carlisle, had got back as far as Barnet when he heard the news. 'I shall never forget our chagrin,' he says. 'We were full of confidence that all was going well, and that we were winning, when we saw the evening paper contents bills announcing that the strike was over. We simply couldn't believe it, and were convinced that the pass had been sold in London.' In Lewisham Leslie Paul put up on Wednesday morning a notice denying the rumours that the strike was to be called off, and was making a list of meetings for Wednesday evening while the BBC was broadcasting the news that the strike had ended.

In many places it was felt that the only possible interpretation could be that the strikers had won. The Army officer, already mentioned, who had merged with the strikers at Gravesend, attended a big open-air meeting on Wednesday afternoon, and heard the trade union official who spoke begin his speech with the words: 'Comrades – victory.' In several towns victory meetings were held on Wednesday evening.

Disillusionment came on this evening when Baldwin broadcast a message to the nation. He had already said that the end of the strike was a victory for common sense, and now he confirmed that 'our business is not to triumph over those who have failed in a mistaken attempt'. He said also, however, that the strike had ended 'without conditions entered into by the Government'. The *British Gazette* was less discreet. 'Unconditional Withdrawal of Notices by TUC,' it said on Thursday morning. 'Men to Return Forthwith. Surrender Received by Premier in Downing Street.' The *Daily Mail* went further, and announced 'Surrender of the Revolutionaries'. The *British Worker*, in its account of 'How Peace Came', did not mention anywhere the General Council's split with the miners.

It became slowly clear to the men on strike that the General Council had obtained no terms at all for the calling off of the strike: no terms for the miners, nor for the millions who had struck in sympathy with them. A Government statement issued on Wednesday began: 'His Majesty's Government have no power to compel employers to take back every man who has been on strike, nor have they entered into any obligation of any kind on this matter.' In spite of the pious hope expressed later in the statement that all malice and vindictiveness would be put aside, many employers interpreted this statement as an open invitation to re-engage men at lower wages. In many cases strikers were offered re-engagement only on the condition that they tore up their union cards and accepted lower wages. In others an attempt was made to single out and punish ringleaders.

In the House of Commons Arthur Henderson recited a long list of cases in which men were being penalized for taking part in the strike. The Board of Admiralty was proposing that strikers should forfeit from two to four years' service for pension purposes. The Army Victualling Department had denied reinstatement to certain men, and was replacing them by volunteers. The London County Council had reduced the wages of some strikers by putting them on different jobs. The railways were making a particularly determined effort to impose fresh conditions of service, on the ground that the strikers had broken their contracts. In Leeds, Glasgow, South Wales and elsewhere men applying for reinstatement had their names taken, and were told that their applications would be considered. GWR employees were asked to sign a statement saying that they were not relieved of the consequences of breaking their service with the company.

These happenings, in the forty-eight hours after the strike had been declared at an end, alarmed almost equally the Prime Minister and the TUC. Baldwin had a genuine desire for industrial peace that was not shared by some of his colleagues. He was distressed by vindictiveness, and it may be thought that he was almost too good-natured to understand it. On Thursday evening he said in the House of Commons that he would not countenance an attack on the trade unions as such, and that a condition of anarchy in the trade union movement would be disastrous. He was specific: 'I will not countenance any attack on the part of any employers to use this present occasion for trying in any way to get reductions in wages below those in force before the strike, or any increase in hours.' In using these words Baldwin was addressing his own party exclusively and, as an American commentator remarked, 'the Labour Party was merely sitting by to see whether he could drive it into submission'. On such occasions he was never lacking in force, and his parliamentary triumph over the dissidents was complete.

Baldwin's difficulties were trifling compared with those of the General Council. The telegrams sent out on Wednesday afternoon simply said that the strike was terminated, and asked the unions to 'instruct members to resume work as soon as arrangements can be made'. The letter that followed said that each union should make its own arrangements for the resumption of work. When the local Strike Committees discovered the real situation, their anger erupted into outbursts of fury. Representatives of the *British Worker* were asked for explanations which they were unable to give. Swansea forbade the distribution of Friday's issue, and in London some of the voluntary drivers threw the parcels back into the officials' faces. In Glasgow men marched in procession, carrying placards which said 'Down with Thomas'. 'Alarm – fear – despair – a victorious army disarmed and handed over to its enemies,' said the Hull Strike Committee. Telegrams poured into Eccleston Square, at best reproaching the General Council for its timidity, at worst making accusations of treachery.

The decision to allow each union to make its arrangements for going back was, from the General Council's own viewpoint, both unwise and dangerous. Unwise, because it was a denial of the whole idea with which the strike had started, that the General Council had a bargaining power not possessed by individual unions; dangerous, because it was the surest way of putting power into the hands of left-wing forces. Contemptuous of their national leaders, confronted with a variety of humiliating conditions when they reported back for work, the men listened to local leaders and all over the country pledged themselves not to return until all strikers in their own groups gained reinstatement without conditions. Twenty-four hours after the General Council had declared the strike terminated, the number of strikers had increased by 100,000, and their good temper was turning to violence. No doubt this fact, as well as the desire for industrial peace, influenced Baldwin's speech; and it moved the General Council to desperate action. A statement was issued saying that the council had responded to the Prime Minister's appeal for peace, and denying that the trade union movement was beaten or broken. Telegrams were sent to the individual unions which began: 'The General Strike has ended. It has not failed.' The workers were warned not to sign individual agreements, but to stick to their unions. 'Your union will protect you, and will insist that all agreements previously in force shall be maintained intact.'

Brave words, these: but not easily translated into realities. The individual unions had to fight for the best terms they could get, from employers who found more subtle means of victimization than a simple increase in hours or reduction of wages. The very existence of trade unionism as an organized force in Great Britain was at stake in the three or four days after the General Council terminated the strike. Had any considerable proportion of railwaymen, transport workers or dockers gone back on the terms originally offered them, the remainder could hardly have resisted. But the men did not go back. In several places they showed that they remembered what their leaders had forgotten, that in unity was their only strength. In Hull the railway and tram workers, and the dockers, refused to go back on Friday because 150 tramway employees were threatened with dismissal. On the same day a demonstration of 30,000 railway workers was held in Manchester, which affirmed a demand for unconditional reinstatement. On this day the BBC reported that there had been no general return to work, on Saturday railwaymen were still out everywhere although an agreement had been signed on Friday, and not until the week-end were terms of settlement reached for the printing workers and the dockers. These terms were hard enough, compared with the expectations of men who had felt that victory was in their hands: but only the extraordinary unity shown by the rank and file prevented them from being much worse.

On Friday afternoon Cramp sent out a telegram to NUR branches: 'Complete reinstatement secured without penalties. All members should report for duty immediately. Full details to follow.' This telegram was accurate only in so far as the railway companies had agreed to take back strikers 'as soon as traffic offers and work can be found for them', with the loophole that the settlement should not extend to 'persons who have been guilty of violence or intimidation'. In the agreement the trade unions admitted that in calling the strike 'they committed a wrongful act against the companies', and agreed never again to instruct their members to strike without previous negotiation with the companies.

The unions gained the point that the companies agreed to pay wages for the broken strike week, which had previously been withheld. By the final settlement, made a week later, the companies agreed to re-engage all men (with the exceptions already mentioned) and to give them two or three days' work each week until services returned to normal. The employees who had not gone on strike were still allowed to work a full week. The companies found no difficulty in using these terms to force men of supervisory grades into lower positions. Strikers who had occupied responsible positions were treated with particular severity. One district inspector was offered employment as a spare signalman, another as a passenger guard. A goods inspector was offered temporary employment as goods guard, a yard master as passenger guard. There were many such cases. A station-master on the LMS writes:

I and a few more men in 'responsible posts' were sacked outright, an absolutely novel and unheard-of proceeding. Others were banished to far ends of the system, put to humiliation, lectured and reproached by the 'top bosses'. I was reinstated after dismissal, but to a very low-grade job.

The agreement reached by the TGWU for the dockers contained an admission that the unions had broken their agreement, and a promise that the unions would not again instruct their members to strike without first using the existing conciliation machinery. The transport and tramway workers signed an agreement which included guarantees of reinstatement as and when vacancies were available. All these agreements were used by employers to retain volunteers who had served during the strike, or to reinstate men in lower grades than those they had formerly occupied.

The terms imposed by the Newspaper Proprietors' Association included an agreement by the unions that there should be no interference with the contents of newspapers, and that chapel meetings should not be held during working hours. Other restrictions were imposed by individual firms or groups. The London newspapers agreed to unite in resisting lightning strikes in the future, and to lock out all union men if such strikes took place. The *Manchester Guardian* formed a 'company union'. In Glasgow the Outram Press refused to employ any but non-union men. The Stationery Office decided that they would declare an open shop, in which unionists must work beside non-unionists.

The conditions of workers in many industries were worsened as a result of these settlements: but the point being made in this recital of what some will call victimization and others a just punishment is not a moral one. Such a sequence of events was inevitable if the strike was called off without firm conditions of settlement. The astonishing thing is that the General Council was apparently unprepared for what happened. Afterwards some members of the council complained of deceit and trickery, but in truth they had taken their own wishes for horses and tried to ride on them. Yaffle of the *Daily Herald* provided a bitter postscript to their abnegation of responsibility. 'We shall never have another revolution,' he said, 'for Mr Baldwin has announced that the strike is unconstitutional, and so the TUC packed up and went home.'

PART IV
AFTERWARDS

I

THE MINERS FIGHT ALONE

What, in the meantime, was happening to the miners and the Samuel Memorandum? On Thursday evening Baldwin met a miners' delegation in what was to prove an important discussion. Smith asked the Prime Minister directly whether he had seen Samuel and Baldwin replied, with strictly literal truthfulness, that he had not seen Samuel at all during the negotiations, up to half an hour before the visit of the trade union delegation on Wednesday. Baldwin went on: 'I understood from what I saw in the press – it may not be true – that proposals on the lines he advocated were of no use.'

Smith replied: 'I think that would be rather foolish as far as we are concerned, or anybody else, not because he advocated it, because I want to say I have finished with Samuel as far as I am concerned. I want to make that perfectly clear, to say because somebody put something on paper that you rejected entirely——'

Baldwin: 'That is what I wanted to ask you.'

Smith: 'We want to remodel it. I would not sweep any man's ideas aside and say that is no good, because I have to watch his point of view as well as I have to watch my own.'

Baldwin interpreted these confused words as an outright refusal to discuss the Samuel Memorandum. Henceforth he was always able to reply, when the question of its acceptance by the Government was raised, that the miners themselves had rejected it. As the weeks went by his position on this point grew firmer. In reply to a parliamentary question on 15th June he said that he had never accepted the Samuel Memorandum as a basis of settlement.

In a letter published a few days after the strike's end, Bevin and two other members of the General Council accused Baldwin of bad faith and urged Samuel 'to speak and to speak without any reservation. Will he deny that consultations took place between Mr Baldwin and himself on the terms of the memorandum?' We have the words both of Samuel and Baldwin that no consultations took place, although it is obvious that the Prime Minister knew what was going on. Yet he was never committed to the memorandum, and it seems obvious that he never intended to be committed. The Permanent Under Secretary for Mines, Ernest Gowers, wrote a letter to Cook on 17th May which has in it a most revealing phrase:

> [The Samuel Memorandum] has no official existence, and if the miners had accepted it on the understanding that the Government had also done so, an impossible situation would have arisen for all concerned.

As a result of his meeting with the miners on Thursday Baldwin extricated himself and the Government from the 'impossible situation' with speed and adroitness. Had the miners accepted the memorandum as a basis of negotiations at this meeting it is possible only to conjecture what would have happened, for Churchill and his followers would never have accepted such a document: but the obstinacy of Smith and the fiery simplicity of Cook lost the miners a chance of bargaining which they were never to be offered again.

On the following day, Friday, 14th May, the Government issued its own proposals for settlement. They were markedly less liberal than the Samuel Memorandum, for they embodied immediate wage cuts (to be made up for a short time by a £3 million Government subsidy), the introduction of district settlements instead of a national agreement, and substitution of compulsory arbitration for collective bargaining as a means of settling disputes. The miners were bound to reject such terms. The owners, who did not approve of any sort of Government interference, and wanted an eight-hour day, did so too.

Now began for the miners a long travail of misery and poverty. Their case was hopeless, although the Executive for a long time refused to admit it. The other unions, all of them impoverished and some overwhelmingly in debt because of the strike, gave generously to them, but the gifts were grains of sand in the great glass of their needs. The complacent note made by Neville Chamberlain in his diary on 20th June: 'They are not within sight of starvation, hardly of undernutrition . . . they are not living too uncomfortably at the expense of the ratepayer', was not echoed by those who visited the South Wales, Durham and other coalfields.

As the weeks became months the miners made concessions. They would accept the Samuel Commission's recommendations, they would even accept something like the Government proposals: but the owners would have none of it, and Baldwin refused to put any sort of pressure on them. Government interference with industry had always been profoundly uncongenial to him; and besides, he had lapsed now into the strange apathetic state that often succeeded his periods of great effort. What had become of the square deal, the even justice between man and man? Well, Baldwin was always ready, as he said, to help with negotiations: and by way of proving it the Government announced legislation to lengthen the miners' working day. The seven-hour day was suspended for a period of five years under the Coal Mines Bill. The strike remained unbroken.

In July representatives of the churches met the miners, and as a result appealed to the Government to give assistance to the industry and to implement some of the Royal Commission's recommendations. In his reply to them Baldwin was conciliatory, as always; negotiations, as he said, could always be started, and he would be delighted if they were; but the Government could not now possibly see its way to giving the mines a subsidy, whatever it might have done last March. In August the owners and miners met, at last, in conference. The miners' leaders were now desperate; the owners scented a victory completer than they could have hoped. Evan Williams, in a reference to the churchmen who had tried to mediate, and to the Prince of Wales, who was believed to sympathize with the miners, said: 'We have never had any faith in princes or in governments – whether they are princes of the Church or whether they are princes of another kind – as far as industrial questions are concerned.' What the owners wanted, he said, was a reduction of wages, an increase in hours, and the abandonment of the national agreement. They would consider nothing else.

In this sad case the miners appealed to the Government for help. Churchill, whom they saw, immediately said that the question of giving financial help to the industry had 'long passed out of the sphere of practical politics'. There is something pathetic and dignified about Herbert Smith's reply:

> After your statement I do not think we need detain you long. You seem to me to be of the same mind as the employers. I am not here to make a petition. If that is what you think I am here for you are mistaken. I am here to get an honourable settlement. . . . We can carry this fight on a bit further yet.

But they could not carry it on much further. In several districts men were going back to work; and although visits by Cook to the centres of disaffection in the Midlands, Derbyshire and Nottinghamshire sealed the leaks temporarily, they opened again almost as soon as he left the minefields. He coined a new slogan: 'Back to work we go on the *status quo*'; but really it was now a question for the miners of going back on any terms they could get. The opinion of many responsible newspapers was on their side; in the

Manchester Guardian, the *Daily News* and elsewhere, the Government and Baldwin were accused of bad faith, and of deliberately choosing a fight to a finish.

When at last a settlement was reached the miners lost everything for which they had fought. They had wanted to retain a national agreement, but were forced to accept district settlements; the hours worked were longer than before, in some cases a forty-nine hour week exclusive of meal-times; and their wages were often lower than those they had earned for a seven-hour day. By the settlement, also, the owners made sure that wages would be kept down permanently, through the existence of a large pool of unemployed miners; for, as the Samuel Commission had suggested, the effect of working longer hours was to produce cut-throat competition between the European coal-producing nations. Yet the miners had no choice but to accept these terms. The strike had lasted for more than six months, and at the end of it hunger and despair had driven more than a quarter of the men back to work.

II

THE SPOILS OF VICTORY

The strike's failure, and the subsequent defeat of the miners, was a disaster for the British trade union movement. In 1927 trade union membership fell below the 5,000,000 mark for the first time since 1916, from a figure of 5,500,000 before the General Strike, and did not recover for many years; the numbers affiliated to the TUC fell even more steeply. Equally serious for the unions was the way in which the strike had drained their funds. The accumulated funds of all trade unions dropped from £12½ million to £8½ million in a year; and this latter sum was set aside for benefits, so

H

that the unions had no funds left for supporting strikes –
indeed several unions had borrowed money from their
friendly funds, which had to be repaid.

Thomas said that the strike had cost the NUR over £1
million, and Ben Tillett, at the Labour Party Conference
late in 1926, said that the TGWU had spent £1 million on
the strike and the coal dispute, and that they were £500,000
in debt. The plight of the unions was aggravated by the
falling off in trade which came partly as a result of the strike.
They were in no position to ask for wage increases or to support strikes. In the four years before the General Strike
between 400,000 and 600,000 workers were involved in
strikes each year. In 1927 and 1928 the figures were little
over 100,000.

It was not to be expected that the employers would refrain
from exploiting the unions' weakness. They did so through
the Trade Disputes and Trade Union Act of 1927, a measure
which was said by the Liberal Lord Reading to offer no
single ray of light for British working men, and to be 'more
vague, more indefinite, more lacking in precision in respect
of the crimes which it indicates and the penalties which
follow upon them, than any Bill I have ever seen or any Act
of Parliament I have had to construe either as a law officer
or as a judge'. More than any other single measure, the
Trade Disputes Act caused hatred of Baldwin and his Government among organized trade unionists. Its repeal in 1946,
after the refusals to amend it of Chamberlain in 1939 and of
Churchill in 1945, had great emotional as well as practical
significance for the Labour movement.

The Act consisted of eight sections. The first defined all
sympathetic strikes as illegal, confining the right to strike to
'the trade or industry in which the strikers are engaged'.
The funds of any union engaging in an illegal strike were
liable in respect of civil damages. The second protected all
workers who refused to engage in a sympathetic strike. The
third limited the right to picket, in terms so vague that

almost any form of picketing might be liable to prosecution. The fourth attacked the political use of union funds, by substituting 'contracting in' for 'contracting out' on the part of any member who was prepared to allow his subscription to be used for political purposes. The fifth banned civil servants from joining or remaining members of a union which had any political objects or was linked with any other union; its immediate effect was to separate the Civil Service unions from the TUC and the Labour Party. The sixth prohibited all local and public authorities from insisting on trade union membership as a condition of employment. The seventh gave the Attorney General the right to restrain a union from using its funds to support an illegal strike. The last clause made it an offence for any worker to refuse to accept employment 'under a common understanding', when it was offered by an employer during an illegal strike.

This savage piece of legislation was pushed through with gusto by the Government's right-wing. It is possible that Baldwin did not approve whole-heartedly of this way of securing even justice between man and man; but by this time he had lost interest or been overborne: and in June 1927 he called into service the closure, which had not been used since 1921, so that the Government could make use of its overwhelming majority in a vote. A month later the Bill became law.

Its logical consequence was seen in the talks between a group of industrialists and employers headed by Sir Alfred Mond and a sub-committee of the General Council headed by Ben Turner, now chairman of the TUC, to discuss the possibility of industrial co-operation. From the Mond-Turner conferences, as they were called, came the suggestion for a National Industrial Council on which both employers and workers should be represented. The idea was accepted, although it was bitterly criticized by Cook and others on the trade union side, and viewed lukewarmly by the shipbuilding and engineering employers: but before it had a chance to operate in practice, the world slump at the end of the twenties put another Labour Government into power, and the Mond-Turner talks were forgotten.

The end of the twenties saw the British trade union movement almost at the nadir of its power and influence. Many militant trade unionists had joined the Communist Party, feeling that orthodox trade union policies held no hope for the future; some others split away, particularly in the Nottingham coalfields, and tried to form 'non-political' unions which would co-operate with the employers; the great majority stayed in their unions, but lacked enthusiasm for or interest in the policies of the leadership. Of one thing governments, Conservative, Labour or National, could feel happily sure: the trade unionists would never again attempt to engage in a general strike.

III
SIX QUESTIONS ANSWERED

The six questions asked and answered in this chapter no doubt express a personal attitude towards the strike in the conclusions reached, but at least these conclusions are based upon evidence which has already been put before the reader. The moral justification for calling such a strike is a matter of opinion: the questions and answers concern practical details of the strike's origins and effects.

Q. Did the Government want the strike?

A. It is probably true to say that no Government ever consciously wants a strike. But the feeling that, after Red Friday, some kind of showdown must take place between the Government and the trade unions was strong in the Cabinet.

Given that supposition, it was natural to prepare for a strike; natural also that when preparations had been made some ministers were anxious to see the struggle joined on almost any pretext. The way in which the trivial *Daily Mail* incident was used as a reason for breaking off negotiations shows the extremists' strength, and it seems in retrospect unlikely that Birkenhead's formula would have found acceptance, in spite of the hopes that were entertained for it at the time. The ambiguity of Baldwin's own position arose from the fact that his political skill lay less in forming opinions than in guiding those who had formed them. Whatever may have been his personal opinions in April 1926, Baldwin was content to act as the instrument of those who felt that the trade unions' aspirations to power must be destroyed. Thus, although there were individuals in the Cabinet who would have liked to see a negotiated settlement, both before and during the strike, they never provided a coherent opposition to the inflexible attitude of Churchill and Joynson-Hicks.

Baldwin's management of the conflicting forces inside the Cabinet was masterly. The restraint he exerted upon the extremists' desire for drastic action was wonderfully light and dexterous, and to him, more than to any other individual, must go credit for the pacific conduct of the strike. The use he made of the Samuel negotiations was unscrupulous but adroit, and it is difficult to believe that he would really have been placed in a very awkward position (as the General Council afterwards suggested) had the miners accepted the Samuel Memorandum.

Q. Could the trade unions have avoided the strike?

A. Powerful, although intangible, pressures worked upon the trade union leaders to declare themselves in full support of the miners before the strike. Any repetition of Black Friday would have been regarded with horror in the whole trade union movement. The leaders were irresistibly impelled by the forces behind them to support the strike call, however great a distaste many of them felt for the prospect. But in their minds the strike call was not meant to take effect. They hoped for, and expected, a settlement. The union leaders were ignorant of the extent of the Government's plans and over confident of their own strength; there is no other explanation of the way in which the strike call on Saturday morning, which was interpreted by all who heard it as a final, decisive move, was succeeded by the approach made to the Government on Saturday evening. The subsequent meetings of sub-committees from either side, and the attempt to work out settlement formulae, have an air of unreality. If it seems unlikely that the Cabinet would have accepted Birkenhead's formula, it is all but certain that on the trade union side the miners would have rejected it. The persistent self-deception practised by the General Council in relation to the miners' attitude towards hours and wages created many misunderstandings. It is fair to say that the General Council did everything in its power to avoid a general strike which it did not want, and for which it had not prepared. The attitudes of the Government (and coal-owners) on one side, and of the miners on the other, made the strike inevitable.

Q. Could the General Strike have succeeded?
A. The strike was defeated by the adaptability and enthusiasm shown by inexperienced men doing jobs that had always been thought to demand great technical skill. It did much to destroy the myth that the skilled man is indispensable. But it must be added also that the Government used only a fraction of its resources. The armed forces were hardly called upon. Had the Government used at once the severe measures advocated by the extremists in the Cabinet, the strike would have ended more quickly, although with considerable damage to the fabric of British society. There was never any prospect at all of its success since, in spite of what the General Council said and intended, the strike was by its very nature

a political, as well as an industrial, threat to the Government. To enforce rigid picketing of all transport, for instance, would have been a political act from which the General Council shrank: yet such picketing was demanded by the logic of its position. A general strike can be used only as a political, indeed a revolutionary, instrument; and for such a use the General Council and the great majority of strikers were not prepared.

Q. Why did so many of the strikers feel that they had been betrayed?

A. Partly because of their own over-optimism. The strikers almost everywhere interpreted their own solidarity as a portent of victory, whereas it was merely a foundation on which victory might be built. The local and partial picture was almost wholly misleading, since it took no account at all of Government activities. But although the strikers' feeling of betrayal was a natural one, in one case only was the word justified. Most of the leaders worked hard, though with misgivings, to make the strike a success. Only Thomas worked from the start to end it, using whatever lies and misrepresentations came ready to hand. It is difficult to estimate the harm done to the Labour movement by the way in which Thomas conducted his negotiations with Samuel and Wimborne. It was Thomas, much more than anybody else, who was responsible for the idea that the Government had bound itself to accept the Samuel Memorandum, when it had done nothing of the kind. More than any other single person he was responsible for the final capitulation and the consequent split in the Labour movement. The strike leaders numbered among themselves several mules and fools, but only one traitor. It is a tribute to Thomas's limber cleverness that he survived the General Strike as a politician.

Q. Could the General Council have negotiated a settlement?

A. No course could have been more disastrous than the one actually taken. There are grounds for thinking that a settlement might have been reached which would at least have allowed the railwaymen, dockers and printers to return in good order, and without signing new agreements. The strike movement had by no means lost its impetus, and although the Government was in an immensely strong position, it could not have contemplated the strike lasting for (say) another fortnight without some misgivings. Members of the General Council said afterwards that they had relied upon Baldwin's assurances of fair play, but this is the flimsiest excuse. They were sufficiently experienced to know that vague words about fair play are no substitute for a negotiated agreement.

Such an agreement, of course, would not have helped the miners. Here one meets a small mystery of the strike: the fact that throughout its course the two miners' representatives on the General Council, Robert Smillie and Tom Richards, were out of London. Why the miners did not recall Smillie from Scotland (Richards was ill), or nominate two people to take their places temporarily, will never be known: but the result of this ridiculous arrangement was that Smith and Cook remained in ignorance of much that went on, and that Thomas's misrepresentations of the miners' position passed without contradiction. But it is difficult to see how, with the forces balanced as they were, the miners could ever have secured an acceptable agreement. Their leaders had the over-optimism of many strikers. They never realized the Government's strength, or their own weakness. In July 1925 Baldwin accepted the realities of the situation, and persuaded the Cabinet to agree to a subsidy. In 1926 the miners made no such practical assessment of realities. Their total intransigence was a total error. They would have done better to accept the Samuel Commission Report in principle, and try to pin down the Government on its details.

Q. Could it happen again?

A. In the form of 1926, never. Thirty years after, the General

Strike appears hopelessly out of date, in its means and its method. As Amery said, its sponsors took little account of the wireless and the private car; they believed that it was possible to suppress newspapers; they entered the struggle financially and mentally unprepared. Union leaders today are perhaps no tougher than they were then, but they are more canny, and the unions are richer and more powerful. They are careful in choosing the moment to strike and in assessing a strike's implications. They are aware, also, of the fact that a general strike is by its nature a political weapon, and that sympathetic strikes within a given industry are much more flexible and easier to handle. The mystique of the General Strike, once so powerful, was destroyed by what happened in 1926. It was seen to be, from the point of trade union leaders concerned primarily with practical industrial problems, a self-destroying weapon. Unless at some time a movement arises in this country which tries deliberately to use the strike weapon with the object of overthrowing the Government of the day, the General Strike of 1926 will remain a unique event in British history.

APPENDIX I

The following official report of the meeting of the Prime Minister and the TUC representatives at 10 Downing Street was issued on the evening of 12th May:

The following were present: The Right Hon. Stanley Baldwin, MP, Prime Minister; the Right Hon. Sir L. Worthington-Evans, Bart, GBE, MP, Secretary of State for War; the Right Hon. the Earl of Birkenhead, Secretary of State for India; the Right Hon. W. C. Bridgeman, MP, First Lord of the Admiralty; the Right Hon. Neville Chamberlain, MP, Minister of Health; the Right Hon. Sir Arthur Steel-Maitland, Bart, MP, Minister of Labour; Col. the Right Hon. G. R. Lane-Fox, MP, Secretary for Mines; Sir Horace J. Wilson, KCB, CBE, Secretary, Ministry of Labour; Mr E. A. Gowers, CB, Permanent Under Secretary, Mines Department; Mr T. Jones, Deputy Secretary, Cabinet Offices; the Trade Union Congress General Council: Mr Arthur Pugh, Chairman; Mr A. B. Swales, Vice-Chairman; Mr W. M. Citrine, Acting General Secretary; and other members.

THE PRIME MINISTER: Mr Pugh, will you be good enough to make a statement.

MR PUGH: Well, sir, when we separated something over a week ago it was, of course, recognized and expressed on both sides that the ultimate end would be a settlement of this matter by negotiations, and although the conflict has been very much extended and developments have taken place since then, clearly both sides and all sides and all parties have had in view – they must have had – the ultimate arrangements that would have to be made to bring this trouble to a successful end. We, of course, like yourself, have had. Despite whatever developments might have taken place, everybody has had to direct their thoughts in that channel, and to use such opportunities as presented themselves, and such public opinion as existed with a view to effecting a resumption of negotiations. In that respect, sir, your contribution was made in the statement delivered to the people of the country through the wireless stations. That was something which we on our side certainly could not ignore.

On the other hand, we had been exploring other possibilities with full knowledge that, whatever happened, and however long the present position lasted, or whatever might be its consequences, in the long run the process of negotiations would have to be gone through. Well, as a result of developments in that direction and the possibilities that we see in getting back to negotiations, and your assurance, speaking for the general community of citizens as a whole, that no stone should be left unturned to get back to negotiations, we are here today, sir, to say that this General Strike is to be terminated forthwith, in order that negotiations may proceed, and, we can only hope, may proceed in a manner which will bring about a satisfactory settlement. That is the announcement which my General Council is empowered to make.

THE PRIME MINISTER: That is, the General Strike is to be called off forthwith?

MR PUGH: Forthwith. That means immediately. There is just a point about the actual arrangement, but that is in effect what it means. It is merely a matter of the best way to get it done with the least confusion.

THE PRIME MINISTER: I mean there would be a great deal of work for both of us to do. All I would say in answer to that is, I thank God for your decision, and I would only say now – I do not think it is a moment for lengthy discussion – I only say now I accept fully and confirm fully all I have said in the last two paragraphs of my broadcasted message. I shall call my Cabinet together forthwith, report to them what you have said, and I shall lose no time in using every endeavour to get the two contending parties together, and do all I can to ensure a just and lasting settlement. I hope it may be possible before long to make a statement of the lines on which we hope to accomplish that end.

MR THOMAS: Only one or two of us wish to say anything to you, and it will be very brief. You answered us in the way we knew you would answer us – namely, that just as you recognize we have done a big thing in accepting the responsibility, we felt sure the big thing would be responded to in a big way. We are satisfied all too well that it will not be a day or two or a week in which the dislocation and difficulty can be put right, but whatever may be the view of the merits of the dispute now ending there is common agreement that assistance from those who were opposing parties ten minutes ago is essential to rectify and make good and start things on the right road again. Your assistance in that is necessary; our assistance is necessary. We intend to give it, and in doing that we believe you can help. We want you to help us in that direction – I never liked the word war, and I do not want to use it, but we want your help when the dispute is ended. We trust your word as Prime Minister. We ask you to assist us in the way you only can assist us – by asking employers and all others to make the position as easy and smooth as possible, because the one thing we must not have is guerrilla warfare. That must be avoided, and in that both sides have to contribute immediately. Nothing could be worse than that this great decision which we have taken should be interpreted otherwise than as a general desire to do the right thing in a difficult moment for the industry of the nation.

MR BEVIN: I think you will agree in the difficulties we have had before us, at least we have taken a great risk in calling the strike off. I want to urge it must not be regarded as an act of weakness, but rather one of strength. I am not talking of muscle and brawn, but rather that it took a little courage to take the line we have done. I want to stress Mr Thomas's point, and ask you if you could tell us whether you are prepared to make a general request, as head of the Government, that facilities, etc., ready facilities for reinstatement and that kind of thing, shall be given forthwith. The position is this. Some of the undertakings that are affected, of course, are affected by associations which are get-at-able; otherwise they are all over the country. When this goes out in the press it may cause untold confusion, but if you could agree with us to make a declaration it would, I think, facilitate matters. Employers no doubt have been acting at least in carrying out the spirit of the Government during the fight, naturally, and they would no doubt respond to a statement of that character, and I would put it to you very strongly that that is one of the easiest ways of doing things. One of the reasons I want to put it to you is this. In a dislocation of this character it does affect production very much, especially in producing trades, and if there is a resumption with a sort of good feeling then the thing gets back on to its usual footing very rapidly. If there is not, then it does affect the restoration.

I remember after the 1912 strike, when we were beaten, Sir Joseph Brookbank went into it very carefully, and the loss in output of transport was something like 25 per cent for some time until the war. We do not want that kind of thing. We have had a row, and it does upset things, but we are quite willing to co-operate with our men to repair the damage just as much as the employers, but the employers are the people who can facilitate that kind of feeling, and I am sure they would respond to you if you issued that as a statement. It would be very helpful to us before we left the building if we could have some indication in that direction, because we shall have to send telegrams to unions whose headquarters are not in London, with whom we cannot converse, and coupling with it a declaration from yourself would, in a way, give the lead as to how the thing is to be approached.

You said, sir, also you were going to call the parties together in order to effect a just settlement. Now, we have called our show off, and work will be resuming pretty quickly. I do not know whether I am overstepping the bounds, but I would like you to give me an idea of whether that means that there is to be a resumption of the mining negotiations with us, or whether all the negotiations have to be carried on while the miners still remain out.

MR THOMAS: That implies that we interpret your speech to mean what I am sure it did mean.

MR BEVIN: It helped us to rise to the occasion. I thought personally – of course, it is so difficult when you have to take it without conversing – I really felt in the event of our taking the lead in assuring you we were going to play the game and put our people back, that it was going to be free and unfettered negotiations with the parties very speedily, because thousands of our people cannot go back if the colliers are still out, and if the colliers are still out it is going to make it extremely difficult to get a smooth running of the machine. Those are the two points I wish to put to you.

THE PRIME MINISTER: Well, Mr Bevin, I cannot say more here at this meeting now. I did not know what points you were going to raise, or that anything would be said beyond the statement of Mr Pugh. The point you have put is one I must consider, and I will consider it at once. I would only say, in my view the best thing to do is to get as quickly as possible into touch with the employers. I think that the quicker that is done the less friction there will be. You know my record. You know the object of my policy, and I think you may trust me to consider what has been said with a view to seeing how best we can get the country quickly back into the condition in which we all want to see it. You will want my co-operation, and I shall want yours to try to make good the damage done to the trade, and try to make this country a little better and a happier place than it has been in recent years. That will be my steady endeavour, and I look to all of you when we are through this for your co-operation in that. I shall do my part and I have no doubt you will do yours.

In regard to the second point, there, again, I cannot say at this moment what will happen, because I shall have to see the parties. My object, of course, is to get the mines started the first moment possible, and get an agreement reached. I cannot say until I have seen them exactly what the lines will be upon which my object can best be attained, but you may rely on me and rely on the Cabinet that they will see no stone is left unturned to accomplish that end. Now, Mr Pugh, as I said before, we have both of us got a great deal to do and a great deal of anxious and difficult work, and I think that the sooner you get to your work and the sooner I get to mine the better.

MR PUGH: Yes; that sums up the position for the moment.

MR BEVIN: I am a little persistent. I do not want to take up your time, but shall we be meeting on these two points soon?

THE PRIME MINISTER: I cannot say that, Mr Bevin. I think it may be that whatever decision I come to the House of Commons may be the best place in which to say it. I cannot say at the moment whether the better thing would be to do it there or meet again; but we are going to consider right away what is best.

The proceedings then terminated.

APPENDIX II

The complete text of Sir Herbert Samuel's letter to the Prime Minister, which was written but not sent.

11th May 1926

DEAR PRIME MINISTER,

I think it is advisable at this stage that I should inform you of the steps which I have taken since my return to England.

I left Italy as soon as I knew that negotiations had been broken off, and reached London on Thursday evening, 6th May.

During the last four days I have been engaged in an almost continuous series of conferences and conversations. I have seen the Negotiating Committee of the Trades Union Congress four times, the conferences lasting two or three hours on each occasion. At the last of these meetings the representatives of the miners were also present. I have also had several conferences with my late colleagues on the Coal Commission and have seen yourself, Sir Arthur Steel-Maitland, Colonel Lane-Fox, Mr Evan Williams, Lord Weir, Sir Alan Smith and others. The matter which is of chief interest concerns my conversations with the trade unionists, and it is that to which I shall confine myself in this report.

I made it perfectly clear to them beyond possibility of misunderstanding that I was in no way authorized to speak on behalf of the Government; that I could convey no message to the Government; nor express their views in any form upon any of the matters at issue prior to the termination of the General Strike. I do not think it possible that any difficulty should arise subsequently on this head unless someone tells a deliberate falsehood with regard to the facts.

I also made it clear that in my view there were three essential conditions which governed the situation:

(1) It was useless to attempt to exercise any pressure upon the Government to discuss the conditions on which coal negotiations should be resumed prior to the termination of the General Strike. I stated that in my opinion the attitude taken by the Government was the only one which was possible for them to adopt.

(2) It was useless to re-open negotiations on the coal question so long as a veto was imposed by the miners upon any wage reductions in any circumstances. The question of limits to be imposed upon such reductions or conditions to be attached to their acceptance were matters which might conceivably form the subject of discussion, but no one would begin negotiating on them unless it was quite clear beforehand that a deadlock on that point would not again occur.

(3) It would be useless to suggest any renewal of the subsidy for longer than a brief period on the lines stated in your public declarations.

It would be plain that those three conditions which appear to me to be essential do not leave very much room for accommodation. However, it was necessary to explore every avenue that was open within those limits.

The present situation results from not one deadlock, but two. In the first place, the Government say that they cannot resume negotiations on the coal question until the General Strike is ended, while the TUC say that they cannot end the General Strike until they know that the negotiations will be resumed and lock-out notices withdrawn so as to enable them to proceed under free conditions. No one, therefore, is able to discuss how these divergent views are to be reconciled since there is no means of negotiation between the two parties. I do not myself regard this as the more serious aspect of the situation, because if the conditions of the nego-

tiations themselves could once be settled it is plain enough
from the Government's public declarations that on the ending of the strike you would be willing to renew the subsidy.
This renewal could only be for the purpose of enabling the
mine-owners to continue working the mines during the
interim period on the conditions of employment that prevailed before 30th April. It would therefore automatically
follow that the lock-out notices would be withdrawn meanwhile.

The second deadlock is the real crux of the situation, and
that is the impossibility of reopening negotiations on the
coal question so long as the miners' veto on any form of
wage reduction remains, and it is with this aspect that I
have been mainly concerned during my conferences.

The Trade Union Committee at our first meeting gave
me the definite assurance that the miners' attitude had
changed and that if the point was put to them in a reasonable way and in a palatable form a satisfactory answer
would be obtained. I was given the impression that the
principal difficulty was the intense suspicion of the miners
that while wage reductions would be a certainty the reconstruction of the industry would prove in fact dilatory and
doubtful. If that suspicion could be removed the wages question would fall into the background.

The matters so raised were explored in every direction
and I made several suggestions which the TUC received
most cordially. Finally the principal desiderata were formu-
lated as the following:

(1) Since it is hopeless to expect any lasting settlement by
    means of negotiations between the mine-owners and the
    miners left to themselves it is essential to establish a
    Mines National Board, consisting of these two parties,
    together with a neutral element and an independent
    chairman. This was suggested in a tentative form in the
    report of the commission (page 153). It is now con-
    sidered that the suggestion should be pressed; that the

powers to be conferred upon the board should be enlarged; that the wage question should be referred to such a board for decision; and that the board should also be charged with the duty of ensuring that the reforms, so far as they are to be effected from within the industry, should really be carried out with vigour and completeness. So far as the reforms involve Governmental action the Advisory Committee which had been suggested by yourself should be established for the same purpose.

(2) After these points had been agreed, the Mines National Board should proceed to the preparation of a wage agreement which should:

  (i) if possible, be on simpler lines than those hitherto followed;

  (ii) not affect in any way the wages of the lower paid men;

  (iii) fix reasonable figures, below which the wage of no class of labour should be reduced in any circumstances.

I expressed my own view that these were proper proposals.

I have ascertained that my late colleagues on the Royal Commission strongly support the adoption of the National Board principle as the means of solving the wage difficulty. The protection of the lowest paid men is already embodied in the report. The further protection suggested under subhead (iii) above may be found to be necessary owing to the excessive reductions proposed by the employers which have caused great alarm and which may prevent the miners agreeing to what is in effect an arbitral tribunal, unless some limit is placed beforehand upon the decisions which it may give.

If the miners, then, could be induced to accept these lines as those on which the negotiations might proceed, they could request the TUC to terminate the General Strike and the remaining difficulties would at once disappear, but up to the present the miners have not been so induced.

I spent three hours yesterday afternoon with the TUC and the miners together. Subsequently I understand they debated the point among themselves. Next the miners discussed it separately for two hours and finally there was another joint meeting which lasted till one-thirty this morning. The outcome so far is negative.

Both the miners and the members of the TUC spoke very frankly during these conferences. I am not of course free to record their views, but I think I may give you my general impressions. The TUC would be glad to settle on the terms suggested. They are, however, convinced that their constituents would violently resent any desertion of the miners. Whatever might be their own views as to the probable outcome of the strike and as to the hardships and dangers which it brings they are not in a position to end the strike without the miners' concurrence. So far as the Miners' Federation is concerned it is Herbert Smith and not Cook who is the dominating influence and his position is up to the present quite immovable. The TUC were deceiving themselves when they informed me that there was no longer an absolute veto upon any kind of reduction in any circumstances. My clear view is that the veto remains exactly the same now as it was throughout the negotiations. This is due not only to the suspicion, which is undoubtedly a real one, that reconstruction will not eventuate to any full extent or in the near future, but also to the conviction that the miners' wages are already low and are not susceptible of any further reduction at all.

The TUC have expressed a wish to meet me again this afternoon at three o'clock, when the outcome of our conferences of yesterday will no doubt be discussed.

The solution of the coal question continues to be a choice between the same three alternatives that have offered from the beginning. I do not discuss the question of hours because that would only complicate the issue and I feel quite certain that no section of the Labour movement would accept an alteration of hours at the present time. There are also the fundamental objections that longer hours would involve an enormous increased output and that they would probably be countered by an increase of hours in Germany. The three alternatives then are the following:

(a) To cover the losses of the industry out of the National Exchequer. This solution has been definitely ruled out, and in my opinion should in no circumstances be re-considered;

(b) to leave wages as they are; to allow those mines who are able to continue working to do so; to acquiesce in the remainder being closed; to accept a large increase in coal prices and a rise in the cost of living and the loss of export markets; and the handicap to the iron and steel and other industries which would follow;

(c) to continue the contest until an assent is secured to the wage reductions on the scale suggested in the report. These would still leave a large gap between costs and proceeds in several districts which might partly be met by some rise in prices, but would certainly result in the closing in any case of a considerable number of mines.

If this last alternative is held to be the only one which is feasible – and I believe myself that it is – no course can be pursued other than the one which is now being followed, and the essential point is to explain to public opinion the reasons for the proposals in the report and the extent of their scope. The wage scales offered by the employers, which involve reductions going far beyond anything contemplated by the commission, have certainly tended to enlist sympathy for the standpoint of the miners. If and when a settlement is reached on these lines, the fact that a number of mines will still remain closed in districts like Northumberland, Durham and South Wales may possibly induce the men themselves to reconsider their attitude on the subject of hours, and perhaps permit an increase of half an hour a day, which would bring our working period up to a level with that in the Ruhr. It may be that economic conditions at that time would not cause the market to be glutted by the increased production that would ensue.

Since all my conversations have been of a confidential character I would ask that this communication should be similarly regarded.

Yours very sincerely

(Two hours after Samuel drafted this, at some time before a suggested meeting on Tuesday afternoon, he received a message from the TUC that they were proceeding without the miners.)

BIBLIOGRAPHY

OF BOOKS AND PRINTED SOURCES

L. S. AMERY. *My Political Life*, vol. ii. Hutchinson, 1953.

R. PAGE ARNOT. *The General Strike, May 1926: Its Origin and History.* Labour Research Department, 1926.

R. PAGE ARNOT. *The Miners: Years of Struggle.* Allen & Unwin, 1953.

R. K. A. BELL. *Randall Davidson, Archbishop of Canterbury.* Oxford University Press, 1938.

A. J. BENNETT. *The General Council and the General Strike.* Communist Party of Great Britain, 1926.

ARNOLD BENNETT. *Journals, 1921–8.* Cassell, 1933.

ARNOLD BENNETT. *Letters to His Nephew.* Heinemann, 1936.

MARGARET BONDFIELD. *A Life's Work.* Hutchinson, 1949.

ROBERT BOOTHBY. *I Fight to Live.* Gollancz, 1947.

LORD BRABAZON OF TARA. *The Brabazon Story.* Heinemann, 1956.

FENNER BROCKWAY. *Inside the Left.* Allen & Unwin, 1942.

EMILE BURNS. *The General Strike: Trades Councils in Action.* Labour Research Department, 1926.

THE COAL CRISIS. *Facts from the Samuel Commission, 1925–6.* Labour Research Department, 1926.

J. R. CLYNES. *Memoirs.* Hutchinson, 1937.

G. D. H. COLE. *A Short History of the British Working-Class Movement, 1789–1947.* Allen & Unwin, 1948.

A. J. COOK. *The Nine Days.* Co-operative Printing Society Ltd.

DUFF COOPER (VISCOUNT NORWICH). *Old Men Forget.* Hart-Davis, 1953.

W. H. CROOK. *The General Strike.* University of North Carolina Press, 1931.

HUGH DALTON. *Call Back Yesterday.* Muller, 1953.

R. PALME DUTT. *The Meaning of the General Strike.* Communist Party of Great Britain, 1926.

G. G. EASTWOOD. *George Isaacs.* Odhams Press, 1952.

HAMILTON FYFE. *Behind the Scenes of the Great Strike.* Labour Publishing Co., 1926.

THE GENERAL STRIKE. *The Story of a Great Folly.* Anti-Socialist and Anti-Communist Union, 1926.

E. T. HILLER. *The Strike. A Study in Collective Action.* University of Chicago Press, 1928.

ALLEN HUTT. *Post-war History of the British Working Class.* Gollancz, 1937.

SIR WILLIAM JAMES. *The Eyes of the Navy. A Biographical Study of Admiral Sir Reginald Hall.* Methuen, 1955.

THOMAS JONES, C.H., LL.D. *Lloyd George.* Oxford University Press, 1951.

J. M. KEYNES. *The Economic Consequences of Mr Churchill.* Hogarth Press, 1925.

JACK LAWSON. *The Man in the Cap. The Life of Herbert Smith.* Methuen, 1941.

KINGSLEY MARTIN. *The British Public and the General Strike.* Hogarth Press, 1926.

R. J. MINNEY. *Viscount Southwood.* Odhams Press, 1954.

J. T. MURPHY. *The Political Meaning of the General Strike.* Communist Party of Great Britain, 1926.

HAROLD NICOLSON. *King George the Fifth. His Life and Reign.* Constable, 1952.

FRANK OWEN. *Tempestuous Journey. Lloyd George, His Life and Times.* Hutchinson, 1954.

EARL OF OXFORD AND ASQUITH. *Memories and Reflections.* Cassell, 1928.

LESLIE PAUL. *Angry Young Man.* Faber & Faber, 1951.

RAYMOND POSTGATE and others. *A Workers' History of the Great Strike.* Plebs League, 1927.

RAYMOND POSTGATE. *Life of George Lansbury.* Longmans, Green, 1951.

RED MONEY. *A statement of the facts relating to the money raised in Russia during the General Strike.* Labour Research Department, 1926.

J. C. W. REITH. *Into the Wind.* Hodder & Stoughton, 1949.

VISCOUNT SAMUEL. *Memoirs.* Cresset Press, 1945.

OSBERT SITWELL. *Laughter in the Next Room.* Macmillan, 1949.

SIR HENRY SLESSER. *Judgment Reserved.* Hutchinson, 1941.

PHILIP VISCOUNT SNOWDEN. *An Autobiography,* vol. ii. Nicholson & Watson, 1934.

GEORGES SOREL. *Reflections on Violence.* B. W. Huebsch, 1922.

J. A. SPENDER and CYRIL ASQUITH. *Life of H. H. Asquith.* Hutchinson, 1932.

STRIKE NIGHTS IN PRINTING HOUSE SQUARE. Privately printed, 1926.

VISCOUNT TEMPLEWOOD. *Nine Troubled Years.* Collins, 1954.

J. H. THOMAS. *My Story.* Hutchinson, 1937.

BEN TURNER. *About Myself*. Cayme Press, 1930.

L. MACNEIL WEIR. *The Tragedy of Ramsay MacDonald*. Secker & Warburg, 1938.

FRANCIS WILLIAMS. *Ernest Bevin*. Hutchinson, 1952.

EARL WINTERTON. *Orders of the Day*. Cassell, 1953.

THE YORKSHIRE POST AND THE GENERAL STRIKE. Yorkshire Conservative Newspaper Co.

G. M. YOUNG. *Stanley Baldwin*. Hart-Davis, 1952.

Other Printed Sources

Newspapers and Periodicals of the period.

Reports in Hansard.

Report of the Samuel Commission on the Coal Mines.

The Mining Situation: Report of Special Conference on Executive Committees held from 29th April to 1st May 1926.

Mining Dispute National Strike: Report of the General Council to the Conference of Affiliated Unions, 25th June 1926.

Statements of the Miners' Federation of Great Britain.

Report of Proceedings at National Strike Special Conference held on 20th and 21st January 1927.